POPE PIUS XII LIBRARY, ST. JOSEPH COL.

3 2528 12026 2144

D1521167

Classics of Modern Japanese Thought and Culture

The Ways of Thinking of Eastern Peoples
Hajime Nakamura

A Study of Good
Kitaro Nishida

Climate and Culture: A Philosophical Study
Tetsuro Watsuji

Time and Eternity
Seiichi Hatano

Studies in Shinto Thought
Tsunetsugu Muraoka

The Japanese Character: A Cultural Profile
Nyozekan Hasegawa

An Inquiry into the Japanese Mind as Mirrored in Literature
Sokichi Tsuda

About our Ancestors: —The Japanese Family System
Kunio Yanagita

Japanese Spirituality
Daisetz Suzuki

A Historical Study of the Religious Development of Shinto
Genichi Kato

Japanese Spirituality

Japanese Spirituality

by

Daisetz Suzuki

translated by

Norman Waddell

compiled by

Japanese National Commission for Unesco

Greenwood Press
New York • Westport, Connecticut • London

Library of Congress Cataloging-in-Publication Data

Suzuki, Daisetz Teitaro, 1870-1966.
  Japanese spirituality.

  Translation of: Nihon-teki reisei.
  Reprint. Originally published: Toyko : Japan Society
for the Promotion of Science, 1972.
  1. Pure Land Buddhism—Japan—History. 2. Buddhism—
Japan—History—1185-1600. I. Nihon Yunesuko Kokunai
Iinkai.
BQ8512.9.J3S8913 1988   294.3'42   88-21945
ISBN 0-313-26554-2

British Library Cataloguing in Publication Data is available.

© Ministry of Education, Japan, 1972

All rights reserved. No portion of this book may be
reproduced, by any process or technique, without the
express written consent of the publisher.

Library of Congress Catalog Card Number: 88-21945
ISBN: 0-313-26554-2

First published in 1972

Reprinted in 1988 by Greenwood Press, Inc. jointly with
Yushodo Co., Ltd., Tokyo with the permission of the Ministry of
Education, Japan

Printed in the United States of America

The paper used in this book complies with the
Permanent Paper Standard issued by the National
Information Standards Organization (Z39.48-1984).

10 9 8 7 6 5 4 3 2 1

FOREWORD

The Japanese National Commission for Unesco has been carrying out, since 1958, a project of translating Japanese philosophical works into foreign languages and publishing them with a view to introducing Japanese thought to the people of other countries. Under this project, we have so far brought out nine titles, and the present title is the tenth of the series.

It is our hope that this edition will be of use for those who are engaged in the studies of Japan and its culture in deepening their understanding of Japanese thought.

We are greatly indebted to Professor Shōkin Furuta of Nihon University, and Professor N. A. Waddell of Otani University, for their valuable contribution in many ways to our project.

Kikuo Nishida
Secretary-General
Japanese National Commission for Unesco

TRANSLATOR'S NOTE

Japanese Spirituality, in Japanese, *Nihon-teki reisei*, was first published in 1944, written, as the author writes, between trips to the air-raid shelter during some of the heaviest bombing of the war. It was followed by three other works on the subject of "Japanese spirituality": *Reisei-teki nihon no kensetsu* (The Building of Spiritual Japan, 1946), *Nihon-teki reisei-teki jikaku* (The Awakening of Spiritual Japan, 1946), and *Nihon no reisei-ka* (Spiritualizing Japan, 1947). In 1948 an additional study of the Myōkōnin was published, and in 1967, *Myōkōnin Asahara Saichi shū* (The Works of Myōkōnin Asahara Saichi).

When possible, I have attempted to utilize Dr. Suzuki's own English renderings of terms and passages, found in his many works in English. For the footnotes, it has likewise seemed desirable to quote at some length from two of the author's works concerned with Pure Land Buddhism [*A Miscellany on the Shin Teaching of Buddhism* (Kyoto, 1949); *Mysticism: Christian and Buddhist* (New York, 1957)] in order to clarify for the Western reader some of the terminology of the Pure Land tradition. All the notes (the Japanese edition has virtually none) not marked 'Translator' have been composed in this way. A glossary of terms that occur repeatedly in the text will be found at the end of the volume.

I have needed, and fortunately had, much help and advice in the course of translating this book. Gratefully I acknowledge my debt to those who have given freely of their time to answer questions; above all, to Rev. Shōjun Bandō and Miss Sumiko Kudō, who read the translation at different stages of completion and offered many helpful suggestions.

Japanese Spirituality represents a side of Suzuki Daisetz unknown to Western readers familiar only with his English works. It was directed to the Japanese at a time of growing uncertainty and despair. But in attempting to show them their true, unmilitary, might, it lays open for all readers the thought and wisdom of one of the spiritual masters of our time.

Norman Waddell, 1969

PREFACE

This book was written to consider what I call Japanese spirituality. It is meant as a preliminary essay, and although it is not a systematic and ordered study, I do believe it is able in some measure to elucidate my intentions.

Portions of the second chapter dealing with Pure Land thought are based on a shorthand transcription of a talk that I gave during the summer of 1942 at the Higashi Honganji Branch Temple in Kanazawa. The lecture was arranged by Kaneda Reidō, then the head of that temple. I have completely rewritten and revised the transcript, so that its present form bears little resemblance to the original lecture.

I have tried to trace the imprint of the central idea of this book, namely Japanese spirituality, in the history of Japanese religious thought. To describe this in a methodical manner has not been possible in the time and space allotted. I hope for another opportunity to deal with the subject, but since I do not know when that occasion will arise, I should like to take this opportunity to offer the present work as a kind of prelude.

Daisetz Suzuki
Yafūryū-an, Kita Kamakura,
the beginning of summer, 1944

CONTENTS

Foreword vii

Translator's Note viii

Preface by the author ix

Dr. Suzuki; His Life and Works .... Shōkin Furuta 1

Introduction 11

Chapter 1. Japanese Spirituality and the Kamakura Period 27
    I. The Emotional Life 28
    II. The Awakening of Japanese Spirituality 46

Chapter 2. Manifestations of Japanese Spirituality 59
    I. Buddhism and the Germinal Impulses of Japanese
        Spirituality 59
    II. Spirituality 75
    III. The Autonomy of Japanese Spirituality 93

Chapter 3. Hōnen and Nembutsu Shōmyō 127
    I. The Fall of the Heike 127
    II. Aspects of Pure Land Thought 134
    III. Nembutsu and 'The Unlettered' 144
    IV. Nembutsu Shōmyō 154

Chapter 4. The Myōkōnin 167
    I. Dōshū 167
    II. Asahara Saichi 177

Glossary of Select Terms 214

Index 219

DR. SUZUKI: HIS LIFE AND WORKS

1

In life's journey there is a direct road and a sideway. Dr. Daisetz T. Suzuki's academic career is a unique example of one who took the by-path all through his life. He left the university before graduation and went to the United States to study, but did magazine editorial work instead of attending college or university. He set his mind on study in his early days, yet was unable to take the main road from the beginning due to family and other circumstances. The Meiji and Taishō periods produced many learned Buddhist scholars. Contrary to the favourable backgrounds enjoyed by many of them, Daisetz Suzuki was raised in a poor family.

While doing editorial work for the *Open Court* magazine, he continued his study of Buddhism. This resulted in an English translation of *Açvaghosha's Discourse on the Awakening of Faith in the Mahayana*, published in 1900, which won the nameless young Japanese scholar recognition in Western academic circles.

In 1889, Suzuki left Ishikawa High School and went to a primary school at Iida, Noto, as a teacher of English. Already, no doubt, he wished to improve his English, to use it as a means of promoting his study. His efforts led him to the United States in 1897, and three years later resulted in the translation of such a difficult work as the *Awakening of Faith in the Mahayana*. Granting his linguistic gifts, it was his strong will and a determination to negotiate the sideway that was his destiny that made him realize his special abilities and made him persevere in his efforts. During his thirteen year stay in the United States he completed a translation of *T'ai-Shang Kan-Ying P'ien* (Treatise of the Exalted One on Response and Retribution), and wrote *Outline of Mahayana Buddhism*. The latter in particular established his reputation as a unique and outstanding scholar unaffiliated with the universities.

In 1908, a year after the publication of his *Outline of Mahayana Buddhism*, he travelled to Europe from the United States, and in April 1909 returned to Japan after a fourteen year absence. Upon return he was invited to the Peers' School, where he taught English till 1921, when he moved to Ōtani University, Kyoto, at the request of its president, Gesshō

Sasaki. Even after his return home, he continued to tread the sideway as a Buddhist scholar. For years he was given no more appropriate position than that of language teacher. While at the Peers' School, Suzuki taught also at the University of Tokyo for a while, but his post there again was as an instructor of English. During this period, however, he published in London *A Brief History of Early Chinese Philosophy*. He was not destined to remain a language teacher: he continued his unique studies in Buddhism based on his Zen experience.

D. T. Suzuki was 52 years old when he was invited to Ōtani University and finally entered scholarly life. The great number of his writings tell of his scholastic achievements, especially the significant number of books in English. His previous study of English was thus the foundation of his later achievements, with his ten year role as a language instructor the basis for a remarkable literary output. The post offered, however, professor at a private university, in Japan was, after all, a by-path, away from the more established academic posts at the imperial universities. Thus his new scholarly life did not improve his situation as much as it might have, except that he could now afford more time for his Buddhist studies.

After he left Ishikawa High School he graduated from no other school. Unsatisfied with his possibilities in Japan, he went abroad, and took up his studies again on his return. The very fact that he remained on the sideway throughout his life may be said to be all the more impressive. Not only scholars, everyone wants to take the high road, in whatever field, and may very well do so, if given the opportunity. However, if one judges the sideway from the viewpoint of advantages and disadvantages, and refuses to take it because it does not pay, I would have him consider Suzuki's life. To take the sideway is not always disadvantageous; it can be a very worthy way too.

2

D. T. Suzuki's academic work has, briefly speaking, six intellectual peaks. The first is Kegon philosophy, which developed in connection with his study of Zen thought around 1934, the year his *Essays in Zen Buddhism, Third Series* was published in London. The second peak is apparent around 1935 with his studies on Bodhidharma and his thought. His study of Bankei's *Fushō* (Unborn) Zen around 1940 constitutes the third intellectual peak. From 1939 to 1942 he wrote on *"mushin"* (no-mind), and this is the fourth peak. This had important connections with Pure Land thought and later developed to a greater degree. The fifth was the great summit of *Japanese Spirituality* which was first delineated around 1944. His profound study of "Rinzai's Person" around 1947 was the sixth peak.

Throughout these high points, there is one common element, namely, the great intellectual by-path to his studies in Buddhism. It was this that made his respective intellectual peaks so unique and creative. What was this by-path? His philosophy derived from the Zen experience he personally attained through his Zen training under Masters Imagita Kōsen and Shaku Sōen. This training started when he was 22 years old, a student at Tokyo University. He scarcely attended school, but spent his time at Engakuji Monastery, Kamakura, in Zen training and discipline. In other words, D. T. Suzuki did not take the main road of the student. He took the sideway of Zen training, and this enabled him to make unique studies of his own.

This academic pattern did not change even after he took leave of Tokyo University and went to the United States as a working student. As a professor in the Peers' School upon his return, and later as a Buddhist scholar at Ōtani University, he was never apart from Zen training, while thus steadily and calmly carrying on his studies in Buddhism. He did not regard Buddhism merely as a subject of research; his approach to Buddhist philosophy was always based on his Zen experience. His was a very serious approach, and proceeding was not easy. It was obviously a sideway which required much digression.

Among his early writings there is a book entitled *Zen to wa nanika* (What is Zen?), in which he speaks of the ideal of Mahayana Buddhism as follows:

> *"It is not in words; the ideal of Mahayana Buddhism is not in the words written in holy and respected scriptures, but the very life of Shakyamuni Buddha itself clearly represents it. Buddhism does not consist of teachings spoken by Buddha based on his wisdom alone; we have to look at his actual life which was*

3

based on his religious experience." (Chapter 3: "Bukkyō no kihonteki gainen" The Basic Ideas of Buddhism)

As this quotation reveals, he insisted on taking up Buddhism in the domain of actual experience. When this book was published in a popular paperback edition (Sōgen Bunko and Kadokawa Bunko), I wrote some comments for it, a part of which I would like to quote here instead of speaking of the book itself. It shows how Suzuki emphasized the importance of Zen experience:

> There are two things necessary for correct understanding of this book.
>
> First, we should note the depth of D. T. Suzuki's Zen experience which underlies all his writings. Those who do not know what Zen is will no doubt fail to understand it when they first read the book. Yet, if they finish it without taking this point into account, they will have gained nothing from having read it. To read this book properly, one should first read it through, to get a general idea of Zen. Then in order to know this is not a book of philosophical argumentation about Zen, he should read it once more, and read into the depth of Zen experience. What is the depth of Zen experience, one may ask. I am not able to fully explain it. I can only say that one can only know what Zen is by seeing into the depth of Zen experience.
>
> When books are written in an easy style, people are apt to skim over them. The fact that this book is easy to read shows that it is a good introductory book, but it does not necessarily mean readers will thereby easily discover what Zen is. For readers to realize the depth of the Zen experience that underlies this book will not be easy. For them not to overlook such essential points as these, they should be prepared to read it with careful and sincere attention.
>
> Second, it must be understood that is not enough just to know of Suzuki's Zen experience. For instance, his interpretation of "Namu-Amida-Butsu" is his own, based on his religious experience, and he is not bothered with the traditional interpretations. "I am interpreting "Namu-Amida-Butsu" from a Zen viewpoint, and the

4

Pure Land interpretation could be different from mine. If one does not look at them dualistically as two different interpretations, but takes it based on the religious experience itself, he should be able to find his own free interpretation based on his personal experience, no matter what people might have said, or what might have happened in the past. The criticism or evaluation is left to you."

Readers should clearly understand the significance of these words. Suzuki is here being neither dogmatic nor self-assertive. When he speaks of the "non-dualistic religious experience itself," he does not assume a synthetic view of Zen and Pure Land. He speaks out of the Zen experience he personally attained. It does not matter whether the experience itself is Zen or Pure Land. As we cannot discuss anything without referring to certain views, the so-called Zen viewpoint or Pure Land viewpoint is presumed. But whether it is called Zen or Pure Land, the fundamental standpoint itself does not change. Needless to say, it is not a mixture of the two. They are different and yet the same. Here Suzuki's Zen experience is deep-rooted, and readers should correctly understand it. He tells us not to worry about what people have said in the past or what is written in books, but to have one's own interpretation and understanding. Though this may sound somewhat self-assertive, let me remind you that to understand Suzuki's interpretation means no other than for each reader to have his own understanding; D. T. Suzuki's own free interpretation based on personal experience is each person's own free interpretation. Haste in this matter, however, carries with it risk of forming a dogmatic interpretation. We should not forget that it is possible only for those who go through the long training in Zen that Suzuki himself underwent.

D. T. Suzuki's experiential grasp of Buddhism as seen in this book underlies all of his thought and ideas. It is the basic source of his thinking. I have broken down his scholastic achievements into six thought-peaks, the basis of each being his fundamental experience. In a sense, each thought-peak just represents a different aspect of the non-dualistic, experiential truth. In his *Essays in Zen Buddhism, Third Series* (the Chapter "The Desire for Enlightenment" [Bodhicittotpada]), he says that any teaching in Buddhism, not in Zen alone, has to be understood and accepted

5

on the basis of the personal experience of each individual. On Bodhi-cittotpada he writes:

> The Bodhicitta rises from a great compassionate heart, without which there will be no Buddhism. This emphasis on Mahākarunā is characteristic of the Mahayana. We can say that the whole panorama of its teachings revolves on this pivot. The philosophy of Interpenetration so pictorially depicted in the Gandavyūha is in fact no more than the outburst of this life-energy. As long as we tarry on the plane of intellection, such Buddhist doctrines as Emptiness (sūnyatā), Egolessness (anātmya), etc. may sound so abstract and devoid of spiritual force as not to excite anyone to fanatic enthusiasm. The main point is to remember that all the Buddhist teachings are the outcome of a warm heart cherished over all sentient beings and not of a cold intellect which tries to unveil the secrets of existence by logic. That is to say, Buddhism is personal experience and not impersonal philosophy.

Thus, Suzuki insists that Buddhism should not be treated as a philosophy apart from actual experience. He took an early interest in Kegon thought. Starting his study in this direction with such basic work as the editing of the *Gandavyūha* chapter of the Kegon sutra in Sanskrit. Later he had a grand wish of making a correct translation of this sutra. Although unfortunately this unique work was not completed during his lifetime, his Kegon study developed into other achievements which constitute important elements of his work.

His second thought-peak took its form in his *Zen shisō-shi kenkyū, II* (Studies in the History of Zen Thought, Vol. II), in which he took up the Zen of Bodhidharma and the Sixth Patriarch Enō, as well as other masters of the same period. As it can be clearly noted in this book, his study of Bodhidharma was neither historical nor philosophical, but was based on his Zen experience. He writes in the Introduction to this book:

> What is Bodhidharma's Zen? What is Enō's Zen? How did it develop into Koan Zen? It is said that Bodhidharma transmitted the Lankavatara Sutra to Eka, and that Enō attained satori while listening to the Diamond Sutra. How did they become one with

6

the 'sound of one hand clapping'? We have such verses:

> *Lotus leaves are round and smooth,*
> *Even more so than a mirror;*
> *Thistle leaves are sharp and pointed,*
> *Even more so than a gimlet (Daie)*

and

> *Rain is gone and clouds are still thick;*
> *The day is about to break.*
> *Mountains are blue and soaring*
> *So picturesque indeed are they! (Setchō)*

On the other hand there are Indian expressions like 'Prajñā is non-wisdom, and is at the same time wisdom.' How should we understand these expressions? What experiential basis do they have which makes them declare that these apparently quite different statements express one and the same Zen truth? Such questions arose one after another. The desire to somehow solve them from the standpoint of the history of Zen thought, from their aspect as unique Zen expressions, and also in line with deepening of Zen experience, never left my mind.

As he himself writes, he always approached the history of Zen thought from the standpoint of deepening Zen experience. In his study of Zen from the time of Bodhidharma to Enō, or Zen after Enō, the questions he proposes are unique, without parallel in any other writings dealing with Zen history. For instance, he introduces an interesting theory as to how Bodhidharma's idea of *anjin* (peace of mind) developed into the idea *mushin* (no-mind). Doubtlessly, a long period of experiential thinking and philosophizing was needed for him to attain a clear and definite outlook during this second thought-peak, for the deeper one studies it, the higher he will find this peak to be.

The third peak was his study of Bankei's Unborn Zen. Its value may be judged from the fact that it was solely due to his work that "Unborn" Zen assumed a proper position in the history of Zen thought. The two major writings in this regard are: *Bankei no fushō zen* (Bankei on the 'Unborn'), and *Zen shisō-shi kenkyū, I* (Studies in the History of Zen Thought, Vol. I). In the former, he deals with Zen experience from beginning till end. In the latter, the two major themes discussed

7

are *satori* (enlightenment) and *satoru* (to attain enlightenment). He points out that in studying Zen in Japan, it can be classified into three major philosophical types: Dōgen's Zen, Hakuin's Zen, and Bankei's Zen. His study of Bankei's Zen, which had been hitherto unexplored, revealed great enthusiasm. His study of Koan Zen paralleled that of Unborn Zen. Closely related to each other, these form the center of his study of Zen thought based on Zen experience.

His writings on *mushin* (no-mind) mark his fourth thought-peak. His thinking at this time seems to have increased in depth and lucidity. He calmly and steadily trod the by-path, no step wasted, every step made full use of, finally forming one great stream of thought. A representative book of this period is *Mushin to yūkoto* (On 'No-mind'). Though this was transcribed from a lecture, it is one of his great works.

Reading this work, the reader will be reminded of the importance of having the realm and not the thought of no-mind as the foundation of the philosophy. Suzuki warns: "No matter how much I may talk about the realm of no-mind, it will be fruitless unless one actually experiences it." What may appear easy in this book turns to be extremely difficult when it comes to the question of actual experience. Though the thought of "no-mind" was not written in the systematic method of his other books, it developed in various directions and attained great range of thought.

The fifth thought-peak involves the idea of spiritual awakening as seen in his great work *Nihon-teki reisei* (Japanese Spirituality). Spirituality is synonymous with religious consciousness. To awaken to such spirituality is spiritual awakening or realization. Spirituality as he refers to it is latent in the inmost recesses of what is generally called spirit or psyche, and here again he is trying to deal with the domain of religious experience. *Japanese Spirituality* describes the awakening process of religious consciousness of the Japanese during the Kamakura period. It can well be called the history of Japanese religious thought based on spiritual experience. Insofar as this is a book of the history of thought, it shares the same standpoint with *Zen shisō-shi kenkyū, I & II* (Studies in the History of Zen Thought, Vols. I & II), though the approaches and questions proposed in them are quite different.

An outstanding characteristic of *Japanese Spirituality* is the unusual interest in Pure Land Buddhism it reveals. This interest is a continuation from his previous work *Jōdo-kei shisō-ron* (Studies in Pure Land

8

Thought). It seemed to have taken a definite form in *Japanese Spirituality*, wherein Suzuki used the term "spirituality" with positive significance for the first time.

Lastly, in *Rinzai no kihon shisō* (The Fundamental Thought of Rinzai) we find D. T. Suzuki's sixth thought-peak, where his thought reaches such heights of lucidity and profundity. In 1943 he wrote *Shūkyō keiken jijitsu* (Facts of Religious Experience), another fine work. The result of his study in seeking the "facts of religious experience" in Rinzai's thought was *The Fundamental Thought of Rinzai*. In the first chapter, entitled *"Konnichi no mondai"* (The Question of Today), he points out as "the question of today" that studies in Rinzai's Zen had not developed at all from the traditional interpretations of *Rinzai-roku* (Saying of Rinzai) by past Zen masters. He insists that the only way to grasp Rinzai alive is to inquire into his religious experience, apart from which there could be no worthwhile discussion. He writes: "By 'The Question of Today' I mean the facts of religious experience."

In the succeeding chapters, on *"Rinzai no taiken"* (Rinzai's Experience), and *"Taiken no seishitsu"* (The Nature of his Experience), he stresses the importance of Rinzai's *"Nin"*-thought. He writes that *"Nin"* (Person) is spirituality and that Rinzai's experience was his spiritual awakening. He devoted himself completely to writing this book, and in it his great enthusiasm can be clearly traced. This naturally moves the reader. D. T. Suzuki's thinking attains particular profundity here, where all his previous thought is concentrated to make a great towering monument. *The Fundamental Thought of Rinzai* might belong to the same category as *Bankei on the 'Unborn'* since they possess common elements. Suzuki's interest in Rinzai's Zen and in Bankei's Zen might be said to be more or less identical. I myself, however, think that D. T. Suzuki's thought in his study on Rinzai is deeper and wider, that his sixth thought-peak does not yield to the fifth or to any other.

To sum up, D. T. Suzuki's thought always developed in his endeavour to grasp Buddhism through actual experience. With Bankei, or Rinzai, or the rest, he wanted to find out experientially what experience gave birth to Bankei's, or Rinzai's, thought. He did not study their thought outwardly or superficially, but inquired inwardly, into their inmost sources. Needless to say, such an approach is by no means easy; it takes a man who is prepared to tread a great by-path, step by step, slowly and

9

steadily.

Contemporary Buddhist studies made remarkable progress from Meiji through the Taishō and Shōwa periods, and we should not fail to appreciate the significance of the work done behind this progress, by people like D. T. Suzuki who steadily carried on their inner-directed seeking without dispersing their attention on outward aspects. In his private life and academic career, his way was never easy, and often he must have felt keenly the disadvantages of such a route. Yet patiently and serenely he went his way. Not only in Buddhist studies, but in any field, without a handful of sincere scholars willing to undertake such a course, shrewd productions will probably appear, but they will be superficial, with everyone hastening to dash up the main road.

Let me borrow from "The Question of Today," from D. T. Suzuki's *The Fundamental Thought of Rinzai,* and remark that the question of today's Buddhist study is that it neglects the experiential approach to Buddhist studies based on religious experience.

Though universally known as a Zen scholar, D. T. Suzuki was also an authoritative scholar of Pure Land Buddhism, another representative Buddhist thought in Japan. This book will give readers some idea of his interpretations of Pure Land thought.

The first edition of *Nihon-teki reisei* (Japanese Spirituality) had a fifth chapter, "*Kongō-kyō no zen*" (Zen in the Diamond Sutra), which was omitted in the second edition. As this translation was based on the second edition, the fifth chapter has not been included here. I should mention however that "Zen in the Diamond Sutra," though it remains untranslated, is an outstanding example of the author's work on Zen thought.

Shōkin Furuta
Director, Matsugaoka Library
Kamakura, Japan
1969

10

JAPANESE SPIRITUALITY

INTRODUCTION

1. The meaning of seishin (精神)

Before discussing Japanese spirituality I first should draw a distinction between *seishin* (psyche; mind; spirit) and *reisei* (spirituality; spirit-nature). *Reisei* is not commonly used, but *seishin*—especially recently—is often heard. I think once we clarify the meaning of *seishin*, *reisei*'s meaning will become clear as well.

Since *seishin* is employed with such a wide variety of meanings there is a great deal of confusion surrounding it. When I was a child, in the early years of the Meiji period (1868–1912), the saying "if the *seishin* is firm, nothing is impossible," was common. Then, *seishin* had the meaning of *will:* to the possessor of an unbending will all things are possible. Since basically will—using the word in its broadest sense—could be called the essential creative force of all things in the universe, when it is manifested in us, in each individual human being, it can be understood in the psychological sense of "will power." Any task can be accomplished if only this will power is strong enough.

The Sung Dynasty Confucian Chu Hsi properly emphasized the power of *seishin* when he said, "Where emanates the spirit of *yang*, even metal and stone can be penetrated." In the Buddhist scriptures it is written that "If the mind is controlled in one place, there is nothing that cannot be accomplished." This is because the will is finally none other than the power of attention. *Seishin*, then, may be called the power of concentration. But concentration or will power does not seem to be implied in the words "Japanese *seishin*" that have resounded in our ears in recent experience. That is because power of concentration, will, is not connected with Japan, China, Judea, or any other one country.

Originally, both *sei* 精 and *shin* 神, which together make up the compound word *sei-shin*, probably had individual meanings of *kokoro* (心 mind; heart). But since the word *kokoro* is itself replete with problems, saying that *seishin* is *kokoro* brings us no closer to understanding *seishin*.

We find in the *Tso Chuan* (the 25th year of the Duke of Chao)[1]: "The *seisō* 精爽 part of the mind is what we call the soul (*kompaku* 魂魄)."

11

Yet here *sei* 精 of the compound *seisō* means *shin* 神. Thus it seems that even though *sei-shin* 精神 is a compound word, it reverts finally to the meaning of the single character *shin* 神. Inasmuch as *shin* is the opposite of (bodily) form 形 and (material) objects 物, it may be said to be the same as *kokoro*.

In a book entitled *"Dialogues between a Fisherman and Woodcutter"*[2] we read: "While alive, *kon* 魂 functions; when the body returns to earth, *haku* 魄 remains; *kon* ascends to heaven, *haku* returns to the earth."[3] In this light it should not be too difficult to see the three words *kompaku*, *seishin*, and *kokoro* as having a similar meaning. It would perhaps be profitable to delve into this sort of thing using detailed examples (to clarify the currently popular meaning of the word *seishin* would be extremely useful), but since I cannot now pursue that course I will satisfy myself with a look at how the average Japanese of today understands the compound word *seishin*.

Stated briefly, *seishin* is *kokoro*, *tamashii*, the nucleus of things. Yet in the word *tamashii* are contained meanings which would not hold for *seishin*; this would be true of the word *kokoro* as well. When we speak of the samurai's *tamashii* or of *nihon-damashii* (the *tamashii* of Japan), it would not follow that their meanings are directly transposable to the meaning of the samurai's *seishin*, or *nihon-seishin*. There may well be situations in which they are the same, but *tamashii* is imbued with concreteness, while *seishin* carries with it more of an abstract quality.

This is perhaps because *tamashii* is originally a Japanese word, while *seishin* derives from Chinese literature. All such "Japanese" words seem to be weak on the abstract, general, conceptual side. *Tamashii* brings to mind a round object rolling before one's eyes. To me, *seishin* suggests vastness and shapelessness. When we speak of the "fullness of *seishin*," there is something quite concrete and sensitive, but it does not give the sense of actually seeing something before one's eyes. Therefore, we speak of the "spirit (*seishin*) of the age"; for some reason "*tamashii* of the age" does not ring true. I wonder if the original meaning of *tamashii* did not have some implications pertaining to the individual. As has been seen, in China *seishin* could have a meaning of *kompaku*, but this was not necessarily so in Japan.

One could not say that *seishin* and *kokoro* are one; mental science is not only psychology. The "*seishin* of law-making" could not be replaced

12

by *kokoro*, where the meaning of *seishin* would include such as advocacy, reason, and even logic.

In Japan, Chinese characters are used in addition to the original Yamato language. Moreover, Chinese characters have in most cases been given to words borrowed from Europe and America. The modern Japanese language therefore has become strangely and highly complex.

Before the classical Japanese language, that is, Japanese culture, was able to achieve independent growth, there began an influx of continental literature and thought, and the Japanese were obliged almost to limp their way along. Then from the beginning of Meiji, European and American culture rushed on in waves, and there were really not enough days in which to make up, helter-skelter, all the new words for all the many new things people had crammed into their heads. Such is the condition that has continued to prevail to the present. So, without stopping to consider whether *seishin* meant *kokoro* or *tamashii*, the Japanese have combined characters and coined new words indiscriminately, under pretext that the old forms were euphonically uninteresting, etc. Indiscriminate new word combinations have been and still are being manufactured, consciously and unconsciously, in all cultural quarters. Once they are coined—even though they might have been intended for just a short period of use—vested interests form around them which become highly difficult to remove. Though they might be inconvenient or even inappropriate, their power to live on becomes more and more tenacious as time passes.

The two characters that form that word *sei-shin* have thus come to contain many meanings. Generally, however, I think it is justified to understand it in the following way. *Seishin*, in the phrase "Japanese *seishin*," is an idea or ideal. An ideal does not necessarily have to be recognized as such; historically hidden, it may follow the occasional changes that accompany the trend of the times. If it rises to consciousness, it is *seishin*. It has not actually stayed within the consciousness of the Japanese people since the beginning of the national life, nor has it always appeared in the same guise throughout history.

Although when we speak of an ideal we are concerned with the future or with objectives, previous existence seems rather to be implied in *seishin*. In reality, however, *seishin* always comes to consciousness swelled with the future.

13

Were it unrelated to the future and capable only of celebrating the past, it would not be living, and thus not truly be *seishin*, but merely the blind love and devotion of a mother clinging to the body of her dead child. Japanese *seishin* has to be called the ideal of the Japanese people. It also has an ethical nature, for an ideal must always possess a moral foundation.

When we speak of something having the quality of *seishin*, it assumes a nature diametrically opposed to substance. It is of course not limited to matters of a religious character.

A man of the spirit (*seishin-ka*) is one who is not attached to forms, not slave to formalism or to philosophies which stress the pre-eminence of the material. He carries one moral idea with him and tries to apply it to all things.

A history of *seishin* would have the same meaning as a history of culture. It would deal with the separation of man from nature, and with all the human productions that have been superimposed upon nature. Restricted to the area of thought, a history of thought would be more limited.

To conclude, it may be said that when we speak of *seishin* we conjure up an opposition between it and the material, between it and form. In other words, dualistic thought is always held within *seishin*. If *seishin* is not in rivalry against the material, it holds a position of superiority over it. It never holds the material within it. Still less can the notion that *seishin* is material, or that material is *seishin*, ever be stated from the side of *seishin*. Where *seishin* is not at odds with the material, it is certain either to tread over the latter, or else to manifest a clear disposition to do so. Where dualistic thought does not exist, neither does *seishin*. Herein is discerned the singularity of the concept *seishin*.

2. *The Meaning of Reisei* (霊性)

Now it is perhaps time to explain what I mean by spirituality. Although as was noted before, the word *reisei* is seldom used,[4] I wish to have its meaning encompass things not included within the word *seishin*, or within the more commonly used *kokoro*.

In a view that sees *seishin* (or *kokoro*) in opposition to substance, *seishin* cannot be contained within substance, and substance cannot be contained within *seishin*. There is something more which must be seen at the innermost depths of *seishin* and substance. As long as two things oppose each other contradiction, rivalry, mutual suppression, and annihilation will be unavoidable. Where this occurs man's existence cannot continue. What is needed is something that somehow sees that the two are really not two, but one, and that the one is, as it is, two. It is *reisei* that does this. For the heretofore dualistic world to cease its rivalries and become conciliatory and fraternal, and for mutual interpenetration and self-identity to prevail, one must await the awakening of man's *reisei*. In a sense, another world opens up on the far side of the world of *seishin* and substance, where the two of them must come to harmony, though still remaining mutually contradictory. This is possible through spiritual insight, the awakening of spirituality.

Reisei might be called religious consciousness, except that misconceptions tend to arise when we speak of religion. Japanese do not seem to have a very profound understanding when it comes to religion. They think of it as another name for superstition, or that religious belief can support something, anything, which has nothing to do with religion. Consequently, I do not speak of religious consciousness, but *reisei*.

Yet basically, to the degree one does not raise a consciousness toward religion it is not understandable. This could probably be said about most other things as well, and with the ordinary consciousness a certain amount of sympathy and imagination is allowable.

Only when it comes to religion it is absolutely necessary if the operation of *reisei* is to come into play: that is, religion is understood only with the awakening of *reisei*. I do not mean to suggest *reisei* possesses an ability to perform some special activity, but that its *hataraki*, or "operation," is different from that of *seishin*. *Seishin* has an ethical character which *reisei* transcends—although this transcendence does not imply negation or denial. *Seishin* is founded in the discriminatory consciousness; *reisei* is non-discriminatory wisdom. Again, that does not mean *reisei* is produced by discarding or ignoring intellectual discrimination. *Seishin* does not always function as an agent in thought or in logic. It sometimes presses on by means of will power and intuition, another area in which it closely resembles *reisei*. Yet the intuitive power of *reisei* is based on a higher plane than that of *seishin*. *Seishin*'s will power is not able to transcend the self unless it relies upon the support of *reisei*. There is an

15

impure residue in *seishin*-power by itself. This residue is the self, or the various forms the self assumes. As long as it exists, the true meaning of Prince Shōtoku's words, "Harmony is to be valued,"[5] cannot be penetrated.

3. Spirituality and the Growth of Culture

A people cannot awaken to spirituality until they have proceeded a certain degree up the cultural ladder. In a certain sense, the existence of spirituality cannot be denied even in the consciousness of a primitive people, though it would have to be of an extremely primitive nature. It would be a mistake to regard it as the same as genuine and refined spirituality itself.

Even after a culture has advanced to a certain point, it still cannot be said that its people as a whole have awakened to, and are in possession of, spirituality. In speaking of the Japanese of today it cannot be asserted that all have awakened to spirituality, or that this or that person has a true understanding. A great number of Japanese today as well have not emerged beyond a primitive religious consciousness. They would even pursue true spirituality within such a primitive consciousness. The awakening of spirituality is an individual experience, replete with concreteness. It accompanies the advancement of national culture and manifests itself in the individuals within that culture. These people transmit their experience to others, and others may follow in turn, but the people as a whole do not have this type of experience. Some do not encounter the opportunity to experience spirituality's awakening. Others do not have sufficient inner preparation even though provided with the opportunity. Thus even though they are capable of having a yearning and a liking for a primitive religious consciousness, they may not be able beyond that to touch spirituality. Poetry is read to one who understands it, while wine is to be taken with one who knows you. Those who cannot see the interest in these things could not understand them even were they given extensive explanations about them. The mind's consciousness is controlled with extreme firmness and tenacity by a primitive mentality.

4. Spirituality and Religious Consciousness

Although I think the concept of spirituality can be understood from the

16

discussion to this point, there might still be some who would consider placing spirituality outside of *seishin*, making one more confrontation in addition to the one between *seishin* and substance. This placing a head on top of the one you already have is extremely diffusive, so briefly let me state once again, that spirituality is the operation latent in the depths of *seishin*; when it awakens, the duality with *seishin* dissolves. *Seishin* in this true form can sense, think, will, and act. What is generally called *seishin* is unable to touch its own subjectivity, its own true self.

In religious terms, we could say that man's *seishin* experiences the awakening of its spirituality. Religious consciousness is the experience of spirituality. If *seishin*, when it opposes substance and thereby becomes all the more enfettered, has an opportunity to come into contact with spirituality, the troubles of this antagonistic rivalry will fall away of themselves. This is religion in its true sense. Religion is commonly regarded by Japanese as something organized or institutionalized, whereby something or other manufactured by the group consciousness is added to the foundation of the individual religious experience. Although spirituality can sometimes be found there, in most cases this degenerates into mere formality. Even though religious thought, ritual, systems, and sentiment appear, they are by no means religious experience. It is to this experience itself spirituality belongs.

5. *Japanese Spirituality*

I believe now my definition of spirituality should be generally understood. Clearer also, I hope, is the conceptual sphere which surrounds spirituality and *seishin*. Moreover, it should be evident that the awakening of religious consciousness is the awakening of spirituality, and that this also means that *seishin* itself has started to move at its roots. One can understand that because of this, spirituality has universality and is not limited to any particular people or nation. To the extent the Chinese, Europeans, Americans, or Japanese possess spirituality, they are similar. Following the awakening of spirituality, however, each have their respective differences in the patterns or forms in which the phenomena of *seishin's* activity manifest themselves.

What then is the Japanese character of spirituality? In my own opinion, it exists in its purest form in Jōdo (Pure Land) thought and in Zen. The reason for this is simple. Jōdo and Zen are schools of Buddhism. As an imported religion, Buddhism might appear dubious in a role either in the awakening of a purely Japanese spirituality or in the expression of that spirituality. But since in my view Buddhism is not primarily an imported religion, I feel that neither Zen nor Pure Land possesses a foreign nature. Of course, Buddhism did come from the continent, probably during the reign of the Emperor Kimmei (539–571), but what entered was Buddhist ritual and its trappings. This importation did not bring with it the awakening of Japanese spirituality. Though it is said there was opposition to its importation, this opposition was colored with political overtones and could have had nothing to do with Japanese spirituality itself. Buddhism began to make itself felt in the realm of architecture as well as in other arts and sciences, yet this again had no relation to Japanese spirituality, being rather the assimilation of various spheres of continental culture. The spirituality of the Japanese people had not yet come into operation—there was no living connection between it and Buddhism.

Through the catalytic influence of Buddhism a genuine religious consciousness came to the fore among the Japanese; that its expression took Buddhistic form was but a historical accident. We must penetrate this fortuity in order to discover the true marrow of Japanese spirituality beneath. Although the sects of Shinto might be regarded as transmitters of Japanese spirituality, Japanese spirituality does not appear there in a pure form. Those traditions labelled Shrine Shinto, or Ancient Shinto,[6] being fixations of the Japanese people's primitive conventions, did not touch spirituality. Of Japaneseness they had more than enough, but the light of spirituality had not yet emerged from within. No doubt others would hold that spirituality was there in abundance, but I cannot concur with such a view. In certain areas the question of spirituality allows no room for discussion, for the matter would only end in futile argument.

6. Zen

Zen typifies Japanese spirituality. This does not mean Zen has deep roots within the life of the Japanese people, rather that Japanese life itself is 'Zen-like.' The importation of Zen provided the opportunity for Japanese spirituality to ignite, yet the constituents themselves which were to ignite were fully primed at that time. Zen arrived in Japan riding the wave of Chinese thought, literature, and art, but Japanese spirituality was by no means seduced by these trappings. It was nothing like the entrance of Buddhist literature and thought that took place during the Nara period (646–794). The Buddhism of the Nara and Heian periods was merely tied conceptually to the life of the upper classes, whereas Zen put down its roots in the midst of the life of the Japanese samurai. It was cultivated and it budded in that which existed at the depths of the samurai's *seishin*. These buds were not foreign clippings but developed from the very life of the Japanese warrior. I said it put down roots, but that is not quite the correct expression. It would be better to say the spirituality of the samurai was on the verge of breaking through to the surface, and that Zen removed all the obstacles from its path. This was the occasion, the exact moment for "breaking out of the shell"; the mother hen pecks from the outside of the shell at the same time the chick pecks from within. Thereupon, although the Zen Sect of Japan was content to allow the supremacy of Chinese literature, the Zen life of the Japanese came to full flower in Japanese spirituality.

Because of this Shinto, which is considered the essence of Japanese-ness, came under the influence of Zen. This "Zen-ization" reveals all the more, because it was unconscious, the Zen character of Japanese spirituality. Shintoists would consciously deny this "unconscious" process beneath the surface, but those acquainted with the special characteristics of human consciousness will readily discern that this denial is essentially none other than affirmation.

7. *Jōdo (Pure Land) Thought*

To gain an understanding of Japanese spirituality in Pure Land thought, and in Shinshū belief in particular, it is necessary to distinguish distinctly between Shinshū the Shin Sect, which is a group entity, and Shinshū experience, which is the foundation of this group. Unless this distinction is sufficiently understood, one might be led to conclude that there is nothing less Japanese than Shinshū belief. That is because the thought of all Pure Land schools is based on the accounts of the Three Pure Land Sutras,[7] which, it will be said, are wholly and decidedly Indian in nature as well as in fact. Yet such an idea sees only the surface of things;

19

it does not, it must be said, penetrate even the thinnest of paper.

Shinshū followers give scriptural authority to these three sutras. Why, then, did something like the Shin Sect not unfold in India or China? Although the growth of the Pure Land school took place in China during the Six Dynasties period (A.D. 222–589), since that time 1500 years have elapsed. In spite of this the Chinese Pure Land school of 1500 years ago is the same as the Pure Land school of today. It did not produce the ōchō ("leaping sideways")[8] experience of the Shin Sect, nor the absolute *Tariki* ("Other-power") view of Amida's salvation.[9] In Japan, Hōnen made the Jōdo Sect independant of Tendai doctrine, and tried to clarify its significance as a separate sect. Scarcely had he finished when from among his disciples appeared Shinran, who effected great and rapid progress in his master's Pure Land thought. The activity of Japanese spirituality during the Kamakura period would not allow a stop even at the Pure Land thought of Hōnen; it was not satisfied until it had produced Shinran.[10] This occurrence should not be considered accidental. Had it not been for Japanese spirituality, the progression of this transcendental experience would not have born fruit within Pure Land thought.

Pure Land thought existed in India as well as China, but only in Japan did it assume, via Hōnen and Shinran, the form of the Shin Sect. That sequence of events must be said to have been dependent upon the active manifestation of Japanese spirituality, that is, Japanese religious consciousness. Had this happened with Japanese spirituality as merely a passive player, probably such a movement would not have occurred, and Pure Land thought no doubt would merely have been accepted as it was, foreign importation or whatever. Japanese spirituality's awakening, and the external means which provided the chance for that awakening, must be considered separately. Even a passivity which does nothing but receive has to have some active element; but in this case—the case of the ōchō experience of Shinshū faith—an active nature alone would not have sufficed. It was absolutely necessary that the influence of a great and powerful force emerge from within Japanese spirituality. When this influence was expressed through Pure Land thought the Pure Land Shin Sect was born.

Shinshū experience is really nothing else than the exercise of Japanese spirituality. That it emerged within a Buddhist context was a matter of historical chance—it does not prevent in the least the essential quality

20

of the Shin Sect from being identified with Japanese spirituality.

8. *Zen and Jōdo—Directness*

Pure Land experience is manifested on the affective or emotional side of Japanese spirituality; on its intellectual side appears the transformation to Zen of Japanese life. Distinctions such as intellectual and emotional are not very satisfactory, their very existence breeds confusion. But I will nevertheless use them for the moment. The emotional development of Japanese spirituality points to the unconditional Great Compassion of the Absolute One. It transcends good and evil and brings its all-pervading Light to all beings. The *Tariki* thought of Hōnen and Shinran makes clear with the utmost boldness and surety the reason for this. The Great Compassion of the Absolute One, Amida, is neither hindered by evil nor broadened by good; it is absolutely unconditional, it transcends all discriminations. It cannot be experienced without Japanese spirituality. Shinran, for this reason, points in particular to Prince Shōtoku (573–621) as the spiritual head of Japan. Although Shinran's awakening to Pure Land thought was thanks to Hōnen, he attained an unmistakable grasp of the absolute *Tariki* experience about which Hōnen had not spoken exhaustively. Tracing back from Hōnen until he reached Prince Shōtoku, he was obviously conscious of the Japanese character of his own spirituality. Should not the fact that this consciousness was not produced in India or China, and was possible in Japan alone, encourage us to seek here something of the special characteristics of Japanese spirituality?

It is impossible in the world of dualistic logic for beings to have a connection to the highest reality without the intervention of some intermediate condition; yet Japanese spirituality accomplishes this connection directly, without any difficulty. This is a wonder that can also be discovered in the Zen character of Japanese life. Zen's singularity rests in its emphasis upon "going-straight-ahead-ness," finding itself on this point in the same orbit as Shinshū experience. The Zen master Bukkō Kokushi aimed at this when he told Hōjō Tokimune, in answer to the latter's question as to how he should rid himself of his cherished self: "Shut out all your thoughts!" It may also be seen in the words the master Minki spoke to Kusunoki Masashige (1294–1336), when the latter came to a Zen monastery at Hyōgo as he was about to meet the overwhelming army of Ashikaga Takauji. Masashige asked him: "When a man is at the parting of the ways between life and death, how should he behave?" Minki answered, "Cut off your dualism and let the one sword stand serenely by itself against the sky!"[11] Between these two a mediator cannot enter. Although the "purity" of the Japanese spirit lies in possessing nothing at all, just thrusting oneself as is into the bosom of the "other," it can be discussed in the realm of spirituality as well. Where this purity has begun to work in its most fundamental aspect spirituality appears. When the 'bright and pure heart' of the Japanese ceases to work on the surface of consciousness and begins to move submerged in its deepest parts, when it is moving unconsciously, with non-discrimination, without thought, then Japanese spirituality can be understood. The singularity of Japanese spirituality is manifested in this feature of "no-thought"; it can be seen in various aspects of Japanese life. This is usually termed the permeation of Zen thought, but it would be better to say that viewed from the standpoint of the Japanese people, Japanese spirituality makes its word and deed speak through the form of Zen.

While Zen arose in China, it did not penetrate deeply the practical life of the Chinese people. Because Kegon (Hua-yen), Tendai (T'ien-t'ai), Yuishiki (Wei-shih), and so on were not at all assimilated by the Chinese people, Chinese Buddhism was made to take the form of Zen and Jōdo. With the Zen development of Buddhism, the School of Reason of the Sung Confucians was brought to completion,[12] and the Ōyōmei (Wang Yang-ming) school of the Ming Dynasty arose.[13] Yet Buddhism did not permeate the ordinary life of the Chinese people in the form of Zen, but prevailed instead as a doctrine of karmic retribution. For the Chinese, guided by the thought and feeling of a northern people, a doctrine of good actions leading to good rewards, which has about it a logical nature, would probably be more effective than the Zen-type thought of the south. For this reason too, Pure Land thought could not have been conceived as a Shinran-like ōchō experience. There is, after all, a foundation in the Japanese character which must be called the way of thinking or way of feeling of the southern Chinese tradition. In this, Zen and the Japanese people seem to possess naturally the inclination for a ready and close friendship. The paintings of the Chinese Zen artist Mu-ch'i (Mokkei) were not appreciated in their native country. That they were preserved only in Japan may be explained by the above remarks as well.

22

Motoori Norinaga (1730–1801) was displeased by this inclination to the logic of the Chinese mind.[14] He avowed he chose to accept things directly and naively in their natural appearance as they were bequeathed by his Japanese ancestors. This was due finally to the points of disparity between the northern and southern traditions in their ways of thinking and feeling. The phrase *kannagara*[15] must fall into the same tradition of thought as the "Shut out all your thoughts!" of the southern school. Here perhaps is the reason as well Shinto thought tends to a Taoistic vein. Yet Zen is not just "no-thought"; there is also its Chinese generation and Indian roots. And we must not overlook the fact that there was a certain speculative refinement added to plain *kannagara*.

Zen traces its source to the Indian thought of the southern tradition. It materialized within the northern tradition as seen in the Chinese people, where nurtured by a northern temper, it possessed a quite positive and practical nature. Going eastward across the sea, it touched the southern tradition as present in the spirituality of the Japanese people. Japanese spirituality thus on the one hand accepted the practical, logical nature of the Chinese people; but more than that, it perceived in Zen what should be termed the intuitive nature of the Indian people as well, with its southern character. The Japanese felt a kind of satisfaction when they saw the shape of their spirituality reflected here. From the beginning there has been something in Japanese spirituality that could be regarded as "Zen-like." Since this was awakened by the chance appearance of Zen, it would be confusing cause and effect to say that Zen is foreign.

This explains why Zen sympathized so directly and deeply with the mentality of the Kamakura warrior class. This meeting occurred during the Kamakura period in particular because until that time Japanese spirituality had been in dormancy. The relation between the people and the earth first became close in Kamakura times, and the breath of spirituality was interchanged between them. Hōnen and Shinran arose abruptly during this age, and the samurai became frequent visitors at the Zen monasteries. On through the Muromachi period (1336–1568) Zen seems to have become an increasingly deep expression of Japanese life. (A more detailed treatment of this topic will have to wait for a future time. Some areas are touched upon in my *Zen and Japanese Culture*, and [in Japanese], *Studies in Pure Land Thought*.[16])

23

NOTES

1 左伝昭公二十五年
2 *Yü ch'iao tui wên* 漁樵対問 by Shao Yung 邵雍 (A.D. 1011–1077) of the Sung Dynasty. Trans.
3 As this passage indicates, the soul or spiritual part of man—represented here by the compound *kompaku*—is divided into two elements: *kon*, which death separates from the body; and *haku*, which remains with the body even after death.
4 In a postcard written in 1947 (*Suzuki Daisetz Zenshū*, Vol. 29, Tokyo, 1970, p. 409) Dr. Suzuki stated that he felt "spiritual" an inadequate rendering of *reisei*. Since, however, there is actually no appropriate English word for *reisei* in the sense it is used here, I have chosen for want of a better alternative to render it as "spirituality" throughout the remainder of the translation. It may be said to be generally synonymous with "religious consciousness," used elsewhere in this work. Trans.
5 "Harmony is to be valued" comprises the first article of the so-called Seventeen Article Constitution, a document which, according to the *Nihongi* (Chronicles of Japan), was issued by Prince Shōtoku (572–622) in 604. See *Zen and Japanese Culture* (New York: 1959) pp. 274–276. Trans.
6 Shrine Shinto (Jinja Shinto) or Ancient Shinto refers to the pre-Buddhist Shinto centered around the ancient Shinto shrines (*jinja*) that is said to be Japan's native religion. It is sometimes called Kokka (State) Shinto as differentiated from Sectarian Shinto. Trans.
7 *Sambu-kyō* (三部経), the 3 main sutras of the Pure Land schools: 1. The *Sukhâvativyūha Sutra*, which treats of the Land of Bliss inhabited by Amitābha Buddha, and of the 48 (forty-three in the Sanskrit text) vows of the same Amitābha; 2. *Sutra of the Meditations on Buddha Amitāyus*, in which Queen Vaidehī is instructed by Sākyamuni to practice 16 forms of meditation regarding the Land of Bliss and its Lord; and 3. The *Sutra of Amitābha*, which is generally known as the *Smaller Sukhāvativyūha*, as it also describes the Land of Bliss. Amitāyus (Eternal Life) and Amitābha (Infinite Light) refer to one and the same Buddha.
8 *Ōchō* 横超. Shinran, the founder of the Shin branch of the Pure Land school, teaches that the way to be absolutely assured of one's rebirth (Ōjō) in the Pure Land is to accept wholeheartedly the Original Prayer announced by Amida, and that this acceptance is effected when one has what Shinran designates as a 'side-wise leap' or a 'leaping cross-wise' (*ōchō*). Instead of following a continuous logical passage of ratiocination, he tells us to abandon all our intellectual calculations and to jump right down into what seems to be a dark bottomless abyss of the absolute, when the white road to the Pure Land opens up before us.
9 *Tariki*—"Other-Power" 他力: Shin makes the distinction between *Tariki* and *Jiriki*. *Jiriki* 自力 means "Self-Power," or depending on one's own virtue for rebirth in the Pure Land, while *Tariki*, literally "Other-Power," is to put oneself in a state of complete passivity and lose the self altogether in the Other, i.e., Amida.

24

According to Shin Zen is *Jiriki* and Shin is pure *Tariki*.

10 The Jōdo 浄土 and Shin 真 sects (Jōdo-shū and Shin-shū) both belong to the Pure Land school. Jōdo means the "Pure Land" and the official title of the Shin sect is Jōdo-Shin and not just Shin. Shin means 'true' and its devotees claim that their teaching is truly *Tariki* whereas the Jōdo is not quite so, being mixed with the Jiriki idea; hence Shin ('true') is added to Jōdo.

The main points of difference between the Jōdo and the Shin teaching are essentially two: 1. Jōdo fully believes with Shin in the efficacy of Amida's Prayer but thinks that Amida's Name is to be repeatedly recited, whereas Shin places its emphasis upon faith and not necessarily upon the Nembutsu, which is the repeated recitation of the Name. 2. Jōdo encourages good works as helpful for the devotee being born in the Pure Land, whereas Shin finds here a residue of the *Jiriki* (Self-power) and insists that as long as the devotee awakens his whole-hearted faith in Amida, Amida will take care of him unconditionally, absolutely assuring his entrance into the Pure Land. Whatever Nembutsu he may offer to Amida it is no more than the grateful appreciation of the favor of the Buddha.

11 Literally, "Cut off two heads, and let one sword stand cold against the sky."

12 Li-hsüeh (理学: J. Rigaku).

13 Ōyōmei is the Japanese rendering of the name Wang Yang-ming (王陽明), the Chinese Neo-Confucianist of the 16th century who became the most important advocate of the School of Mind, opposing the school of Reason (Principle) of Chu Hsi and the Sung Confucianists. It became an important school in Japan, espoused by men such as Nakae Tōju (1608–1648) and Kumazawa Banzan (1619–1691). See *Sources of Japanese Tradition*, compiled by Theodore De Bary, Donald Keene and Tsunoda Ryusaku, New York 1958, pp. 378–392. Trans.

14 Motoori Norinaga-本居宣長 the great classical scholar of the Edo period who argued for a return to primitive Shinto and a rejection of Chinese ideas (Confucianism). Trans.

15 *Kannagara*—a composite term: *kan*, that is, *kami*, is "deity" and *nagara* is "in accordance with," "in conformity with," or "as it is." *Kannagara* thus means "in accordance with the gods," or "such as the gods are;" more fully, it is "in conformity to the gods'will," or "to follow the gods in such a way as they are in themselves," or "to be like the gods," or "to reflect in oneself the image of the gods." Shinto is called "the Way of the Gods," *kannagara*, or *kannagara no michi*. See *History of Philosophy: Eastern and Western* (London: Allen Unwin, 1952), Chapter XXV, p. 596.

16 *Jōdo-kei Shisō-ron* 浄土系思想論, Kyoto: Hōzōkan, 1942. In Vol. 6 of *Suzuki Daisetz Zenshū*.

CHAPTER 1　JAPANESE SPIRITUALITY AND THE KAMAKURA PERIOD

Here I will attempt to explain the first awakening of Japanese spirituality in the Kamakura period. This was originally entitled, "One Phase of Japanese Spiritual History."[1] *It first appeared in the magazine* Shindō *published by the Shindō Kaikan of Nagoya, and was later included in* Culture and Religion.[2] *My original intention was to write a general history of the Japanese* seishin. *This has given way to an extremely broad description of the Kamakura period (1185–1333). It appears here in a more or less revised form. The term "religious consciousness" has at times been used in addition to "Japanese spirituality," because at that time I saw Japanese spiritual history mainly from this direction. Because many readers had considerable interest there, I limited Japanese spirituality, that is, the rise of religious impulses or religious consciousness, mainly to the area of the Pure Land sects.*

*　　　*　　　*　　　*

To begin I will give my conclusions. The ancient Japanese, a simple, natural, and child-like people, really had no religion. Through the Heian era to the Kamakura, religious impulses for the first time stirred their spirituality, and the awakening of Japanese spirituality began faintly to appear. These impulses resulted in the rise of Ise Shinto on the one hand, and on the other brought about the Buddhism of the Pure Land tradition. During this period the Japanese first awakened to religion and perceived their own spirituality.

27

I. THE EMOTIONAL LIFE

1. The Manyōshū

A look at this collection of verse will, I think, yield general agreement that the ancient Japanese lacked a strong religious consciousness. The Manyōshū[3] was compiled around twelve hundred years ago. Its poems give us a nakedly sung record of the spiritual life of the ancient Japanese. Since poems were collected from the palace and from the populace as well, we are given, on the whole, very fine data with which to see the ancients' spiritual life. Briefly, this life could be described as simple, honest, and natural; love of the mountains, love of the rivers and streams, the sorrow of parting, bravery in battle, the love of man for woman and woman for man, yearnings, grief for the dead, respect for the Emperor, fear of the *kami*, and on and on; all the feelings of the natural man are sung. Here man's inherent emotions are just as they are, as yet not having passed even once through any great trial. The people of these poems have not wholly emerged from their child-like nature. Theirs is the life, often referred to by religious scholars, of a soul yet to experience rebirth.

From ancient times the Japanese people have been lovers of the beauties of nature. Yamabe Akahito's famous

> *To the beach of Tago*
> *I come, and, behold,*
> *In pure whiteness enveloped*
> *There rises Mount Fuji—*
> *Snowing it seems above us!*

and

> *The tide flows into Waka Bay,*
> *And the cranes, with the lagoons lost in flood,*
> *Go crying toward the reedy shore.*

are truly representative of the Japanese taste.

The ancient Japanese loved the plum blossoms, the cherry blossoms, and the moon. This is a poem composed at a plum blossom-viewing party:

28

The plum blossoms fall in the garden;
Are they really snow-flakes
Floating from the sky?

This is a bit fanciful. The first line speaks of plum blossoms, then the poet wonders if they might not be snow-flakes falling in the garden. And yet that is no doubt how the situation was actually experienced.

Even at this early date the association of plum blossoms and the *uguisu*, or Japanese bush warbler, was already established.

Lamenting the plum flowers falling in the garden,
I hear the sad cry of the uguisu.

The next poem was written at a poetry-composing party. The subject is snow.

Looking at the brightness of the new-fallen snow
Now covering everything under heaven,
My heart is filled with awe.

It is natural that Love Songs should occupy a large part of the collection. Love between man and woman is an emotion of the greatest strength and the ancients sang of it with especial openness. The theme 'Love' was one of those used in later times for training in poetical composition. Even monks who had supposedly renounced the world wrote love poems which were chosen for inclusion in Imperial poem collections. But such was not yet the case in *Manyō* times. The actual emotions were simple and honest. What could be called the "arts of love" were really not in evidence. Happiness at seeing one another, the sadness of parting, yearning for the deceased, etc.—these were merely subjects. Reflections or speculations on the sorrow that comes from love itself do not appear anywhere in the *Manyōshū*. Nowhere is a child-like and natural love exceeded. Though love's tragedies are one of many opportunities that may drive man to religion, man must be mentally ripe for it.

Those who are unable to proceed as far as religion when faced with disappointment, discontent, or despair sometimes soak themselves in wine. Wine, in a toxic, psychological way, temporarily presents a face of

29

life-affirmation. In a certain sense, it smacks of religion. The ancient Japanese, however, do not seem to have considered it in such a light. The renowned wine-drinkers of ancient China are placed within a religious setting. The religion of the Persians praised the virtues of drink. This is not the case with the Japanese. Since the wine-drinking poems in the *Manyōshū* only imitate the tradition of the Seven Wise Men of the Bamboo Grove and the Eight Sage Drinkers of China, they lack any real spiritual depth. The pleasures of wine-bibbing do not transcend the emotional level of the Heian nobility's, "Today, once again, I pass the time away, shading myself with a spray of cherry blossoms."

The next poem is one of thirteen written in praise of wine by Ōtomo Tabito.

> *Rather than spend thought on unavailing things,*
> *Better to drink a cup of wine.*

The meaning here is just as it appears on the surface, with no deeper spirituality to be found.

The poetry of the *Manyōshū* is not entirely without ideas of life and death. References are made to after-life and the like, but they remain somehow on a speculative level with no evidence of deep religious reflection:

> *We who are made of impermanent stuff,*
> *Must quickly go the way of our kind.*
> *And so, following the course of my fate,*
> *I dare to enjoy life while I am able.*

> *If I could but be happy in this life*
> *What should I care if in the next,*
> *I became a bird or worm.*

The first poem is concerned with the transience of living beings, the second with thoughts of the six paths of transmigration,[4] yet the way in which they affirm present existence reveals but an attitude of sensuality.

Besides sorrow, the Elegies of the *Manyōshū* reveal feelings of transience, with expressions like "such is the way of impermanency," "when the bubbles are gone, no trace is left." But none are really deep-seated. The mysterious nature of death, eternal life, existence transcending life and death, a longing to stay the wax and wane of the shining moon, the struggles or agony of trying to grasp the unknown—such things are not to be seen in the *Manyōshū*. Only the ubiquitous lines about "my lover who may be awaiting me," "my lover I have finally met," "my lover I may not see again," about the "loneliness of lying alone at night," or the "constant grief of mornings and nights away from you," etc. These, though no doubt pretty sentiments, are but secular, sensual, pleasure-seeking, temporal emotions. There are no cries from the depths of the soul for the eternal feminine. In the case of the *sōmonka*—the exchange songs or love letters in verse—where we might expect to find something transcending sexual love, we do not. It is the same with existence itself, towards which the poets of the *Manyōshū* indicate no real religious profundity. The following are typical of their view of life and death.

> *As if to foreshadow*
> *The transiency of our life,*
> *This bright moon waxes and wanes.*

This is an elegy on the death of Prince Kashiwadebe, in which the poet apparently would bring about an awareness as to the transitoriness of all things by having us watch the wax and wane of the moon. The style is perfunctory, and the poem sounds like an example drawn from some textbook.

> *Like the bubbles on the waters*
> *That run echoing by the hill of Makimuku,*
> *Frail human thing, am I.*

This too is speculative and colored by a dream-like, foam-like, illusory nature. No appearance is there of a will to locate something that does not disappear into the vanishing foam.

We find in a poem by the Buddhist novice Manzei the words,

> *To what shall I compare this life?*
> *To a boat unmoored at dawn,*

31

Which disappears and leaves no trace.

Since Manzei is said to have entered the priesthood upon retirement from office, he probably had some elementary understanding of Buddhism. Yet it is nothing more than that; there is no religion here.

The following two verses show some aspiration for Nirvana. They are said to have been inscribed on the face of a koto kept in the Buddhist temple of Kaharadera. Perhaps they give a glimpse of some monk's sincere spiritual aspirations.

> *Loathing both seas of Life and Death,*
> *How deeply I long*
> *For the upland of Nirvana,*
> *Untouched by the tides of Change!*

> *Living long in the temporal hovel,*
> *I remain complacent, and ignorant*
> *Of the way of life of that land*
> *I have yet to reach.*

This is typically Buddhist thought. It has not, of course, attained the state of *prajñā*-wisdom, but a heart that turns away from the world, a heart searching for the "other shore," is the way to denial of the world. Without denial religion cannot enter a final affirmation. When denial is deep and thorough-going, a religious—spiritual—life is possible. It must be said that the great majority of the *Manyō* poets, whose hearts were not so weary, who were not searching for the "other shore", were not in contact with the inmost workings of man's mind. Their *kami* did not develop into the *kami* of Ise Shinto until the Kamakura and Muromachi periods. And this was to be expected. The *kami* hidden in the clouds, in their palaces above the overhead thunder, are the personifications of physical phenomena, the incarnations of might and authority. Yet even so, when they do not assist one in having his own will, even offerings once given may be taken back. Today as then, people pray for worldly advantage, in exchange for which they give *torii* to the Shinto diety *Inari*.

> *Give back my offering to the shrine, o kami—*
> *You did not grant my prayer to see my lover.*

32

Kept from seeing his lover, someone shows his malice towards the *kami* by withdrawing his offering. Such a *kami* is apparently no higher than man. Though he appears to possess more power than man, his heart is won, and things are possible, on the level of exchange. Although sometimes it is a matter of calling on the *kami* when one is in distress, prayers are invoked to the *kami* whenever the need arises. Since the *Manyōshū* poets were particularly keen on love, it is to this the *kami* are summoned.

> *Day after day*
> *I pray that I may meet*
> *My love again.*

But when this petition is not granted, the petitioner reverts to violent statements and deeds. He becomes desperate to the point of cursing the *kami*, threatening to resort to whatever retaliatory means necessary, even in disregard of his own life and name.

> *Since even the propitious kami*
> *Has dealt me such a blow,*
> *What care I for useless life?*

> *In deepest disillusionment*
> *I will dare to cross*
> *The sacred fence of the shrine.*

These both have an attitude of self-abandon. There is no concern at all even with the sanctity of the *kami*. Here there is absolutely no religion. There are expressions of the 'inexpressible' or 'recondite' *kami*, the *kami* 'beyond speech'; of the *kami* as ineffable, or 'infinitely awesome,' but when reciprocal benefits do not accrue the petitioner is even willing to give up his life in confrontation with the power of the *kami*.

Such *kami*, awesome and beyond speech, are simply gods of power. Religion must have something of another dimension.

> *Though I went to the shrine*
> *To pray for him*
> *Offering wine,*

Yet he has passed away.
(to reign in the world above.)

Since this is an elegy rather than a love poem, we find neither the sexual element nor the abandon, the desperate nature without care for life or reputation, we saw in the other poems. There is no outburst that would violate the sanctity of the Shinto shrine. But as in the previous poems, the element of reciprocity is clearly betrayed. The religious thought of the people of *Manyō* times usually does not go beyond this level. It is a level of "religion" that appears as well today, however. Prayers are given, "I wish help for my son even if it means shortening my own life"; "I am abstaining from something of which I am very fond, please do this, please do that." The mind of *Manyō* times is all but that of today. Some may call it religious, but such people do not know what true religion, spiritual awakening, is.

Although this short section will not allow a thorough study of the religious thought of the *Manyōshū*, I would like to touch upon the *Manyō* poets' ideas concerning life after death with the following poem as representative. It is an elegy written by Okisome Azumabito for Prince Yuge, a son of the Emperor Temmu:

> *Our lord and prince, rule in peace.*
> *Child of the Bright One above,*
> *Kami as he is, has taken*
> *His divine seat in the Heavenly Palace*
> *Far above; we, awe-stricken,*
> *Lie prostrate and weep,*
> *Day after day, and night after night.*
> *And to our weeping there is no end.*
>
> *ENVOY*
> *Our lord and prince, because he is a kami,*
> *Has gone to dwell unseen,*
> *In the five hundredfold clouds of heaven.*

The Prince has gone from this world, and "*kami* as he is," has taken his divine seat in the palace beyond the five hundred fold clouds. We, "the

34

awe-stricken," lament and weep day and night without end, still we cannot express our hearts' boundless grief: such seems to be the meaning. The "Heavenly Palace" apparently is placed somewhere above the clouds, but, probably because of an insufficient knowledge of Heian literature on my part, I do not completely understand what "*kami* as he is," means. Does "Seated with the *kami*" mean seated together with the *kami*, or seated as *kami*? Somehow or other Prince Yuge has deigned to hide himself from this world and now dwells in the Heavens. Yet is this the same for everyone, or is it limited solely to princes? And is it possible for his common subjects left behind, grieving "day after day, night after night," to communicate their feelings of grief to him who now "has taken his divine seat . . . dwelling in the Heavenly Palace?" Are these personal feelings of grief? Do the grievers grieve knowing they reach by some means the object of their emotion? What manner of life is this celestial life? These are some of the things I find it very difficult to comprehend. Yet this is the way Okisome Azumabito wrote it. Can it be called religious? It does have the germ of a religious spirit, and this does not seem to have been derived from Confucianism, Taoism, Buddhism, or to be their imitation. It is unquestionably expressive of what our ancestors genuinely felt as Japanese. Shinto developed from this, though its beginnings are at this point only faintly visible; it had yet had no chance for a full step forward. This 'grief' must be much more refined, it must undergo trial, for it is not religious in the true sense of the word. Okisome Azumabito had not yet even taken the first step beyond what is a traditional and primitive sentiment. This can be understood from a look at some other *Manyō* poems of the same period: for example, the twenty-three poems of lamentation written at the death of another of the Emperor Temmu's sons, the Crown Prince Kusakabe. They were composed by members of the Crown Prince's retinue, yet they display a mere tearful wailing in place of religious introspection, without even a reference to the "*kami* in the Heavenly Palace." There is nothing but the lamentations of the mourners, whose lachrymose chest-drummings do not transcend the stage of 'artlessness and purity.' We even suspect that the tears and such are a courtesy, probably the behavior expected of loyal subjects.

Besides the lamentations, Okisome Azumabito's elegy establishes the whereabouts of the dead Crown Prince. "Our lord and prince, because he is a *kami*," the *kami* dwelling beyond the celestial clouds, the *kami* existing in the form of "*kami* as he is," are not in the least introspective; they were merely traditional notions circulating within the mind of Okisome Azumabito. "*Kami* as he is" presents difficult problems of interpretation, but death signifies going out of sight behind the clouds, that is, above in the "Heavenly Palace," ruling in Heaven.

But what is *kami*? What does it mean, "He has ascended the Plain of Heaven, and is seated on the Heavenly Throne?" What is the relation of this to the mortal body with its soft skin that remains behind after the ascension of the *kami*? Elsewhere in the *Manyōshū* there is mention of "eight hundred, one thousand, myriads of *kami*, assembled in high council on the shining beach of the Heavenly River." These are the protective *kami* of the "Rice-Abounding Land of Reed Plains" [an ancient name for Japan], but since they do nothing at all, what is the act of 'divine protection'? Can it include things besides those which are political, racial, material, and ethical? Of course, the *Manyō* poets keep their mouths closed about these and other questions. In short, religion had not yet entered into their spiritual world, and the opportunity for contemplative introspection had not yet penetrated what Shinto calls the "pure and clear" heart of the Japanese people. The naturalization of foreign thought into the climate of Japan was still in the future. Japanese spirituality had not yet awakened.

The "religious" thought of *Manyō* times underwent a lengthy education throughout the period of the Heian, accommodated an increasing ability for deep reflection, to arrive for the first time at a Japanese religious awakening in the Kamakura period, to which I would like to turn my attention in following sections.

2. Heian Culture

The Heian era was a long one (794–1185). Excepting its early stages it did not receive the influences of foreign culture, making it a period during which elements characteristically Japanese evolved above all. The center of Heian culture was localized in Kyoto, gaining its sustenance from the rest of the country, which was still not fully developed. Kyoto had the government, the literary and fine arts, religion, learning, and so on; culture unfolded brilliantly in all directions. But the creation, enjoyment, and appreciation of these cultural assets were limited to the upper classes of society—a very few people. The whole of Japanese culture at this time consisted of a nobility clustered about a central court. Therefore, although in certain areas it reached a high degree of refinement, it was influenced by the decadant spirit of a materially favored noble class that lived by the support of the rest of the country. Most will agree that the predominant traits of the Heian are delicacy, effeminacy, elegant refinement, and sentimentality—characteristics summarized in the word 'courtier'. Within these traits dwell the traces of formal stiffening.

If the *Manyōshū* could be said to characterize the Japanese temper of the period prior to Heian, the *Kokinshū* could probably be said to reflect the mood of the Heian people. Of the twenty "books" which make up the *Kokinshū*, six are of nature poems (the 'poems of the four seasons'), and five of love poems. This aristocratic life, so materially blest, was pervaded by a pleasure-filled, playful spirit. But how abundantly their tears flowed! Their eyes would dampen at the slightest pretext, leaving their long flowing sleeves constantly wet. The *Genji Monogatari* is called an unexcelled literary work. But for all merits, to make it representative of the Japanese spirit is, I think, regrettable. *Genji*, filled with the love complications, sensual pleasures, and literary and rhetorical pastimes of the aristocratic life, is to my mind best not overly applauded. Although I wish to show admiration to the author as a woman, beyond that I would not go The same is true regarding the *Pillow Book*.[5] Compared with the composure and dignity of the *Tale of Genji*[6] it is keen and quick-witted—but that is all. There is little to learn from its thought, passion, spirit, or religious or spiritual aspirations. Heian culture, as represented in these ladies, as well as by the authors of the various diaries and *monogatari*, is elegant and refined, but with the reservations noted above, I frankly can attach little merit to it.

The reaction against the culture of Chinese characters and language that produced the culture of Japanese writing and language was no doubt a welcome occurrence. But the Japanese language aside, the *kana* syllabary is a delicate and effeminate instrument. Given the feminine rule of Heian culture, these feckless court nobles were probably inevitable. They are nonetheless quite astonishing. There is no reason men have to strut around all the time in attitudes of defiance; still some intelligence and depth is desirable. Profound creation seems to be, all things considered, a masculine affair.

The masculinity of the Heian era was completely hidden away in the rural areas, while the center of culture passed through the soft hands of the young nobles. Learning and the arts, not to mention government · itself, naturally stiffened and became formalized. The so-called diaries of the period are the records of precedents, being used as reference books for ritual and ceremony. Nothing resembling active politics existed. The whole of the "government" was nothing more than investiture proceedings. All this was tightly bound up in a patriarchal system. It is surprising it lasted for almost four hundred years. That it came into being at all is probably due to the fact of Japan's insular confinement, without ties to other nations and supported by the large areas of untapped land still at her disposal.

Religion does not exist in a world that affirms epicureanism. The period of the *Manyōshū*, with its primitiveness still intact, was unable to generate religion. Coming to Heian times, the Japanese might well have turned to religion if even to a small extent, but the cultural educators of the capital were worldly to an excessive degree. Lacking the needed outside stimulus, the opportunities for introspection were also lacking. Because there was no material want, there was growth on the artistic side—but there was no depth. Indeed, from their very beginnings the Japanese seem to have had an elegant and refined disposition, but to have lacked something in the way of strength and depth.

In any case, in Heian times the development of a religious consciousness did not appear. The awakening glow of Japanese spirituality had not yet started to shine forth.

It is not because there is a word—religion—that the reality of religion exists. When Buddhism entered Japan, about the time of the Emperor Kimmei (539–571), the origins of what was to become Shinto were already present, but religiously the Japanese people did not at that time have spiritual awakening. In the Nara period (672–780), temples were constructed, Buddhist scriptures were read, recited, and studied, Buddhist images and allied objects were fashioned, and there was wide observance of Buddhist ritual. Later, in the Heian period, Kūkai (Kōbō Daishi) and Saichō (Dengyō Daishi) appeared along with many other excellent Buddhists and Buddhist scholars.[7] Still I would have to say the Japanese did not yet understand Buddhism. They still did not possess in themselves

38

that which they were to employ later in its mastery.

Religion could not arise, spirituality could not spring up, from within cultural forms completely monopolized and congealed by a materially rich nobility that had easy access to political power, even though this power meant for them nothing more than change—upward progression—in court rank. The disappointment when a beautiful girl was not born who could be given to the Emperor and thus bring one closer to the power and prestige of the throne; the anguish of not being able to swagger with pride because a promotion was not forthcoming; the pain of not being sought by the opposite sex because of a lack of literary skill or good looks—such ordeals will never bring about the rise of religion. It is in the nature of religion, it is true, to deny the existing world. But this is something that must be experienced in the depths of the soul, and the stirring of spirituality must appear. All the melancholy, transience, *mono no aware*,[8] and so on that we find in the numerous *monogatari* and poetry collections of the Heian period are without depth. The cry that comes from the ground of the human soul is nowhere heard.

Religion does not spring from prayers for worldly gain. Neither is there a direct relation between a life of spirituality and the welfare of the nation. Generally speaking, in Heian times religious observance in the secular world was tied to the group life. Even though yearnings were expressed for the Pure Land and love for Amida was manifested in thought and form, these were no more than an emotional aestheticism, or a conceptional extension of the secular world, and as such they were merely ideological pastimes. For the people of Heian, the Pure Land was an extension of their own world. The imperial courtiers and ladies pictured the bodhisattvas as being much the same as themselves, spending all their time simply wandering in and around the imperial palaces. The bodhisattvas that appeared in their entertainments were in fact themselves.

Religion is not merely concerned with future existence. Religious life —spiritual life—covers the three periods of past, present, and future existence, and future life is only one part of it. Though some think that without an after-life there is no religion, they are mistaken. In truth, religion has a time-transcending nature, and in this sense it can be said to include the future. Shinto never goes beyond a temporal and spatial nature, in which there is of course neither future nor past. Consequently, even the present is not the present in the true sense of the word.

Though religion is said to come from heaven, its essence exists in the earth. Spirituality arises with its roots in the earth. Its sprouting buds point to the sky, but its roots are buried deep in the soil. For lack of this, Heian culture was devoid of religion. Its nobility did not set foot on the earth. The earth that supported Kyoto was distant from it. To set out on a trip from the capital was an unwelcome duty for the courtier, and departures were, to say the least, reluctant. To quickly conclude a distasteful burden and to return to be with the people and pleasures of the capital was the prayer of the local official. The great bother even today's Japanese seem to find it to go abroad might well have its source in Heian times.

The Heian spanned an extremely long period of nearly four hundred years. Separated from continental Asia, though Japan was small, her men of culture still had plenty of resources to draw from, and thus enjoyed their "cultural life" in Kyoto much as they pleased. However, since they had no roots in the earth, it is no wonder their lives lacked spirituality, the life of religion.

3. The Nature of the Earth

The sun is a blessed thing. Without it there would be no life. All life points to the sky, but its roots must be in the earth. Life that has no connection with the earth is not really alive, in the word's true sense. We should be awed by the heavens, and be intimate with and love the earth. No matter how much we trample over, strike or pound it, it does not anger. Life begins from the earth and when we die we return to it. We must revere the skies, yet our bodies are not received there. Heaven is distant; the earth is near. In every respect it is a mother, and we feel a corresponding affection for it. Nothing is more tangible or concrete, and religion cannot truly come into being save from this concreteness. The deep recesses of spirituality exist in the earth. Although the people of Heian felt a sympathy with the beauties of nature they did not know of labor on the soil, the intimacy of the earth, or its reassurance. They were consequently incapable of feeling its boundless love, its tolerant, catholic nature; they could not touch this mother of all things.

The sun decomposes death's remains and leaves unsightly remnants.

40

The earth receives all this without so much as a murmur, and resurrects it with a new breath of life as things of beauty. The Heian people embraced beautiful women but forgot the affectionate mother able to embrace even a dead child, and this is an essential reason why religion is found nowhere in their culture.

The earth is where one experiences the blending of man and nature. He adds his power to that of the earth, and with industry harvests its products. It assists him in his work in proportion to his exertion. He is able to measure his own sincerity according to the degree he is helped by the earth. It does not falsify or cheat or delude, nor will it be deceived; it reflects man's heart as honestly as a mirror reflects his face. It does not hurry, knowing that summer can come only after spring. If the sown seed's season does not come, the sprout does not appear. Without the appearance of the leaf, the branch does not lengthen, the flower does not blossom, and therefore the fruit does not come forth and ripen. It does not disrupt this order in any way. Man learns from this the order of things, and is taught the need for patience. The earth is man's great educator and his great disciplinarian. How much of his own excellence he has attained because of it.

Man knows the blessings of the sun by means of the earth. Without it, the great power of the sun would not be felt. The earth immediately heeds man's call, the sun, being distant, cannot be reached. Man can offer up prayers, but beyond that his power does not extend. He is in a completely passive relation to heaven. Heaven is not dear to him to the extent he respects it, for vis-à-vis heaven man can know only a crouching fear. Even were we to grant the possibility of an intimacy with heaven's love, it would have to come to us through the medium of the earth. The direct relation between heaven and man lies nowhere but in man's accepting the action of heaven's will as it is. If the sun is broiling hot, the heat will burn inexorably an earth unshadowed by foliage. The winds blow, the rains fall; to stave them off there is no protection but outcroppings of rock. In such cases the aid of the earth must be relied upon. The warmth of spring is closely felt in the plants and flowers sprouting up from the soil. If this warmth is felt merely in one's own body, the blessings and virtues of the sun cannot have universality. When its blessing is received in conjunction with the earth, the sun goes beyond the individual human being and affirms the impartial nature of its love. The inclusion of both oneself and others in the depth of the individual is essential for genuine love, and it is there religion and the life of spirituality are found.

The sun does not by itself awaken religious consciousness, rather it must pass via the earth, where man and the earth are joined in full and unfettered communion. One can understand neither the sun's blessings nor anything else without these ties, merely floating in mid-air. The sun comes, in varying degrees, into man's direct and tangible experience via the earth upon which his feet rest and upon which he works with his hands. In this way the actions of heaven come to have a connection to him that is dependant upon the earth. Religious consciousness with regard to heaven, quite simply, will not be brought forth by heaven alone. When heaven descends to earth man can feel it in his hands; he has knowledge of heaven's warmth because he can actually touch it. The potential in cultivated land derives from heaven's light falling to earth. For this reason religion bears its greatest authenticity when it appears among peasants and farmers who live and work on the soil. The courtiers did not and could not know the land except as an idea or concept, a shadow they approached only in their poetry and *monogatari*. The emotions of Heian times are as a result far from religious. Even among the so-called Buddhists, religion was merely an agency to eminence: it did not become a guide, pointing the way into the deep recesses of one's own heart. Nara and Hiei Buddhism lacked human authenticity because it was without the direct experience of the earth.

The four hundred years of Heian rule was a long hibernation, rendered inevitable by historical, political, geographical, and other considerations. Still, the sleep was not without advantage.

On the one hand, the Heian period permitted its courtiers the tender sweetness, sorrow, and elegance of love within a 'world of ideas', but on the other hand, in the country areas, the areas away from the cities, it allowed the samurai and the peasants a continuous and extremely direct connection with the earth. Hence the latter confronted life full face. The Heian nobility were to be superseded both politically and intellectually by the class that directly controlled the farmers and peasants—the samurai. Only those grasping the reality of life can become the leaders of the group life. Although it is said that those who did not or could not realize their ambitions in the capital went to outlying districts, these ambitions referred to include becoming a high government official or minister. Therefore, those with even a little of the "spirit of the Japanese male" (*yamato onoko*)—and even in those times it must have existed—probably did not trouble themselves with such trivialities. They no doubt struggled to realize their ardent hopes, even to the point of leaving the boundaries of Japan and going abroad. The taste of the times was single-minded pursuance of pleasure, the men knocking like mud-hens at the doors of their women as the latter composed poetry. To follow such delicacy and refinement is not the way of great men or warriors, who would no doubt wish to live truer lives. In all likelihood they wanted—even if unconsciously—to live closer to the earth. People of this caliber, secluded in the countryside, accumulated visible and invisible influence during the latter part of the Heian period. With the power of the central government doomed to fall, those who would inherit its power would be those firmly entrenched in the earth.

The points I have indicated above are especially true regarding the life of spirituality. Spirituality may appear to be a faint and shadowy concept, but there is nothing more deeply rooted in the earth, for spirituality is life itself.

The depth of the earth is bottomless. Things that soar in the firmament, and things that descend from the sky, are wonderful, but are nonetheless external and do not come from within one's own life. The earth and the self are one. The roots of the earth are the roots of one's own existence. The earth is oneself. The Kyoto nobles and the priesthood hanging in their train continued to lead lives divorced from the earth, and all their artistic taste, learning, *yūgen*, and *yūbi*,[9] separated as they are from real life—from the life of reality—are but castles in the air.

The whole of the Heian era did not produce a single man who can be said to have had a spiritual existence or religious character. Even such men as Dengyō Daishi and Kōbō Daishi did not have sufficient contact with the earth. Their intelligence, virtue, and achievements are truly the pride of the Japanese people. However, they were the products of an aristocratic culture, and thus provide the good and the bad points discernible in that culture. Since they came to prominence in the early years of the Heian era, the distinctive features of Heian culture—the feelings of frailty, sorrow, gracefulness, delicacy, etc.—are not present. They were more continental in character. Their Buddhism—in contrast to Nara Buddhism—had at first a fresh and pure thrust. After a while

43

it came nevertheless to the same road of formalization, ritualization, aestheticization, and artificiality as the other culture forms, and became separated from the essential nature of Buddhism. Without any stimulus from the continent, confined to an island nation, surrounded by the mountains of Kyoto, the nobles lived on the economic support they gleaned from the rest of the country. Passing their lives in refined and unmixed pleasure, they were bent on somehow passing to position and power, regarding this as necessary to uphold the 'pride of family.' The priesthood, next in line, instead of guiding them as monastics, were dragged along with the nobles.

Contemporary observers of Heian culture give us the account of men who followed the lead of their women, taking great pains with their splendid garments and beautiful personal appearance. Anyone who has read the Heian *monogatari* has perceived how rich and beautiful the descriptions of this "masculine attire" are. Men and women, their faces meticulously adorned with cosmetics, freely exchanged and wore one another's clothing. They were also strangely given to tears; so often we read, "my sleeves were wet with tears." The extent of their overt sentimentality can be seen in the following: "By the edge of the swift-running river, the sounds of the falling leaves and the echoing water . . . . are too fierce to be described as nice; it is a lonesome, desolate place."

The personal appearance of the priests, as well as the various religious ceremonies, were obliged to take their keynote from the effeminant tastes of the nobles. There is no limit to the "exquisiteness, beauty, and delight," of the priests reciting the Nembutsu at the Buddhist services. Their attire is described on page after page, and we are finally told their dress is so magnificent it cannot be readily adjectivized. And it is no ordinary aspect we find in the world of smells. The priests are described walking with weary steps, dragging their robes filled with over-powering odors of incense. We read of their faces covered with cosmetics, their voices delicate as the sound of the *Kalavinka* bird, and so on and on. We realize that for them religious functions were spectacles of a wholly sensual nature. Even such a life is not entirely meaningless, but those who tread its path cannot help but keep a highly perilous foothold.

It was inevitable Heian culture would be superseded by a culture coming from the earth. Those representing this culture, with a foothold in the country, were the samurai, who had immediate connections to the peasantry. Therefore the nobility was finally to surrender before the gates of the samurai. This did not happen because of the samurai's physical strength, but because their roots were deep in the earth. Historians may call this economic or material strength (or physical force), but to me it is the spirit of the earth.

The spirit of the earth is the spirit of life. This life always unfolds itself within the individual, who is a continuation of the earth—he has his roots there, there is where he appears, and there is where he returns. The spirit of the earth breathes at the inmost recesses of the individual, so that reality is ever present in him, sharing a pole in opposition to the world of ideas. Heian Buddhism was established within the world of ideas and could not be separated from the pleasure-seeking spirit that followed in the wake of aristocratic culture. In the *Kokinshū*[10] we find this poem:

> *Is this world dream or reality?*
> *I cannot tell—*
> *Because it at once is and is not.*

If they could be satisfied with something like this there is little chance for their attaining the realm of religion; nothing of spirituality is to be found herein. Such words as "melancholy," "loneliness," "world-weariness" are common in Heian literature, and they immediately bring Buddhism to the minds of some people. Regardless, the Heian period had nothing derived from the earth.

As I said above, the samurai's superseding the nobility did not mean force replaced ideas. They did have physical force, yet their strength lay elsewhere, in their relation to the earth. They did not always have their field of operations fixed in the earth. Physical force did exist, for the samurai and physical force were inseparable. But if it had not been entrenched in the earth the physical force would simply have collapsed. Aristocratic culture would perish because of its frail, delicate nature; samurai culture was ordained to fall from its violent, despotic character. Physical force and the earth are not the same thing. Brute force may exist alone. Had even the Heian courtiers taken notice of the earth, there is little doubt their culture would have been different than it actually was. This is a point we should consider deeply. The Kamakura samurai culture which succeeded the Heian had a life of the spirit as well as physical strength. Were it a question of strength alone, the culture that appeared in the Kamakura period in all likelihood would not have evolved. This spiritual life that lived in Kamakura culture was manifested in a religious direction.

The Heian period was an excessively human one. In Kamakura times the spirit of the earth can be said to have returned the Japanese people to their origin.

II. THE AWAKENING OF JAPANESE SPIRITUALITY

On coming to the Kamakura period the Japanese truly awakened to religious or spiritual life. It was then the seeds which had been placed in position by Saichō and Kūkai at the beginning of the Heian, and had subsequently settled into the earth, began to germinate. Until then the Japanese people were unaware of the world of spirituality. In the area of religious thought the Kamakura period produced a spectacle unparalleled, before or since, in Japan's spiritual history.

The four hundred years of the Heian were by no means wasted, for during that time the preparations for the Kamakura era were laid. Thanks to the existence of this kind of root and stem, the springtime of the Kamakura period unfolded, in which the flowers and plants of a beautiful thought began to blossom forth. Today, seven hundred years after, this has come in substance to be the basis for the Japanese character, thought, religious faith, and esthetic taste. With it, I believe in the future there can be constructed something new of world-wide significance. Such is the mission of today's Japan.

What is it that characterizes the thought and belief of Kamakura culture? Beginning with Buddhism, I would first mention the new, Japanese developments in Pure Land thought—that is, the rise to influence of the Jōdo, Shin, and other *Tariki* sects. The source of these developments is primarily to be found in religious belief, from which the life of the Japanese was able to attain depth.

Next is the importation of the Zen sect. Though it came to Japan by way of China, its imported character altogether vanished following its introduction, and it became Japanese. There appears to be an essential rapport between Zen and the Japanese character. The intelligentsia and

46

above all the samurai took to it immediately. In general, it pervaded literature and the arts and came to be the very foundation of Japanese life. We must not forget to mention the rise of the Nichiren sect, which, since its thought had connections with the Mongol Invasions, became imbued with political colorations—patriotic sentiment, nationalism, etc. Given the international spirit current in Kamakura times, the Nichiren sect's emergence was perhaps natural.

On the other hand, *Shinto Gobugaki*, "Five Classics Shinto,"[11] which was to become the well-spring of Ise Shinto, was written. *Ryōbu* Shinto or "Dual-Aspect" Shinto[12] is Shinto as seen from the side of Buddhism; Five Classics Shinto is Shinto seen from the side of Shinto. Both are attempts, within the context of Japanese thought, to unify Shinto with things provided by transmissions from Buddhist and other external sources. I do not know whether this usage of the word "Shinto" is technically correct or not, but in any case I am using it in a practical and general sense.

I believe one of the external factors involved in the elevation of consciousness that stimulated Shinto thought was, once again, the Mongol Invasions. Since Heian times the Japanese had indulged themselves in the dream that they were living in some kind of insular Eden. Suddenly, they saw the approach of an external and hostile force, and this made them take another look at themselves. Of course, prayers were invoked at shrines whose lineages were rich in traditional and historical associations. But the Japanese were also required to reconsider the concepts and ideas that had led to the continued subsistence of such shrines.

It is my opinion that the Mongol Invasions had a remarkable influence upon the growth of Japanese introspective life. Although the often expressed tendency is to treat the Kamakura period solely from a political angle, there is a sore need for a study of Kamakura history that will earnestly try to trace the psychic or spiritual foundations of the Japanese people. In *Manyō* times the Japanese *seishin* was still primitive, manifesting merely a child-like simplicity and artlessness. Heian times were still not favored with an opportunity that would permit the Japanese to discover the spirituality lying hidden at the end of deep self-introspection. But now, because of gravely serious political developments, because of many forces in motion within and without, the psyche or spirituality of the Japanese—which had during this time been gradually nurtured along

47

smoothly and otherwise—experienced a crisis at its roots. The Japanese were obliged to consider whether or not their own resources were really capable of dealing with the impending invasions. The initial pulsations of both *Ryōbu* Shinto and Five Classics Shinto began here—though they were no doubt unconscious. But, not unexpectedly, they were mainly political.

Shinto is an essentially political thought, and strictly speaking not a religious belief. It is not a manifestation of spirituality. The moment the Shintoists tried to turn it that far they ran into 'foreign' thought and feeling, and had to adapt themselves by taking them in. Since this contradictory nature in inherent in Shinto, the danger is always present that it may conflict with other spiritual elements. Yet Shinto displayed a catholic nature in its "Five Classics" form, where it is not yet developed to the point of exclusiveness. Thanks to various domestic and foreign conditions, the existing political aspect was here provided a chance for self-examination, and enabled to deepen and broaden in the direction of religious thought—namely, in the direction of spiritual awakening. Here, faintly, we may see its sprouting in Shinto. Though we must judge it as far from sufficient when compared with the systematic upward turning of the contemporaneous Pure Land thought, it cannot be doubted that Five Classics Shinto was an awakening of the Japanese spirit or *seishin*. A genuine spirituality was soon to follow.

Thus, in the Kamakura period the true significance of religious thought and faith and mood—in a word, spirituality—grew in all directions. When Pure Land thought is discussed in Japan, scholars usually relate it to *masse* (Latter-day) thought.[13] I do not necessarily agree. Latter-day thought must first of all be studied to find whether or not it was prevalent among the Japanese people as the scholars contend. Since the time of Dengyō Daishi this kind of thought had probably circulated among Buddhist scholars, but Buddhist scholars were not all of the Buddhists and certainly not all of the people. What level of familiarity with the Chinese language Buddhist Canon did ordinary Buddhists at that time generally have? To what degree did missionaries spread a Buddhist consciousness throughout the general populace? There were temples and monks (though of course there were—and still are—shameless monks who broke the Buddhist commandments, as there have been at all times, in all Buddhist countries), but how much did the average person have to do with Buddhism? How many of them came to hold the Latter-day thought?

48

Throughout the Heian, Buddhist attainments—if we grant their existence at all—were limited to a few Buddhist scholars. The nobles who came to the temples for memorial services with offerings for the monks had absolutely no understanding of Buddhism, much less belief in it. They regarded Buddhism as a kind of pastime, and the priests usually did not demand anything more from them. Even though the government was decadant, and the peace of society and the lives and property of the populace all threatened, it was not the degenerate Latter-day (*masse*). Buddhism's dissemination was not so widespread as to cause people to be conscious of such things. Buddhism at that time, today as well for that matter, had virtually no connection to the political and social life. If the advocacy and acceptance of Pure Land teaching was owing to the flourishing of a Latter-day thought at all, it was only among a part of the priesthood and probably never had a general dispersal. I would add that even had there been a universal acceptance of Pure Land thought, it would not have been due to *masse* thought, but because the average person was brought by the degeneracy of the times to contemplate the meaning of his existence. From this occurred the awakening of Japanese spirituality.

There has been talk of the Latter-day at all times, cries that the world is at an end, cries of decadence; it is in no way limited to Buddhism. Such calls were heard in China from remote antiquity. Though I do not know if the same was true in ancient Japan, I personally find myself undecided as to whether the transition from the 'age of the *kami*'[14] to the 'age of man' was a progression or a regression. In any case, the idea that the times are degenerate, that the Latter-day has come, would seem to be a universal phenomena. Although we do find such notions in the *monogatari* and diaries, they are only the hackneyed expressions of those of the population able to read and write. The idea of *masse* somehow becomes just one of the various complaints of the effete and tear-drenched Heian nobility. Although I will not now document my belief, I feel that Pure Land thought would not have been capable of spreading among the ordinary people in such a manner. The means by which Buddhism was transmitted to the common people during Heian times are not well understood, and there is a need for detailed and accurate studies into the extent Buddhist faith and understanding were generally comprehended. Since this has not been done yet, I assume that even though priests talked of a Latter-day and the intelligentsia followed them, it was unrelated to the current propagation of Pure Land thought.

Because of their own decadence, there was some meaning to the priests' and intellectuals' talk of a degenerate Latter-day, but because his lot never rose in the world there was no need for the common man to feel the coming of a Latter-day at this particular time—the final years of the Heian period.

What is the meaning of the spread of Pure Land teaching, especially Shin teaching, among the common people? I think there was a simultaneous and mutual response between the fundamental religious truths included in the special characteristics of absolute *Tariki* faith and the initial religious awakening at this time of the spirituality of the Japanese people. This is what I call the awakening of Japanese spirituality.

There is something in the Shin sect able to penetrate straight into the heart of the average Japanese. We may call it pure *Tariki* ('Other-power'), the power of Great Compassion (*mahākarunā*). It is here the doors of spirituality open. It is here the ultimate ground of Pure Land faith must be.

Because the Shin sect fully grasped this it came to be the faith of the common man. Had it not come this far Pure Land faith would not have measured up to its original and primary mission. The essence of the teaching lies in absolute *Tariki* faith, rather than in such teachings as a Pure Land of Infinite Bliss. Its true aim is not that "this land" is impure so let's go to "that land" where we can have a life of purity. Pure Land teaching preaches of the Pure Land because through it one is able to free himself from karmic entanglements and thus enter the way to enlightenment. Pure Land *Ōjō* (birth in the Pure Land)[15] is the means, enlightenment is the end. By way of the Other-power of Amida it is possible to enter into the Pure Land, something impossible for one who is karma-bound. One must have, by means of an absolute Other-Power, an existential grasp of the world that transcends karma. Though 'Pure Land' teaching is thought to have the attainment of the Pure Land as the end object, the real Pure Land is in fact no such place. It is like the waiting-room of a station, where one passes through in transit. The world of the Latter-day and the Pure Land should not be considered antithetical. If there is to be a contrast, it must be between the karmic causation enslaving man and the life of enlightenment which transcends it. Logically stated, to be released from the chains of karma is to acquire the transcendental intuition of *prajñā*, which may be called the logic of *soku-hi*.[16] But stated in terms of religious belief, it refers to great non-discriminative Compassion, that is, the salvation of Amida's Original Prayer.[17] The result of joining the Pure Land to the concept of a Latter-day and arranging it so it is an extension of the present world is not religion. It is merely an easy materialism, an echo of individualism of an extremely inferior grade. Since from this, the spirit of the earth comes to be camouflaged, materialistic people say that religion is an opiate. A man who has truly achieved a penetrating insight to the depths of spirituality—the true essence of Buddhism—would never hold such an idea.

With a genuine *Tariki* faith it does not matter whether the next world be hell or heaven: this is what Shinran stated in the *Tannishō*. This is true religion. Naturally, Pure Land teaching did not come this far in a day. The Pure Land view of the Heian period was without question influenced by an aristocratic culture that made it an extension of the present world. Nembutsu was discussed as a device for entering the Pure Land. The Pure Land of Genshin (Eshin Sōzu, 942–1017) seems still very rich in actuality, and the paintings of the time depicting bodhisattvas descending to welcome the spirits of believers are certainly charged with the qualities of the Heian era. When we come to Hōnen we feel much of religion's essence, but with him also there is a hitch, in connection with *raigō*, the idea of bodhisattvas coming to meet one at death to show the way to the Pure Land. In the *Chokushū goden*[18] Hōnen gives the following explanation to Amakasu Tarō Tadatsuna:

> *Amida's Original Prayer does not speak of good and bad, does not consider the abundance or lack of one's acts, does not choose between a pure and an impure body. Since it takes no account of time, place, or other relationships, it doesn't bother about how one dies. A sinner is a sinner, yet if he calls the Name, he attains the Pure Land; this is the wonder of the Original Prayer. One born to a warrior family, even though he fights and falls in battle, if he says the Nembutsu he shares in the Original Prayer. He must never have the least doubt that he will be met by the coming of the bodhisattvas.*

With the words, "A sinner is a sinner, yet if he calls the Name, he attains

51

the Pure Land; this is the wonder of the Original Prayer," Hōnen strikes home to the true and wonderful meaning possessed by the *Tariki* sects, but the phrase about *raigō* (the descent of the bodhisattvas) seems somehow a remainder of the Heian spirit. Hōnen's real service was his role of building a bridge between Heian and Kamakura times, and as such he is one of the brightest luminaries in Japanese spiritual history.

The one who exemplified most fully the life of the earth and the true spirit of Kamakura times was Shinran. Under Hōnen, Shinran attained spiritual awakening as to the great meaning of *Tariki* (Other-power), but it was his exile to the northern provinces and later his wanderings around the Kanto region that brought this great awakening into contact with the earth. While in Kyoto Shinran would never, no matter what he did, have been able to extricate himself from the idealities of Heian culture.

What is more, had Hōnen spent much more time in the countryside— the areas away from Kyoto—his spirituality would in all probability have been even more brilliant. This he was unable to do owing to his advanced age, but Shinran was young, and was able to assume his teacher Hōnen's mantle. The characters of these two are inseparable; one coming first, one following, like beads on a rosary string.

Had it not been for Shinran's many years of exile and wandering in rural areas, he would not have been able to penetrate to pure *Tariki*. His exile provided him with the chance to propagate Buddhism among the people of remote areas, which was a blessing for them; yet Shinran himself would have been the first to admit that it was a windfall for himself as well. Because he went and lived there, his own religious experience assumed an added profundity. Not being a specialist I do not know the external historical reasons he did not return directly to Kyoto on his release from exile, but viewing him from the point of view of his inner life, there is no doubt in my mind that his life in the country close to the earth caused him to have an increasingly deep and existential appreciation of Amida's Great Compassion. His collection of letters, *Shōsoku shū*, (消息集), written for a people who were intimate with the earth, reflects, I think, the cultural spirit of the Kamakura period.

His twenty-year life in the eastern provinces must not be viewed as mere historical chance. It should not be difficult to imagine the effect of this long period in Shinran's life upon the development of existing Shin sect thought. It was certainly great. The Shin sect never forgot the country, and one can easily understand that the reason its foundations exist in the country even today is due more to its faith emanating from the earth than to doctrine. Japanese spirituality and the earth are inseparable.

Those who make Nembutsu the prime consideration in the Shin sect, or say Shinshū teaches birth in the Pure Land (*Ōjo*), or things to that effect, have not grasped the true meaning of Shinshū faith. The stronghold of Shin Buddhism rests in the belief in Amida's Original Prayer, which means reliance upon Amida's boundless Compassion. I myself believe the religious life of the Shin sect consists in one throwing oneself into the unobstructed Light of Compassion which, thus set to work, enables one to transcend karma and free oneself from karmic effects and all things that accompany it. Whether it happens or not, entrance into a Pure Land that is an extension of this earth is not a matter of concern.

It is enough if one realizes that he is embraced within the Light. The Nembutsu appears from this realization. To say that the realization appears from Nembutsu is wrong. First, one must once be absorbed in boundless Great Compassion. This absorption can be experienced when one realizes his profound ties to the earth. One must perceive the truth that both the sorrows and hardships of the world come from attempting to live by oneself cut off from the earth. The desire to travel to some 'Pure Land' because this world is difficult is not in accordance with the true faith of Shin Buddhism, nor is it a characteristic of Japanese spirituality. It is the popularization of faith, the faith of *Weltschmerz*, and is not the true form of *Tariki*. It is the residue of aristocratic culture.

The 'certain hell' often spoken of by Pure Land people does not exist beyond life and death. It should not be thought that hell any more than the Pure Land is situated at some distant point beyond innumerable Buddha-lands, the Pure Land lying to the west, hell to the east. That implausible notion is a handdown from Heian culture. I am not saying that both heaven and hell exist in this world, but such a viewpoint does occur, and it comes from an incomplete understanding of this world. If our thoughts progress in a direction isolated from the earth, both heaven and hell there exist; but if they are conscious of their identity with the earth, there, straightaway, is the Land of Purity. The idea itself becomes the earth; the earth is the idea itself. There shines the Light of Great Compassion. Where this Great Compassion exists, is the Land of

53

Bliss; where it does not, "certain hell" is actualized.

This is the culmination of Shinshū belief, and here it must lie. Here, again, is the realization of Japanese religious faith, the awakening of Japanese spirituality. Until this point the cultural process was in a period of preparation. Once there was true awakening it was possible for Japanese spiritual history to proceed in the direction of steady development. (In this Shinshū belief can be said to conform to the Japanese character. But this cannot be understood without fuller explanation, which, together with a discussion of Zen's significance in Japanese spiritual history, will have to be postponed.)

I would summarize by saying that Japanese spiritual history demonstrated its true significance for the first time upon reaching the Kamakura period. At that time Buddhism's essential nature came into contact with the life-spirit of the earth. While boundless Great Compassion was manifested on the one hand, intellectual insight was fused into the Japanese character on the other, bringing with it the realization of unique expressions in artistic life. Absolute *Tariki* and Zen, the 'transmission outside letters,' were these two manifestations.

In a mixture with political and patriotic ideas a new Buddhist sect, the Nichiren, was formed. Also, in the production of Five Classics Shinto, developments in political thought based on national and local beliefs were reinforced and stimulated by the acceptance of foreign thought and beliefs in an attempt to elevate the political environment of the times to the level of religious introspection. It influenced greatly the future development of all Shinto thought.

The historical environment of modern Japan resembles quite closely that of Kamakura times, but with even more tenseness and urgency. Not only in international relations, but in various areas, including thought, faith, technology, and so forth, many heterogeneous forces are rushing on in violent assault. Of course, they are not necessarily hostile. Heterogeneity does not have to mean hostility. But precisely because of this heterogeneity the modern situation greatly differs from Kamakura times as well from as the times before and after it when Japanese culture encountered things foreign to it. There should not be a mere blind opposition bred of self-esteem or anti-foreign sentiment, for such attitudes virtually pursue self-destruction. They may for a while promote vigorous activity, yet even though some glimpse of small success may appear, a time of disillusionment is sure to follow. Armed might, the power of the machine, disputes over wealth—these things are finally, and have been since the dawn of history, but small twigs. What does matter are spirituality, and faith, and thought. Spirituality and faith, dependant as they are upon thought and reality, must be all the more refined by means of them. The Japanese Buddhist's mission must not be to accommodate himself to the occasion. He must have a sufficient understanding of the mission of the Japanese in the world, and moreover, he must broaden, elevate, and deepen his thinking. I earnestly hope he will be able to do this.

NOTES

1 *Nihon seishin-shi no ichidanmen.* 日本精神史の一断面.

2 *Bunka to Shūkyō* 文化と宗教, Shindō Kaikan, 1943. (Suzuki Daisetz Zenshū, Vol. 19).

3 *Manyōshū:* an anthology of about 4,500 verses compiled in the late 8th century. The first great Japanese literary work. Trans.

4 The six realms in which sentient beings transmigrate: Hell, the realms of hungry ghosts, animals, *asuras*, men, and Heaven.

5 *The Pillow Book*, by the Heian court lady Sei Shōnagon.

6 *The Tale of Genji*, by Murasaki Shikibu a contemporary of Sei Shōnagon, ca. 1008.

7 Kūkai 空海 774–835, the founder of the Shingon Sect in Japan. Known popularly by his posthumous name, Kōbō Daishi. Saichō 最澄 767–822, the founder of the Tendai sect in Japan. Known by the name Dengyō Daishi. Trans.

8 *Mono no aware* (sensitivity to things), which swept over the minds of the poets of the Heian Period (A.D. 897–1185), sounds somewhat sentimental and the Japanese are a sentimental people. *Mono* mean "things" generally, *no* corresponds to "of," and *aware* is "emotional response" in its broadest sense. The whole phrase thus means "to feel the sentiments moving in things about oneself," and thus may be inanimate objects or sentient beings capable of emotions.

9 *Yūgen* is a term often used in Japanese aesthetics, meaning "obscurity," "unknowability," "mystery," "beyond intellectual calculability," but not "utter darkness." *Yūbi* 優美; another aesthetical term, indicating an elegant, graceful, and refined beauty. Trans.

10 *Kokinshū*; compiled by Ki no Tsurayuki and others around 905. The first imperially commissioned poetic anthology. Trans.

11 *Shinto Gobugaki* (or *Gobusho* 五部書); "The Five Books (or Classics) of Shinto.' These are forgeries purporting to have been composed in remote antiquity but in reality probably dating from Kamakura times. They are concerned mainly with the history of the Ise Shrine, and attempt to set forth a Shinto philosophy and ethics. Trans.

12 *Ryōbu* Shinto—The Shinto of Buddhist-Shinto syncretism; for example, Tendai Shinto, Hokke Shinto. The term is also used with reference to Shingon Shinto, interpreted mainly in accordance with the doctrines of the Shingon sect.

13 *Masse* (末世). It was said that Buddhism would spread through three time periods, the last of which is *mappō*. *Masse* is the world of *mappō*. *Shō-zō-matsu* are the three periods after the Buddha's decease. They are the period of the *shōzō* (righteous law), the period of the *zōbō* (imitative law), the period of the *mappō* (last law): I. The period of the righteous law is the period when Buddhist doctrines, practices, and enlightenment all exist. II. The period of the imitative law is the period when both doctrine and practices still exist, but there is no longer any enlightenment. III. The period of the last law means the

period when doctrine alone is still alive, but there is neither practice nor enlightenment. Trans.

14 As to the "Age of the Gods," Motoori Norinaga writes: "The *Kami* of the divine age were for the most part human beings of that time [ancient times], and because the people of that time were all *kami*, it is called the Age of the Gods (*kami*)." Quoted in Ministry of Educ., *Religions in Japan*, 1963. Trans.

15 *Ōjō* (往生); literally, "to go and be born." Popularly, Shin is understood to teach the doctrine of 'Nembutsu *Ōjō*,' literally 'to go and be born by thinking of calling the Buddha.' By this it is meant that when one thinks of the Buddha, i.e. Amida, with singleness of heart and in all earnest, one after death will go to and be reborn in the Pure Land. In practice, 'thinking of Amida' is pronouncing his Name one or more times. According to Shin, once is enough if it comes from absolute faith in Amida, but Jōdo tells us to say "Namu-Amida-Butsu" repeatedly; and here lies one of the essential differences between Shin and Jōdo. At any rate the 'Nembutsu *Ōjō*' sums up to popular minds the teaching of both Jōdo and Shin. But a closer analysis shows that merely being born in the Pure Land is not what is really promised in the sutras. Rebirth is advised because of the Pure Land being the most favorably conditioned environment for enlightenment which is the aim of the Buddhist life, both *Tariki* and *Jiriki*. The practical outcome of this is the identification of rebirth and enlightenment, and being assured of rebirth means the foretasting of enlightenment. It is for Buddhas alone, the most highly perfected beings, to enjoy Supreme Enlightenment, while what is granted to us ordinary mortals is to experience something of enlightenment and thereby to orient ourselves—this orientation is the foretasting and the assurance of rebirth. Thus according to Shinran, *Ōjō* occurs when one is truly awakened to the meaning of Amida's Original Prayer while one is yet alive, not after death.

16 *Soku-hi* 即非; Dr. Suzuki formulated the logic of prajñā-intuition as "A is not A and therefore A is A"; this he called the logic of *soku-hi*. See *Studies in Zen*, p. 119 ff. Also *The Eastern Buddhist* (New Series), Vol. II. No. 1, p. 80: "The formula is: A is A, because A is not-A; or A is not-A, therefore A is A." Trans.

17 Original Prayer—Amida made forty-eight vows or prayers at the beginning of his career as a Bodhisattva which are detailed in the *Sukhāvatīvyūha Sūtra*, the principal text of Pure Land Buddhism. The most important one of those prayers is the eighteenth, in which Amida, while yet in his Bodhisattvahood, set forth his strong resolution to save all beings without exception, if they call upon his name even only once in sincerity of heart. The term 'prayer' sounds perhaps somewhat unBuddhistic. It has been generally translated as 'Vow' but this is not quite satisfactory. "Prayer" is better if it can be understood as having no specified petitionary object to attain as is often the case with most Christian and Buddhist prayers.

18 法然上人行状画図. This is also called *Chokushu-Goden* 勅修御伝: Hōnen's illustrated life story, authored by Shunshō (舜昌) in 1306 at the imperial command

of Gofushimi: 48 vols. Hereafter referred to as *Hōnen's Life*. It was translated by Rev. H. Coates and Rev. Ryugaku Ishizuka and published as *Hōnen, The Buddhist Saint* (Kyoto, 1925). Trans.

CHAPTER 2

MANIFESTATIONS OF JAPANESE
SPIRITUALiTY

I. BUDDHISM AND THE GERMINAL IMPULSES OF JAPANESE SPIRITUALITY

1. Buddhism and Foreign Thought

Within Japan's cultural resources there is contained something I believe to be of a most world-wide significance. I further believe these cultural forms, as they are, should be spread to the rest of the world. One of these is Buddhism, which is really a manifestation of Japanese spiritual awakening.

To most people, Buddhism is something that formed in India, and since India is not Japan, Buddhism is to them a foreign thing. That foreign importations are not Japanese is a simplistic notion; yet there is also an idea that all things emanating from foreign nations should be rejected as inconsequential. So some would reject Buddhism because it is foreign, regardless of its possible value for the world. Rejection of things on such purely superficial grounds might compel us to glance at our pattern of life today, where things from other parts of the world are appearing in all directions, a great many of which we have indeed imitated. To begin with, you sometimes have to ask whether someone is Japanese or not, with western clothing, hats, and shoes so prevalent. The degree to which something is Japanese or not remains a debatable point. Considered historically, does "Japaneseness" refer to remote antiquity, or to Heian, or Kamakura times; or does it include Edo or Meiji times as well? Or should we include the beginning of the Meiji era, or perhaps the end of Meiji too? It becomes extremely vague and unreliable. As a matter of fact, "Japanese" is not something easily or clearly conceptualized. I feel that if something is useful in life, it is all right to use it. Since everyday life is governed by pragmatism, there should not be much bother about whether something is Japanese or not. But when we come to the questions of thought and feeling and spirituality it is quite another matter. Here, the matter of something's Japanese character should not be thought of only in terms of appearance or location or time. To speak only from the point of time, we find that more than one thousand years have elapsed since Buddhism was introduced into Japan. Though it is a considerable period, in some ways it is not such a long time. When Urashima Taro travelled down to the Dragon Palace beneath the sea, he thought he had been there only a short time, but upon returning home he found all his acquaintances had died.[1] Close your eyes and one or two thousand years pass right by—it is no great matter. Still, being more than ten and less than twenty times the human span of seventy years, it is a long time. Since the time it was first implanted in the Japanese earth, Buddhism has sprouted, flowered, and borne fruit.

I am no great authority when it comes to plants and animals, but since plants are constantly before my eyes, I am able to make some lay observations about them. For example, when the *asagao* (morning glory) is taken and planted in other countries, it blossoms its first year as a Japanese flower, yet the following year its flower becomes smaller and it reverts to being a regular morning glory, smaller than the Japanese variety. A few years ago, some tulips and hyacinths were brought from Holland. Though the first year they were fine, now after two or three seasons all trace of the imported plant has disappeared. Once they became naturalized into the Japanese climate and became a "Japanese" tulip or "Japanese" hyacinth, they remained that way. It takes two to five years for an alpine plant brought down to the lowlands to become a lowland plant.

In Japan, especially in the northern provinces, chrysanthemums are assiduously cultivated. Yet in England last year I found that Londoners raised and exhibited chrysanthemums as well. Naturally, with regard to flowers the tastes of the English and the Japanese differ, so there would be no sense in my trying to assess the success of the exhibition. In the eyes of the English, they were admirable flowers, and they are not, of course, to be judged by Japanese criteria.

Chrysanthemums came originally to Japan from China, but on coming to Japan they became Japanese. When later they were transported to Europe they became European. Because chrysanthemums originated in China there is no need to insist that chrysanthemums grown in Japan are Chinese chrysanthemums, or that those found in Europe are Chinese. If in each place the chrysanthemum simply manifests its own characteristics

60

it can be said to fulfill its chrysanthemum-nature. Chrysanthemums are not to be seen with merely a regional eye, we must be able to see into the life of the chrysanthemum.

With the culture of the spirit the acclimatization period that follows transplantation is not a question of one, two, twenty, or even fifty or a hundred years. There is neeed at the very least for two or three centuries, a period that would vary according to the people. Therefore in view of the thousand years that have elapsed since the entry of Buddhism into Japan, we are justified in calling it Japanese, in spite of its Indian origins. It does not mean we are justified in saying that because Buddhism became Japanized, Buddhism is Japanese.

I wish now to take up Japanese spirituality and then to consider Buddhism within the framework thus established, rather than speaking of Buddhism coming from China, being transplanted in Japanese soil, becoming naturalized, and losing its foreign character. It seems to me that Japanese spirituality existed within the Japanese from the very beginning; when it fortuitously encountered Buddhism, the Japanese manifested within themselves what was their original endowment. There is here a great need to recognize the autonomy of Japanese spirituality. Let me carry through on this point for a moment.

Some twenty-four hundred years ago Buddhism arose in India, where, after a thousand years its expansion and development ceased altogether. It passed on into Central Asia on the one hand, and travelled in the direction of southern Asia on the other. Then it entered China. In other words, Buddhism arrived in China from the south and from the north. But, as might be expected, this Buddhism in an intact Indian form was not accepted in China. When it first entered there was opposition, just as there was when it first entered Japan.

Opposition in Japan to the entrance of things western is well-known. It is said at the time of the Meiji Restoration (1868) some people, seeing telegraph wires for the first time and thinking them to be apparitions of some kind, even manifestations of Christianity, covered their top-knotted heads with their fans before passing beneath them. Strange as such behavior seems to us today, there is no doubt it was an expression of sincere and deep feeling.

Now, roughly seventy or eighty years have passed since the Meiji Restoration and such actions appear silly, so different is our understanding of electricity from that of the Japanese of eighty years ago. It shows us time is not simply something notched off by clocks. In the very tick of a clock the changes in our world view and our view of ourselves are ticked away. Profound indeed is the meaning contained in the ticking of a clock.

Resistance to that which is new is a natural emotion found within people everywhere. But even within this natural emotion there are inherent conservative and progressive elements. The conservative element is large among older people. At some juncture the ways of thinking of old people and young people are bound to clash. Children have an inevitable tendency to rebel against their parents. The struggles of the world may be said to be the struggles of age, yet on the other hand they cannot be said to be regulated by age alone. Because human mentality or natural emotions are so complex, any simple decisions reached concerning them must end in failure. Youth's opposition to age will always exist. But human nature has it that children are also devoted to their parents. They will observe the rules of their parents years after their death. The elderly one with whom one has lived for so long has gone, and his way of doing things is ever so difficult to change. All his articles had to be just so in life, each in its own special place. One wants to keep the ways and things of the departed just as they were. Three, five, even ten years later the predilection remains to do things the way of the parent. Father or mother did it this way, we will do it this way—such is the conservative nature. Practical convenience or inconvenience, logical or illogical, take on secondary significance. Respect for and compliance with a parent's wishes is to my way of thinking not a question of a child-parent or a parent-child relationship; it occurs simply as a natural human instinct.

On the other hand, this sort of thing often happens as well. While living, the parent had prohibited the child from doing something. With the death of the parent there is a feeling of release in the child. What had been forbidden is now at last possible. In one sense this cannot be censured as being wholly bad. Whether it is all right to encourage it is another matter, yet psychologically speaking, we can understand the youth's feeling. On one hand our forbears' conventions go unchanged for three, ten, or perhaps twenty years, on the other they are changed immediately. If in daily life these two tendencies are not wisely seasoned with mutual self-restraint, society's troubles merely continue as before.

The world cannot be thought of as one large family, for such is simply not the case. What may be good and proper for a family might not be right applied to larger groups such as a society or a country. Something practicably applicable to the principle of the household is not necessarily applicable to the larger areas of group life. Even when it may be applicable, there are still many times it should not, or must not, be applied.

Today's societies and nations have highly complicated structures. There is no such thing as an isolated country. When we speak of a nation, there is always at the very least one more nation in relation to it. A nation is such within a nation group; it can never go in isolation. Each of these nations has its own traditions, conventions, history, and other singular features. In relations with others, one nation must not impose its own self-centered tenets upon another. Individual conventions and traditions must be respected.

Yet in the world of men—everywhere it is so—it is regrettable each person merely goes along guarding his own conventions. Since the way of our time is ceaseless and indomitable movement, each person, in addition to safeguarding his own traditions and continuing in his own peculiarities, comes to be affected by things that influence others as well. It is from this situation international problems arise. So when confronted by changes of circumstances—and in certain other cases as well—one must adapt oneself in some way to these problems at the same time he protects his own interests. When the adjustment is not forthcoming, it may happen that one's own traditions cannot be guaranteed. International discussion becomes more frequent by the day, especially with modern scientific advances, developments in mechanized life, commerce, bewildering productions of all kinds of thought, and greatly increased avenues of dissemination. The various entanglements within each individual nation alone are something that would dazzle the minds of Japanese of the past, isolated in their distant ocean. This is not the conflict of a household, or of age and youth, but of nations, and as such, troubles spring up risking the very existence of whole peoples.

2. Buddhism in China

I would now like to turn back to the time Buddhism entered China from India, to try to see how these new wavelets of thought were received by the Chinese, an essentially realistic people with a highly pragmatic nature. This realism and pragmatism does not like to be separated from the land. Cut off from the land, the Chinese would be unable to care for their ancestral shrines. In a nation where ancestor worship is so important, such severance from one's descendants becomes a serious breach of filial piety. In Buddhism, when a monk enters a monastery he undertakes to uphold the precepts of not taking life—not killing living beings—and celibacy. However, since the Chinese custom of ancestor worship makes inconceivable severance from the line of descent, one must marry and produce children, for without children the parents cannot be served by filial piety. To be divorced from ancestral traditions means a lack of filial piety. Indian Buddhist life thus collides head-on with the traditions of the Chinese people. The enshrinement of their ancestors, which is the same even today in China, is a fact, and it involves live sacrifice of animals such as pigs, oxen, sheep, or goats, cooked whole amidst great clamor. If this is not done the service is not considered completed. There is no greater breach of filial piety than to give one's ancestors insufficient ritual. It is thus only natural for the Chinese to have regarded the introduction of something like Buddhism as a disruptive influence. Buddhist logic aside, it is from this point of view the Chinese utterly rejected Buddhism. But, in the realm of Buddhist theory the Buddhist philosophies introduced by the Indian people were not, in the long run, to be resisted by the Chinese.

India is not very interesting politically. Although recently the movement for independence has appeared, viewed politically the national life does not strike one as particularly favorable. I do not know what the future will bring, but to this point Indians have thrown their whole being into religion and philosophy.

So great is the Indian concern for matters religious, when they meet and talk together one of their foremost salutations is 'What is your religion?' The majority of Japanese people asked the same question would probably feel uncertain. After a death in the family, they suddenly ask themselves, "What is our religion. Shingon. Shin. Zen?" and usually end up running to a friend's temple. In the larger cities there are people whose occupation is to go about performing funeral ceremonies in any religion desired. One can see from this that most Japanese are rather indifferent about religion.

Indians are different. Now, with the appearance of Gandhi, they have real cause for pride. Indeed, any country would be proud of producing such a man. His principles—to which he is always consistent—renounce all resort to power, either armed power or power of influence; instead, he resists by means of non-resistence. His own life is that of a true holy-man. Such a person could not have appeared in any country except India. I am convinced that in producing such a man, India now has a role to play which will be of world-wide relevance.

China and India are altogether different. In the spheres of religion and philosophy the Chinese have never been able to match the Indians. They have not, as a rule, either opposed or attempted to refute Indian thought, ideology, philosophy, or religious logic. It was on the practical side the Chinese were extremely antagonistic, when a point was emphasized that would have caused them to violate the canons of filial piety by preventing them from properly honoring their ancestors. Buddhism thus came to China and was assimilated into the thought of the Chinese people. It retained something from its Indian background, at the same time took in elements of a Chinese nature, and thus became sinicized. In this way, Chinese Buddhism came into being.

The Buddhism realized in India fused with the Chinese people, becoming Zen on the one hand and the Nembutsu of the Pure Land school on the other. In China there appeared, among others, the T'en-t'ai (Tendai 天台), Chên-yen (Shingon 真言), San-lun (Sanron 三論), and Hua-yen (Kegon 華嚴) schools, with remarkable men emerging from Kegon, Shingon and Yuishiki (唯識). We of the East should feel proud of such men, but as for Chinese Buddhism itself, it is in a sense preferable to call it an Indian product taken and perfected by the Chinese land, rather than a natural product of the Chinese mentality itself.

Finally, just as the morning-glory ceases after a few years to flower as a Japanese morning-glory once it is taken to another land, so the Kegon Buddhism and the rest perfected in China and elevated among her distinguished men naturally assumed a Chinese flavor, but it retained something of its native Indian character. It was developed by the Chinese earth without losing its original nature. Therefore, Buddhism needed still further transformation to become a complete production of Chinese spirituality. That is why the Buddhism of T'ien-t'ai, Hua-yen, and the rest did not produce the great and talented men needed to follow priests

65

such as Fa-tsang (643–712) and Chih-i (538–597).[2]

Even if we say that Hua-yen and T'ien-t'ai—both splendid systems of religious thought created upon Indian forms—were initially possible owing to the Chinese genius, the fact remains they do not seem to have grown up from Chinese spirituality, and so they did not develop beyond the ideas of their respective founders, Fa-tsang and Chih-i. To attain further development the Chinese would have had to dig deeper, to grasp what was germinating within their own religious consciousness.

People usually think of something being transplanted from without and then putting down roots. I prefer to think that the seeds and seedlings—spirituality—were in the earth from the beginning, and that this began to move availing itself of the opportunity the transplantation afforded. Instead of placing importance on things said to have come from without, would it not be closer to the truth to look to the things already extant within, and say that they became the main constituents? Otherwise, we could not explain the historical fact of the genesis and steady growth of Zen and Nembutsu. Although we may say that Zen and Nembutsu appeared directly from Chinese spirituality, I believe that Zen did not flow in the midst of the national life in China as it did later in Japan because something somewhere in Chinese life could not yet move together in complete harmony with Zen. Were not one aspect of Chinese spirituality unquestionably manifested in Zen, Zen itself would not have been possible in China. Still, in one area of the Chinese mentality there exists a deep-seated belief in *inga* (retribution, cause and effect: 因果). Then there is Nembutsu which, more than Zen, can be said to represent the elevation of Chinese spirituality. Though the sutras connected with Nembutsu originally came from India, what must be called the Nembutsu sects would not have been possible outside of China.

These two schools entered Japan, where Japanese spirituality made them Japanese, and where they both assumed special Japanese characteristics.

3. Japanese Spirituality and Buddhism

Indian Buddhism passed through China and entered Japan. Since at that time Japan had already been exposed to the influences of Chinese culture, it was thought Buddhism would enter without difficulty. But factions divided over the question of its introduction, and controversy and political strife ensued. Although controversy is one thing, the fact that there was conflict is indeed unfortunate. Buddhism, nevertheless, entered Japan and various schools appeared, among them Kegon, Tendai, Sanron, Yuishiki, and Kusha. When we speak of this we must keep in mind that although they did of course come into Japan, their main ideas are today studied as theory and have not found their way into the actual life of the Japanese at all. Their success if any must be said to have occurred during the Nara period (646–794), when they flowed along as the conceptualizations of the pleasure-seeking upper classes.

I wonder how Buddhism would have been received had it been transmitted directly from India. This we cannot know of course, though certainly the reception would have been vastly different from that accorded the Buddhism which came via China. Still, it did come by way of China, and it was thus it was received in Japan.

Yet it was not until long after its importation that Buddhism finally became Japanese. In the interim it assumed the character of Chinese Buddhism. Japanese spirituality had not yet made its appearance through the medium of Buddhism. Although there seems almost to have been some design or meaning in the historical fact that Buddhism entered via China, we probably do not have to go so far as to say that. The fact remains that the Buddhism that settled in Japan did arrive from China via Central Asia, and after it united in harmony with Japan and received the baptismal rites of Japanese spirituality, it was neither Indian nor Chinese but Japanese Buddhism. It is not sufficient to say it became Japanese, for it was the affirmation of Japanese spirituality, and at the same time possessed what we may call Oriental characteristics. That is because the Buddhism developed in India naturally possessed an Indian character; when it passed through Central Asia it took on the nature of that region as well; since it underwent its great change in China there was an abundant store of Chinese elements; finally, upon entering Japan it was transformed into Japanese spirituality. Thus Japanese Buddhism must be said to have a wholly Asian nature. Moreover, since it came through southern Asia too, it contains a southern accent. Japanese Buddhism is therefore endowed with the characters of the northern and the southern peoples, the power of Indian intuition, and the practical-mindedness of the Chinese, all in one. The unique characteristics of each of them were not just arranged within Japanese Buddhism physically and spatially in some confused manner, but grew and worked with Japanese spirituality as their center. It seems to me the thought that binds greater Asia into one, that is, the motive force behind it, exists within Japanese Buddhism. Of course Buddhism as it is probably would not be helpful even were it introduced universally in the world. But the Japanese spirituality that flows along intrinsically within it must be found and promulgated by means of modern thought. Japanese spirituality connotes something which is able to subsist on a world scale. This is a point deserving special discussion. I will leave it for the moment and turn to examine the things that exist within Japanese Buddhism.

Because Buddhism died out completely in India, doubts are sometimes expressed as to the need for such a death-struck thing in Japan. Nothing could be more superficial. It is a type of thinking that sees only the form and not that which moves the form.

In India, where the sects of Buddhism were seemingly extinguished, Buddhism lost political influence by opposing the traditional caste system. That was an unavoidable occurrence. Still today its spirit has been absorbed within the other religious sects. It is really as if Gandhi is one of those living within this spirit today. The primary cause for the broken road Buddhism came upon in India is that it was too abstract and conceptualized, that it became separated from life itself, that is, separated completely from life grounded in the earth.

Spirituality reveres concreteness highest of all. Deciding whether something is concrete or not presents considerable philosophical problems, but here I am speaking in terms of common sense. Mountains seen as mountains, rivers as rivers—this is the concrete way of looking at things. To feel cold water coldly, and warm water warmly, is feeling concretely. Concreteness is what is not divorced from the earth. Being is nothingness, nothingness is being; mind is such, will is such, and consciousness is such —these are abstract. Thoughts dealt with in such works as the *Chūron* or the *Yuishikiron*[3] are conceptual, separated from the earth, and without foundations. In Buddhism, as long as one controls his own acts, that is, as long as he strictly observes the life of the sangha, the Buddhist life is present. If laxity in any sense comes into this life, conceptual diversions will dominate it. Basically, thought is an act too, it is life. In this regard it has a concrete nature. Yet once this thought is severed from

68

its connections with the earth, it becomes like a balloon and for man its force is lost. Here there is a vital manifestation and a death manifestation. Buddhism in India became a death manifestation, but fortunately it travelled to China where it regenerated in the midst of the pragmatism of the Chinese people.

China is the land of the *Four Books* and *Five Classics*.[4] She has no *Vedas* or *Upanishads*, no *Mahabharata* or *Avatamsaka Sutra*. The extravagant imagination and profound speculative powers of the Indian people became functional for the first time when joined with the common everyday path of the Five Confucian Virtues (Benevolence, Justice, Politeness, Wisdom, and Fidelity) and Five Confucian Filial Piety Relationships that existed in China. Usefulness suggests the principle of pragmatism first. Promotion of the public welfare is an ideal of the Chinese people. Buddhism must also be of benefit in this life.

Since Indian imagination and speculative powers, fused to the Chinese way of everyday-mindedness, came to Japan and developed there, it is in a sense correct to say that Japan swallowed up all the choicest parts of the banquet. On the one hand, this developed into Zen; on the other, it was manifested in Pure Land thought and accepted in the form of Nembutsu. The finest essence of the best milk, that is, the finest flavor of all things, is in India called *sarpirmanda*. This is the Zen and Nembutsu of Japanese Buddhism. When we deal with Zen and Nembutsu we cover almost the whole of Japanese Buddhism. It is really in them that Japanese spirituality was incorporated into Buddhism, and through them that it has been giving life to it.

4. *Japanese Spiritual Awakening in the Kamakura Period*

It was not until Kamakura times Buddhism brought about full realization of Japanese spirituality. Had the illustrious sect-founders Kūkai and Saichō not set the proper foundations, I believe the opportunity present in the Kamakura period would not have occurred. Yet Shingon and Tendai did not penetrate to the center in Japan. They were present solely as conceptualizations of an upper class. Shingon (Tendai could be included here too), in a peculiar blend with Shinto, evolved into *Shugendō*, the Way of the Yamabushi or Mountain Ascetic.[5] Part Shinto and part Buddhist, *Shugendō* can be said to touch the surface of Japanese spiritu-

69

ality. In one sense, Shingon holds within it the Japanese religious consciousness, yet its deepest parts are Indian. It is rich in conceptual elements the great majority of Jopanese could not approach. They captured instead its surface features, added a part of Shinto explanation and with that were inclined to feel that an effective spirituality had fully appeared. When with the advent of Kamakura times government and culture lost their distinctively aristocratic and conceptual conventions and took on the qualities of the earth, Japanese spirituality awakened to itself.

The Kamakura period offered a fit opportunity for the entrance of Zen, that is, Zen entered Japan at just the right time. I personally believe that the Kamakura era was an age in which the depths of the Japanese people, where is found their spirituality, were exhibited. Until this time Japanese spirituality had barely come to the fore. Reaching Kamakura times it assumed an autonomy that moved it to its very ground. A look at Japanese history (perhaps the same is true of other countries as well) reveals that when some external or foreign incident occurs, things heretofore unnoticed or hidden away are suddenly found to be inspiring, and the vibrations produced from this are revealed on the face of all things. Without stimulation of some sort a man's heart will weaken, and this is true of the group life as well. For a long time prior to the start of the Kamakura period communications with other countries had been nonexistent. That they then started once again is something that should never be overlooked in the history of Japanese cultural development. When the Heian revealed a collapse of political energy and an overripeness and deterioration culturally, the national spirit, with no stimulation provided, was on the verge of decay and stagnation. It finally reached a point of no recovery. The voice of the earth began to strengthen within a samurai class backed by the common people. There came frequent news of the Mongols, about to attempt incursions into western Japan following their successes pressing back the Southern Sung. Priests visiting Sung China returned to Japan breathing a fresh continental atmosphere. The emotions and thought of the common class—the spirit of the earth—which had until this time been quiet thus came to have a voice through the medium of the samurai. Something like the sound of the Japanese people's spirituality itself must have at this time been heard.

So it happened that the samurai took the way of Zen, and the common people gave rise to a Pure Land thought. With samurai culture sup-

70

planting to a greater and greater extent the culture of the court, the Zen spirit was made to permeate deeply Japanese life and art. On the other hand, Pure Land thought, in an intimacy with the earth, bore fruit as a direct manifestation of Japanese spirituality.

Whatever else is said of it, the Heian was an age of feminine culture, or perhaps it should be termed the period of Court culture, the golden age of the courtier. One facet of what has been praised as the Japanese spirit was given unrestricted play. Had it not passed through the Heian period this aspect might never have emerged. The Heian was indeed delicate and elegant compared with the magnificence and splendor of the Nara period. Even in letters women occupied the throne. The names Murasaki Shikibu, Izumi Shikibu, and Sei Shōnagon[6] are known to all, and are a source of pride to Japanese. They were truly remarkable, going against the formal and difficult Chinese language and literature, developing the *onna-moji* ("woman's writing") and using it freely and unrestrictedly to express their soft and delicate natures. The men followed in their train here as well, writing diaries in the style evolved by the women.

The women thus cultivated a unique world to themselves. It might even seem such things as a delicate awareness of and sensitivity to nature, to the seasonal scenery of the natural world, cannot be grasped except by a Japanese woman. In these areas the ladies of Heian were truly outstanding.

One must recognize fully the extent the development of the Japanese syllabary (*kana moji*) played in the characteristic evolution of Japanese thought. As long as it was controlled by the Chinese style of writing and literature, Japanese thought could not operate in a free and untrammeled attitude. The 'National Learning'[7] that flourished during the Edo period (1603–1868) owes its emergence and self-assertive manner in part to literature written in the Japanese syllabary as well. The Chinese style of writing limited the natural expression of thought for the Japanese, being for them deficient in freedom and flexibility and lacking a close interrelation between words.

The fact that one is bound and shackled by the tools he creates emerges in all of man's acts. Modern thought by creating machines, technology, and science, has lost freedom; instead of aiding man they seem to lead him all the more toward his destruction.

71

Were it not for this *kana* literature I do not believe Japan would have been capable of attaining the great achievement of the Meiji Restoration. Imported literature, thought, and art could all be freely taken into the development of the national psyche because of the linkability and flexibility of the Japanese syllabary. Considering this, we must show ample gratitude in honoring the creative gifts of the Heian women.

There is no doubt the syllabary of *Manyō* times (*manyō-gana*)[8] was incapable of being handed down from generation to generation for an indefinite period. Still I believe without the Heian women's rise to prominence the Japanese syllabary would not have been used at such an early date, and the 'women's literature' as well would not have developed. Even had the literature been entrusted to the men Japanese culture still probably would have been unable to extricate itself from the oppressive influences of Chinese literature. Chinese characters, Chinese style writing, and Chinese literature have a distinctive muscular strength, a charm and beauty, a feeling and color extremely difficult to relinquish. Yet since Japan is not China she should not become an extension of China. The Heian women of this era must be given credit for the promotion of the Japanese spirit.

But the strong point of the feminine culture was its defect as well. Mildness and softness are fine but must not be without bone and structure. Gentleness is all right but effeminacy is not to be overly welcomed. Tears have a certain mystery about them yet to be continually "wet with tears" is absurd. Though the Heian women exemplify perfectly the Japanese emotional character, actual life cannot be emotion alone; intellect is needed, as well as the working of spirituality. Women are replete with the emotional and sensual natures, but lacking in logic and spiritual insight. Logic aside, without spiritual insight the Japanese would be left with nothing to add to the advancement of world culture.

In the Heian period the time was not yet ripe. The progression is from the senses to the emotions, from the emotions to spirituality. It is a route that goes progressively deeper yet inevitably takes time. There remained many political and social trials to be undergone. Feminine culture had a kind of greenhouse atmosphere in the miniature garden in which upper-class Heian Japanese lived. There the most favorable growth conditions existed on the side of the Japanese feminine character. Seedlings raised without being exposed to wind or open to rain are frail and delicate.

For a tree to grow large with deep rootage, exposure to wind and rain is a necessity, in order for its roots to run deep into the soil. Such tenacious root and trunk structure could not grow in the world of *mono no aware*. It needed to pass through one more trial.

The feelings and emotions of the Heian women were still on the periphery of Japanese spirituality. Once its surface is broken through there has to be a wedging-in to the midst of spirituality itself. Then, via the eye of intuition which opens there, the world of the emotions and senses must be reexamined. When that happens the incomplete nature of the world of intuition prior to the attainment of spirituality will be understood. Both emotion and sensory experience have an intuitive nature similar to that of spirituality, and the former are on that account confused with the latter. This is an error that must be very carefully avoided.

During the Kamakura period the outer wall of the Heian's feminine, emotional, sensory nature crumbled and the center of spirituality began to move. That is, the religious consciousness of the Japanese people underwent a self-affirmation. In the Nara period, and previous to it as well, Buddhism moved the people of ancient Japan, giving expression to their artistic sensibilities and feelings in the production of architectural works such as Hōryūji and Tōdaiji, and the construction of the Daibutsu at Nara. Here we witness the manifestation of a feeling that is sometimes sublime and sometimes refined, but still without disclosure of Japanese spirituality. Although there are some things—like the prosperity Buddhism experienced in the early years of Heian—which cast a truly radiant religious light, I cannot help but consider them as being of an abstract and hedonistic quality. The use of Chinese literature was prevalent, Indian thought was discussed on every side, all manner of religious ceremony, ritual, lecture meeting, and the like prevailed, all of which presented the outward appearance of a grand religious scene. But the feeling it imparts of being somehow vague and hollow is irrepressible. The strengthening of Japanese spirituality still had not begun in earnest.

There are perhaps many reasons for the collapse of Heian culture. Political factors, though they might not have been political in the word's strict sense, no doubt played a role. But the real underlying cause is that the very thought that had created the culture ran up against a blank wall. That is to say the court culture—feminine culture, culture of a conceptual nature—floated on the periphery of spirituality because it lacked firm

73

roots in the earth. It could not continue to maintain itself indefinitely along such lines.

Even granting something comes to be conscious of its own capability, it still has to be able once to pass through the moment of collapse, to be capable of surviving chance collisions with external or foreign elements. Kamakura times provided precisely such opportunities and conditions. Even after the decision to discontinue the dispatch of envoys to T'ang China, news was occasionally transmitted by merchant shipping between the two countries. Coming to the Kamakura period, the political situation in China gradually came to be understood from Japanese Buddhist monks who travelled and studied there. Word was no doubt received concerning the serious situation slowly building up in China, as well as information as to when Japan herself might expect invasion. There would otherwise have been no basis for the forebodings of calamity voiced by such men as Nichiren.

With that the case, the strife of Heian's last stages saw political and economic unrest and public ferment. Add to these the anticipation of an impending national disaster and it can be seen why the Japanese could no longer live simply with an appreciation of *mono no aware*.

The Japanese had unquestionably begun to feel deep stirrings of spirituality. Of course such a fundamental thing is not experienced consciously. At such times human beings—especially those yet to have experienced any awakening of religious consciousness whatever—are simply, without knowing exactly why, carried away by a kind of uneasiness. No doubt this insecure feeling simply discovered its outlets through existing means of expression.

Although this cannot be seen unless we take a detailed look at the various records, mainly the literary ones, of the period, I personally believe the great historical event of the Mongol Invasions, the effects of which passed high and low throughout the entire country, spreading in all directions in the national life, probably generated an extraordinary excitement. One of these many agitations, in the psychic realm, caused the Japanese to reflect deeply about their country. There grew up a consciousness of Shinto, the "Way of the Gods." Though this had probably been given consideration prior to Kamakura times, I think it had not previously been related to other nations.

Because of his dissatisfaction with imported Chinese Buddhism, Shinran

74

came to regard Prince Shōtoku as the spiritual head of Japan. And Nichiren's position in all this is well known. Were the history of the spiritual life of the Japanese to be written, I think its center would have to be placed in the Kamakura period.

II. SPIRITUALITY

1. The Negation of Reality

The working of spirituality begins from deep contemplation of the phenomena of the world, progressing finally to a desire to grasp the eternally constant something that is beyond the world of cause and effect. The pressures of karma give rise to aspirations of somehow evading them. If through one's own power this turns out to be impossible, one comes in the end to search at any cost for the absolute Great Compassionate One that will enable him to free himself from the shackles of karmic cause and effect. Unless the weight of karma is experienced the existence of spirituality cannot be felt. Some hold that this is in some way abnormal. But even were that so, unless one has at some time been possessed of this abnormality and undergone subsequent regeneration, all talk of religion, and the circumstances of spirituality, will be totally and unavoidably incomprehensible. Those who say it is abnormal have never undergone the experience themselves.

Although there is little need to be concerned with whether or not it is abnormal, unless one has at one time 'rolled in the swells' of karmic suffering he has no chance to realize spirituality. The people of the Heian age were by nature too primitive and sensual. They entered in some measure the world of emotion but could not touch spirituality. *Mono no aware* still lingers in the realm of emotion, wherein spirituality's stirrings are not discernible. They had not yet penetrated to the basic ground of the self. In a manner of speaking, they had yet to contract the disease or abnormality. They had not gone through the process of self-negation which I have spoken of here as disease. Disease is, generally speaking, denial of the body; through it the body's true existence is encountered. There is a difference in kind in this regard between human beings and other creatures. It is here that religious consciousness first

75

begins to breathe, and unless one is led this far, the weight of karma cannot be felt. As long as he leads an artless and primitive existence man does not leave his infancy. The world of *kannagara*, the Way of the Gods, must once be reflected upon. Once life has transited this reflection and illness, denial and experience, it cannot be included in the category of a primitive or infant nature. Here *mono no aware* is experienced more thoroughly than it was by the Heian poets. The fundamental reality of things themselves is touched.

The Heian poets were still in the shadow of the lamp, still in the state described by the Chinese Zen master Nansen (Case 40 of the *Hekiganroku*):[9] pointing to a flowering plant, he said, "People of this world look at these flowers as if they were in a dream." This manner of understanding, it must be said, is not yet true understanding.

2.   *The* Person *That Transcends Individuality*

Although emotion, the senses, and thought discrimination as well are basically rooted in the working of spirituality, unless they actually encounter spirituality itself they are like rootless water-plants, unable to emerge from a life of floating from one place to another. Such is the life of the individual self, in which audience has not yet been gained to the supra-individual Person that lies at the basic ground of the individual self. Thus stated, it sounds very mysterious, one might even imagine it is a world of the mind existing apart from the world of things. For this reason it is absolutely necessary this point be clearly understood.

Usually, men look only upon the world of the individual self. Even principles that esteem the whole are not yet freed from the individual self. One is completely bound by the world of the individual self. Because the supra-individual Person transcends individuality, it is not within the realm of the individual self. Thus, even though I speak of *Person*, it is not a person functioning in the individual self. And yet neither is it a person that remains excluded from the things of the world, for such a person would still be the person of the individual self.

The supra-individual Person is not without a relation to the individual self; there is a deep, in fact inseparable, relation between them. Though we cannot say that the Person *is* the individual self, still the Person cannot exist apart from it. The Person that transcends the individual self

76

is truly a wonder, a "true man of no title" to use Rinzai's words, or in the terms of another master, "a solitary body revealing itself amidst the myriad phenomena." *Mono no aware* as experienced by this Person is the rhythmic movement of Japanese spirituality. The supra-individual Person is the genuine individual, the "one individual person, Shinran," in the following passage:

> *When I reflect deeply on Amida's Original Prayer which issues from his meditation for five long kalpas, I realize that it was solely for the sake of this one individual person, Shinran.* (Tannishō)

This Person appears as well in the *Hyakujō hōwa zuimonki* (百条法話随聞記)[10]

> *I alone in this world am evil, I alone will go to Hell, I alone will go to heaven. In all things, I realize, it is each one alone, one by one.*

Shin believers who thoroughly embody this Person understand experientially the movement of Japanese spirituality.

Different tendencies or directions in the movement of Japanese spirituality are noticeable between Shin (and the other Pure Land sects) and Zen. The former always sees the supra-individual Person in the direction of the individual self, while the latter sees the individual self in the direction of the supra-individual Person. Rinzai thus speaks of a "true man of no title," words of an intellectual cast. With Shin, the shape of the individual self is manifest in the previously cited, "one individual person, Shinran," and in "I, alone." Of course, in Zen too the individual appears above the shouts and blows, and even Shin says 'Just Namu Amida Butsu!' But in the overall nature of their teachings, Zen inclines its experience in intellectual—though this is different from ordinary word usage—directions and Shin experience tends towards the emotional sphere. A more or less conceptual element comes to be added to the intellectual situation; the emotional aspect clings to each concrete phenomenon. In my view the man of Zen does not ordinarily understand Pure Land thought, thinking its end to be the recitation of Nembutsu which results in rebirth in a Pure Land or Paradise. Even if he does understand this aspect he is usually unable to understand that the Original Prayer is for the sake of "this one individual person." But not to dwell too much on the side of differences; it is enough to understand the following: all that is needed in regard to spirituality is the realization that the supra-individual Person is at the same time the individual self.

The realization that the supra-individual Person is none other than each individual, and that these individuals one by one are none other than the supra-individual Person, was experienced only by Japanese spirituality. Although the Pure Land thought developed in India became the basis for the formation of the sect in China, even after the passage of over a thousand years it did not evolve into a Pure Land thought comparable to that of the Shin sect. There did not sufficiently appear in the Chinese mentality something capable of grasping the reality that supra-individual self is individual self and individual self is supra-individual self. Of course the Chinese did understand this, grasping it either as thought or as a kind of insight, but they were not fully conscious of the one by one character of rebirth the Pure Land. Teachings such as "the Dharma-body preaches the Law"[11] and "your body itself is the Buddha"[12] of Chên-yen (Shingon) thought come very near to Shin Pure Land thought, yet still fail to grasp the emotional side, the feeling of emotional insight that signifies the supra-individual experience of the individual self. Since this experience is a phenomenon that can only occur in the individual self, the supra-individual self might even be regarded as meaningless. But because it simply cannot arise in a consciousness limited to the individual self it is never felt unless one tries to accommodate the supra-individual self. The reason it is called *faith* and differentiated from ordinary *knowing, comprehending*, or *realizing* is found here. In other religions it is said Divine Revelation is beyond human intelligence and must be accepted just as it is. The passive nature of religious consciousness indeed lies here. Be that as it may, Japanese spirituality possesses considerable emotional or affective qualities, and its operation always inclines in their general direction.

3. Japanese Spirituality

That Japanese spirituality possesses something that works within the emotional nature of the individual self, is seen in the fact that the development of imported Chinese Pure Land thought soon advanced along such lines in Japan. Soon after Hōnen said he would establish a new Pure Land sect, Shinran began consciously to draw elements from within it. As long as Amida's Original Prayer did not emerge from the confines of generality Japanese spirituality did not adequately respond to it. Japanese spirituality had not yet broken open its shell and emerged from within, because that 'one by one' most primal and concrete element was not yet at work. "Primal" may be thought to be some abstract, general, or conceptual supposition of a logical nature; but that is only because things are considered objectively. When "primal" is emotional, when it is the individual self, there is nothing more concrete. Then it is "one by one," "for the sake of this one individual person, Shinran." It is highly significant someone like Shinran did not appear in China but in Japan; also meaningful is the fact that his emergence followed closely upon Hōnen's. In fact, we are probably quite right in viewing Hōnen and Shinran as one. That Shinran did not have a thousand-year Chinese Pure Land thought behind him and did have the thousand-year development of Japanese spirituality is meaningful, for such was the situation present in the Kamakura period. It obliges us to find the meaning Kamakura times has in Japan's spiritual history.

Had Shinran's appearance in Japan parallelled that of Chih-i or Fa-tsang in China, his teaching would probably have died out like those of T'ien-t'ai and Hua-yen. Though we of the East may well be proud of Chih-i and Fa-tsang as great religious thinkers, they had not completely shed their Indian mantles. Is there not sufficient cause for us to say that their thought was not an indigenous growth from the psyche of the Chinese people themselves? Because Shinran's experience of 'one by one' came from the spiritual life of the Japanese people—from spirituality itself—it began to work deeply within the Japanese mentality, and is working there even today. Because Hōnen's and Shinran's spiritual experience was acquired from the earth, we may say that is where its absolute value exists. In this context, this spiritual activity imbued with the qualities of the earth was only possible in the Kamakura period.

There is little question Japanese spirituality began to stir somewhat through the religious genius of men like Saichō and Kūkai. But it still lacked sufficient concreteness in that it did not possess a close enough relation to the earth. The individual self remained unawakened to the essential origin of its own existence through contact and union with the supra-individual self. This first was possible in the world in which Shinran lived. Although he was to some extent the product of an aristocratic culture, his individual self awakened to its original ground while he was in Echigo. He received his initial baptism in Kyoto owing to Hōnen, but that did not yet bring forth the Person of the supra-individual self, which only was actuated when he took up life in a remote area untouched by Kyoto culture. Dwelling among the rural people of Echigo in northern Japan, who lived with the earth as a concrete reality, he came into contact with their spirituality thence derived and experienced via his own individual self something beyond the individual self. No matter how much faith Hōnen might have instilled in him, had he not gained the chance to pass beyond the cultural influences of Kyoto it is extremely doubtful whether the Shinran of the *Tariki* Original Prayer would have gone beyond either Saichō or Kūkai. Certainly he would have been unable to attain full maturity in Kyoto, for although Buddhism did exist there, it did not possess the experience of Japanese spirituality.

4. *Japanese Spiritual Awakening in the* Tannishō

The characteristics of Shinran's sect are thus not found in his *Kyōgyō-shinshō*, but in his letters, *Wasan* (Buddhist hymns), and above all in the *Tannishō*.[13] Although it is natural for Shin scholars to regard *Kyōgyō-shinshō* as supreme sacred book, Shinran's true heights are not to be met with there. Rather we feel them intuitively in the openhearted utterances contained in other of his works. *Kyōgyōshinshō* exhibits a residue of aristocratic culture, a sectarian philosophy, and a scholarly air; it does not form his substance. Compelled to judge him by this work alone it would be difficult to refrain from stating that his spiritual awakening was still incomplete. Let us take a look at the following excerpt from the *Tannishō*.

> *Your intention in coming here, after a long journey through more than ten different provinces even at the risk of your lives, was simply to hear from me concerning the way of rebirth in the Pure Land. You would, nevertheless, be greatly mistaken to assume I had some knowledge of being reborn in the Pure Land other than saying the Nembutsu, or that I possessed knowledge*

of some secret religious texts, and envy me on that account. It would be better, if that is what you believe, to go to Nara or to Mount Hiei, where you will find many learned scholars of Buddhism, and learn from them the essential means of being reborn in the Pure Land. As far as I, Shinran, am concerned, the only reason for saying the Nembutsu lies in the instruction of my good teacher who made me realize that the only condition for Amida's salvation is to say the Nembutsu. I do not even know whether the calling of the Name will take me to the Pure Land or to Hell. Even if my teacher Hōnen is deceiving me, and I am sent to Hell by the calling of the Name of Amida Buddha, I shall never regret calling the Name. Those who have practiced enough to attain Buddhahood may regret calling his Name when they are sent to Hell and find that they were deceived. But I am far from doing enough for the attainment of Buddhahood. Hell may be my proper residence. If the Original Prayer is true, the teaching of Shakyamuni cannot be untrue; if the teaching of Shakyamuni is true, the commentaries of Zendō cannot be untrue; if Zendō's commentaries are true, the teaching of Hōnen cannot be untrue; if the teaching of Hōnen is true, how is it possible for me, Shinran, to utter untruth? In short, such is my faith. Beyond this, you must decide for yourselves whether to believe in the Nembutsu or discard it altogether....

This shows that the concrete foundation for Shinran's sect exists in the earth, in the rural areas among the peasants and farmers, directly opposite intellectual discrimination. Here is where they rise and here is where they fall. That the earth has political and economic significance goes without saying. That by virtue of this the earth is man's very body should also be comprehensible. But in Shinran's sect the earth itself is its religious significance, its spiritual value. This value did not, and could not, emerge from a superficial, Kyoto-bound, aristocratic culture. The words of the *Tannishō*, "Your ... coming here after a long journey through more than ten provinces even at risk of your lives..." are not mere verbiage. If we can imagine these rural people traveling the great distances from homes in far-off Hitachi to Kyoto, we can grasp the idea that their relation to Shinran was not in the least conceptual, metaphysical, or verbal but was bound to the earth. What does not appear among the 'scholars of Nara and Hiei'[14] must be said to exist here. Shinran's heart would not have been so deep-seated in the earth had he not had the chance to leave Kyoto.

I often wonder what kind of life in exile Shinran led when he found himself away from the capital for the first time. Surely he did not reside in the near-by Tendai or Shingon temples. He probably did not even have a small hermitage. We may suppose he led life as a layman. As for his livelihood during this period, it would seem there was not much for him besides farming. At any rate, he did not exist as a mere begging monk among the farmers. Can we not imagine him attempting to polish and refine in this practical life the faith he had acquired thanks to Hōnen? It is not likely he tried to test his faith in writing as he had done before when he had lived and studied on Mt. Hiei. He seems to have held no ambition to publish writings such as his *Kyōgyōshinshō*. Did he, who had nothing save the path of attaining *Ōjō* in the Pure Land through the practice of the Nembutsu, probably not try to practice this way in an everyday life in touch with the earth, with the plow and hoe, a life of a Buddhist layman, eating meat and taking wife? I do not think he was capable of engaging in a life of trade, or of being a hunter or a fisherman. I do not suppose he possessed the temperament to try life as a craftsman. There was not even the opportunity for him to teach the villagers to read and write, as might have been the case had he lived as a lordless samurai in Edo times. Villagers in the Kamakura period probably as yet would have had little need for such things. Furthermore, there is no evidence he had any dealings with the regional authorities or local samurai classes. It is perhaps most appropriate to think that Shinran attempted to live a quiet life as a farmer, saying the Nembutsu as one common man among others. We must remember those who came to Kyoto to see him from the Kanto region were not intellectuals, they held no influence or power at all. At a remote rural site in Echigo Shinran took the first steps in his lay buddhist life, as a *gutoku*, a bald-headed, simple-hearted man. He continued this way of life during his stay in the Kanto area, a course said to have been suggested to him by the example of a Pure Land devotee of the late Heian period named Kyōshin. (Mention might also be made in this connection of Zenshōbō. See the chapter on Hōnen.)

5. *Japanese Spirituality and the Earth*

The life of the earth is the life of reality, the life of faith that does not permit deceit, the life of Nembutsu. There seems little doubt, therefore, that given the opportunity his exile provided, Shinran attempted to test the Nembutsu faith he had acquired from Hōnen where the life of the earth was actually found. Life in Kyoto would never have given him this opportunity. He took advantage of his exile to put his own faith to the trial. He already possessed the experience that 'Nembutsu alone is true,' so he did not spend his days merely mouthing empty Nembutsu. His was a true Nembutsu bound to the earth, and for him to live among those who worked the plow and hoe and not to use them himself as well would have turned his faith into the kind of "gibberish and nonsense" he himself condemns in the *Tannishō*. His life in Echigo was in direct and immediate conformity with the earth. The reason he did not content himself with continuing in the 'spotless' life of purity he had been leading to this point—rich in ideality alone, possessed of nothing positive—was because he wished to put the Nembutsu to work in man's ordinary life. Otherwise, it would be difficult to comprehend his reasons for eating meat and marrying in disregard of the Buddhist precepts. He made no attempt to draw distinctions between *Shōdōmon* (the "Holy Path," leading to salvation through self power, or by works; *Jiriki*) and *Jōdomon* (the "Pure Land Path," bringing salvation by means of Amida's grace; *Tariki*) merely in terms of whether one ate meat or practiced celibacy, or whether one repeated a continual Nembutsu or not. He tested in the actual life of the earth whether he could experience the Buddha's grace or favor in ordinary human existence. Here one cannot help but see the earnestness of his faith. He did not differentiate between priest and layman, and though he was unable to extricate himself completely from the ideologies of his time, he had already withdrawn from his previous existence of saint-like purity, both in his view of Nembutsu and in his awareness of faith. For him "raging passions" and "certain Hell" were not matters that could be said merely to relate to forms external to life; for this reason he discarded a conceptual life without hesitation. I think Shin believers who have come after him still lack a firm realization of this. His central thought is absolute faith in the Original Prayer of Amida. Of other matters, even though they might be highly praiseworthy according to the pronouncements of traditional Buddhism, he took no notice.

The following passage comes from a book entitled *Roankyō* (驢鞍橋 literally, "Donkey-Saddle Bridge"), which records the words and deeds of the Tokugawa Zen teacher Suzuki Shōsan (鈴木正三 1579–1655).

> *In the eighth month of the year 1652, the master [Suzuki Shōsan] arrived at Hoshōzen-ji, a temple at Hatogaya in Bushū of the Kanto district. Scores of farmers from all the neighboring parts came to hear his Buddhist teachings. The master said, "Farming is the work of the Buddha. Do not search outside of it. Each of your bodies is the body of Buddha. Your hearts are the heart of Buddha. Your work is the work of the Buddha. But since your minds are inclined to evil, you will fall into hell even with all your good qualities [roots]. Isn't it regrettable, dreaming up all kinds of wickedness in oneself—hate, attachment, stinginess, greed, and so on—agonizing day and night in this life, and in the life after falling into the evil courses eternally? But with farming you can exhaust bad karma, thus kindling the power of the Great Prayer. Farm, repeating the Nembutsu hoe-stroke by hoe-stroke. . . . you will then surely attain Buddhahood . . . (Part I, 98)*

He does not mean evil karma can be exhausted by the repetition of thousands of hoe-strokes. With the Namu-Amida-Butsu of each hoe-stroke the bad karma of incalculable ages past comes to naught. It is not a question of how many hoe-strokes or Nembutsu are required for so much bad karma. One hoe-stroke up, one hoe-stroke down . . . that is the absolute, it passes into the Original Prayer itself. No, it *is* the Original Prayer. In the rise and fall of the hoe is heard the soft whisper of the Original Prayer. Because Shōsan is a man of Zen he uses a Zen vocabulary, but his unconscious consciousness penetrates deeply to the marrow of Shinran's sect. There is not the least doubt that his Nembutsu appears from and returns to the earth. The five or six years Shinran spent in Echigo enabled him to attain this realization.

Upon receiving a pardon, Shinran proceeded to Hitachi instead of returning to the capital. It is not known whether this had any connection with his relatives there or not. But is it not probable he went to this area, where books were obtainable, to find evidence in the Buddhist scriptures for what he had attained—the unattainable.

Later on, we may see recurring in him the passion of his youth—hence the *Kyōgyōshinshō* came to be written. But on the other hand, the light of his faith in Amida, flowing over from his personality and life could not help but have influenced those near him. There began to materialize around him a kind of religious order during the twenty years he lived in the eastern provinces. This would never have happened without his sojourn in Echigo.

6. The Sincerity and Depth of Spirituality—The Person

The Heian courtiers experienced *mono no aware* but were unable to penetrate to its truth. It was Shinran in the Kamakura period who saw and penetrated the "truth of Nembutsu." The former sang of their yearnings in the beauties of nature, the latter came to embody the truth by living in intimacy with the earth. Although the courtiers could not transcend the region of sensation and emotion, Shinran was able to plunge to the center of spirituality. Before the advent of the Kamakura period the Japanese were unable to go beyond sensory or emotional insight. The ancient Japanese, as can be seen throughout the wealth of Heian literature, displayed a wonderful sensitivity in many intuitive directions; yet they were, finally, feminine and aristocratic, and lacked reality in the real sense of the word.

The bitter taste of decline and fall must once be known. Just such an experience resulted in the regeneration or rebirth of the Kamakura period. Here there was a testing that plumbed the depths of Japanese spirituality: sensory and emotional insights deepened into spiritual awakening, and *mono no aware* deepened into the "truth of Nembutsu." This was indeed brought about by the spirituality of one man, Shinran. The Person of the supra-individual—in this case Amida's Original Prayer —always affirms itself through the spirituality of the individual. This is the experience of "for the sake of this one individual person, Shinran," and the religious consciousness in the words, "I alone will go to Hell; I alone will go to the Pure Land." It is a region the Japanese did not even dream of prior to Heian. "Only when the skin is shed does the one real substance appear": here the one real substance is the Person itself.

This Person may best be symbolized by the earth. The concreteness of the earth and the concreteness of the Person are identical, and cannot be replaced by anything else. The beauty of the natural world embraces the four changing seasons, and this movement acts in concert with the mentality of *mono no aware*. But within it there is nothing possessed of the imperturbability, the constant unchangeableness, the indifference to season, of the earth. With the earth's momentary changes of aspect man's sensitivity stirs and his emotions rise—this is the poetry-composing heart of the courtier. Unless this heart is broken asunder spirituality does not appear. Spirituality shines forth when one encounters the earth that sustains the beauties of nature. The concreteness of the Person is at the same time the Person's reality. This is existentially understood only when man returns to the earth. Where the courtiers lived there was no earth. It was found where the common people walked. It was in their hearts and minds that spirituality flowered.

It was essential for Shinran of the capital to become a humble *gutoku*, a bald-headed, simple-hearted country man. When he was sent into exile he was divested of his priesthood and given the secular name Fujii Yoshizane. For him the assumption of this name meant not disgrace, it was the title that was to awaken his spirituality. Shinran built no temples. A thatched cottage was suitable for a simple man, not the Nara or Kyoto temple-complexes. The common people of the countryside had nothing to do with the extremes of magnificence and splendor wrought by those ensconced in Kyoto. For the Nembutsu a thatched hut is most appropriate. A Nembutsu that seeps out from under great roof-structures carries with it much falsehood. Amida does not lend his ear to choruses of empty Nembutsu. Here there is a universal but no individual, and the individual—the Person—is the object of the Original Prayer. In a *gutoku's* faith there is nothing so useless as palatial buildings. Edifices like the present-day Honganji Temples[15] are far removed from the intentions of the sect founder. Within the ancestral halls of their main temples the *gutoku* is not to be found. The "one individual person, Shinran"— if he is there at all—no doubt cries in the shade of the candle-light. But although the true nature of Shinran's sect disappeared from the opulent structures of Kyoto, it has continued to live in the humble thatched dwellings of the Myōkōnin, with their worn and leaky roofs. Myōkōnin— surely there is no more honored name in the sect of Shinran. The Person always lives in him. The authoritative and learned scholar-priests were not the inheritors of Shinran's faith and belief.

'The truth of Nembutsu,' Shinran's Person, the Person of the supra-individual self, Japanese spirituality—all these intuitively respond to the absolute nature, the 'one-by-one-ness,' and concrete finality of the earth. Here is the insight that plunges into the realm of spirituality beyond all sensory and emotional insight. It does not stop at *mono no aware*. The particularly Japanese character of spiritual insight is discernible within the earth or masculine culture of Kamakura that opened up a vista apart from the aristocratic or feminine culture of Kyoto. The essence of this spiritual insight is readily perceived within these words of Shinran:

> *I do not even know whether the calling of the Name will take me to the Pure Land or to Hell.... In short, such is my faith. Beyond this, you must decide for yourselves whether to believe in the Nembutsu or discard it altogether.* (Tannishō)

This certainly is a straightforward disclosure of Shinran's true face. It would be impossible even in the dreams of a tear-drenched Heian poet with his *mono no aware*. Shinran was truly a man of spiritual insight, for the above declaration could never have issued from someone living within a conceptual world. Here we see the aspect of the Kamakura samurai spirit communicated in such utterances as "Shut out all your thoughts!" and "Go right straight ahead!" And certainly Shin belief has underlying Zen-like elements. It is in such beliefs the characteristics of Japanese spiritual insight can be found.

There is an absolute truth, the truth of spiritual insight, in Shinran's enunciation of the "one individual person." Although we readily speak of truth, truth is not nearly so easily attained. Only when sensory and emotional truth are illumined by the light of spirituality are they capable of Truth. Since in the former's case truth is still on the plane of a sub-ject-object duality, it is relative and as such cannot be called absolute. The absolute nature of truth is seen when the individual self is broken through and the Person of the supra-individual self is encountered face to face:

> *A figure between Heaven and Earth—solitariness itself,*
> *Standing alone before an infinitely expanding vista.*

87

This is the domicile of Shinran's Person. Because it cannot be replaced it is absolute. Nothing could exist that is more true. In the 13th book of the *Manyōshū* the following verse is found:

Were there another like you in this land of reeds,
Then why should I continue this constant longing?

This is a love poem, but even with its emotional intent the fact of there being two people who are the same is denied. The truth of love lies in this inadmissibility. If there were two, one would have to be false. It goes without saying that this meaning holds much greater importance for spirituality.

Shinran had absolute trust in the teachings of Hōnen because their origin existed in spirituality. From Amida's Original Prayer to the statements of Hōnen and then to Shinran's own words there is a connection through the absolute nature of truth, inasmuch as they are all rippling the waves of spirituality. Too often we find those of the Shin sect using exceedingly roundabout expressions where a Zen-man would exclaim with no beating about, "Confront it face to face!" Shin tends to see time as a straight-line, probably because it always wants to operate within sensory and emotional spheres. Hence even Pure Land *Ōjō* comes to signify something that takes place after death. Opposed to this, Zen tries to insist on a circular view of time, so that all things are immediately settled in this absolute instant. But to the discerning eye the straight line holds true as well as the circular. Did not Shinran himself teach *ōgen-nisō ekō*,[16] rebirth in the Pure Land and return to this life to dedicate all one's merits toward the enlightenment of one's fellow-beings? Truth, in any case, can only be discovered in the world of spirituality, the world of the Person.

7. The Awakening of the Unlettered to the Person

It was his exile and his everyday experience with the common people that enabled Shinran to become the first person to awaken to Japanese spirituality. Japanese spirituality is extremely concrete, realistic, and personal; it is "I alone." Only when this was experientially understood was the fundamental truth of Japanese religious consciousness established.

Until then preparations were obliged to advance along in a conceptual order based upon the original Indian Buddhism that had entered via China. The many eminent priests and scholars that appeared starting with Saichō and Kūkai were essential; the virtue, learning, and art of Genshin in the closing years of the Heian were especially indispensable. It is difficult to judge the extent his *Ōjōyōshū*[17] influenced the common people of the time. In all likelihood it was merely circulated among the Buddhist scholars of Nara and Hiei. His ideas on morality probably did not reach a wider audience. But inasmuch as his paintings appealed to the sense of sight, anyone with the opportunity of seeing them must have received an exceptional impression. Moreover, his art probably gave rise to many imitators. Sculpture aside, ink-drawings in the form of *e-makimono* or handscrolls were copied and transmitted to many areas. From the close of Heian times to Kamakura's beginnings, the 'Torments of Hell' were depicted a great deal. Even those unable to understand Chinese writing and without access to eminent priests could not only see something that was drawn on paper, they could not fail to be moved by what they saw as well.

Prior to Shinran's arrival such preparations existed among the common people. After Genshin came Hōnen, and without these two Shinran might never have appeared. Hōnen, who came later than Genshin, was for that reason alone much easier for people to approach. Although Genshin is a figure very much in the style of the holy-man, Hōnen has a very familiar air about him. In his *Ichimaikishōmon*[18] especially, Hōnen shows a feeling for the earth that is only one step this side of Shinran. Hōnen, like Shinran, underwent the bitter experience of exile, and because of it his latter years took on a particularly strong spiritual radiance. Had exile come in younger days this would probably have been even more intense. He bequeathed this light to Shinran. The *One Page Testament* still has lingering academic earmarks, but at its roots there is the insight of Japanese spirituality, without however the thorough-going maturity of Shinran. I will devote a separate section to this work in a later chapter.

(Rather than viewing Hōnen and Shinran as two separate individuals I think it would be more appropriate to view them as one. Hōnen appeared reborn in Shinran. Here we may perceive the existence of something vital in the life of Hōnen. Which is to say

89

that Japanese spirituality first awakened in Hōnen, and then was taken over by Shinran. When we read over the records of Hōnen, we can well understand the reason for his persecution by the scholars of Nara and Hiei, men who simply turned out literary documents and kept to a world of groundless concepts. Therefore, seen from the viewpoint of those who would possess the world of success and vanity, men like Hōnen were criminals, utterly ignorant, and totally unacceptable to their circles. Hōnen was a dangerous element. Their persecution of Hōnen and his followers thus had a very rational basis. This point will be taken up again later.)

Although in the *One Page Testament* Hōnen refers to such disciplines as the threefold heart and the four sorts of exercise, that is probably because the *Testament* was written at the request of scholarship inclined disciples. In exile he came into frequent contact with those (in his own words) "simple-hearted, ignorant folk who know not a single letter," who had nothing whatever to do with scholarly endeavor. They repeated the Name of Amida over and over and conducted themselves as "ignorant men and women of simple and honest faith." Hōnen was without question struck by their sincerity, a sincerity he himself finally realized following his lifelong opposition to the oppression of traditional thought and struggle against his own scholarship and intellectualism. When he was exiled to Tosa on the island of Shikoku, he welcomed it as an opportunity to spread his faith to people in remote and isolated regions. It was not necessarily only a matter of influencing others, he probably had some premonition they would be able to teach him as well. Regrettably, he was at the time already declining in years and was unable to pass on to his disciples a more vital and energetic teaching, as Shinran was later able to do. Yet because of Hōnen's life Shinran's own experience became possible. This clearly attests to the fact that spirituality works in the individual, the Person, and that at the same time it is supra-individual.

Hōnen's encounter with a prostitute at Muro-no-tomari in the province of Harima, while on route to his place of exile is an event to be recorded in the annals of Japanese spiritual history. The life and death of millions of human beings in war has its place in such a history and is capable of striking us by its very numbers; yet qualitatively speaking, something able to stir the religious consciousness of a prostitute must possess great and universal truth as well. The problem of karma, of being caught within the web of cause and effect, is not surprising because of quantitative measure. The Zen master Gutei said his "One-Finger Zen" could not be used up in a whole lifetime. It is exactly as he said. It is possible for a single utterance of Nembutsu to bring about changes effecting the entire surface of the world. If the whisper of Japanese spirituality does not reach unto the minds of illiterates as well, then it is a lie. In fact, it is just because they do not know a single word that they are able to hear its voice.

A prostitute might be thought to have an existence quite isolated from the earth. Knowledge of the kind of life such a person led in Hōnen's time is not known to me. I do not know what their place in society was. But they seem to have been included among the 'ignorant men and women of simple and honest faith' Hōnen refers to in his *Testament*. The center of Japanese culture during this period was, as an aristocratic culture, the exclusive possession of the Kyoto court nobles. A prostitute in this remote area of the country would not, I think, even though gasping in the throes of karmic suffering, have considered the reasons behind her condition. But since suffering is suffering, she probably wondered, indeed worried deeply, about how she might possibly escape it. Otherwise she would not have approached Hōnen for advice. As I said previously, I do not know the degree of Buddhism's dispersion during that time, or the extent to which it had been adopted, but its seems certain that Hōnen's "Namu-Amida-Butsu" was warmly welcomed by the rural people. Until this time Buddhism had been based upon benefits in this present world. That the world of the Japanese spirit (which until then had known only such benefits) should, thanks to Hōnen's travel in this remote area, first awaken the spirituality of a prostitute was not simply fortuitous.

Although she was not particularly close to the earth, the gap that separated her was no doubt never even near the size of the one that separated the courtiers from it. Such women did not directly encounter the earth in their daily lives, though the earth was always near at hand and its fragrance undoubtedly surrounded them. Their existence was not conceptual or abstract; indeed, it possessed the raw, direct quality of life's reality, the earth's fundamental quality. In this respect, Hōnen's religion can be said to have found an extraordinary point of communion in Japanese spirituality.

Before crossing the Inland Sea to Shikoku, Hōnen was visited by an elderly fisherman and his wife on the Takasago seacoast, in the province of Harima. It was another chance encounter of Nembutsu with the reality of human life. These people were without learning or political or social standing, the very figures of the ordinary man standing by himself alone on the earth. Provided with the chance to reflect upon the karma of their lives, there burgeoned in them a dread of Hell's torments, and it was no mere mentally conceived idea. This is the process in which a sincere emotional nature penetrates to spirituality. Consequently, Hōnen did not give them conceptual phrases. He taught simply about the Nembutsu and the Compassionate Prayer of the Buddha. The old couple took to the teaching immediately. Japanese spirituality is produced from within precisely the realistic and genuine nature we see in these fishermen. A fisherman's life was not as peaceful as that of farmer working the land, but in having a realistic and untainted character it too is not separated from the earth. Prostitutes and fishermen might appear poetical opposites, but in terms of spiritual life, in their connection to that which conforms to the earth, they both represent the perfect recipient or object for Hōnen's teaching. Their stories were taken from the following excerpts found in *Hōnen's Life.*

> *Upon reaching the seacoast of Takasago in Harima Province, an elderly couple, the man about 70 his wife over sixty, came to Hōnen and said, "We are fishermen of this coast. From early childhood we have taken the lives of fish. This we have done from morning until night. It is said that those who take life will fall to Hell and suffer its terrible torments. Is there any way we might escape this fate?" Hōnen said, "Anyone like you, just by saying Namu-Amida-Butsu over and over again, will attain the Pure Land by virtue of Amida's Compassionate Prayer." Upon hearing this the old man and his wife wept with joy. Thereafter, although they went out to fish as before, they always repeated the Name. After they returned home at night their neighbors were surprised to hear the sound Namu-Amida-Butsu, Namu-Amida-Butsu ... late into the night.*

92

Arriving at the harbor of Muro-no-tomari in Harima, Hōnen was approached by a small boat carrying a prostitute. She said to him, "Many are the ways through the world, what great sin could I have committed in a former life to bring me to such a situation of heavy sins? How may I rid myself of them?" Hōnen replied with great pity, "Truly such a life is heavy with iniquity, the extent of its retribution is indeed incalculable. Try to find some other livelihood if you can and change your ways as soon as possible. If this proves impossible, if the intention to sacrifice your very life in seeking for salvation has not arisen in your heart, then stay what you are and repeat earnestly the Nembutsu. It is for the sake of just such sin-laden people that Amida Nyorai has taken the Vow of universal salvation. Put all your trust and faith in his Original Prayer and do not abase yourself. Place your faith in the Prayer and repeat the Nembutsu and you will certainly be reborn in the Pure Land." Upon receiving this kind-hearted advice she wept with joy. Later, Hōnen told his followers that her faith was very firm and that she was certain to attain Ōjō. When his exile was ended and he was returning home, Hōnen called at the village where he had taught her, and inquired about her. He was told that upon receiving his instruction she had gone to live in a village in the mountains where she had practiced the Nembutsu single-heartedly. Soon after she had died. On her deathbed she is said to have rightly achieved Ōjō. This pleased Hōnen extremely, and confirmed his opinion of her.

III. THE AUTONOMY OF JAPANESE SPIRITUALITY

1. The Advance to Buddhism

We must not view Japanese spirituality merely in terms of deliverance through the Nembutsu and avoidance of Hell. Were it that alone, Japanese spirituality would have existed in China as well, not to mention Japan herself prior to the Kamakura period. Japanese spirituality is not to be regarded as the deepening of a Buddhist religious consciousness which came to allow such ideas as the above to permeate the populace. These explanations would deal only with the popular nature of Buddhism, and would not touch those fundamental ingredients possessed deep within by the Japanese people. Because of the universal relation that exists between spirituality and Buddhism, if we were to speak abstractly about spirituality by itself we would have to settle merely for a discussion of Buddhism's permeability. But what I would like to indicate is how Japanese spirituality influenced Buddhism. First I will set Japanese spirituality apart from Buddhism and try to discover historically what sort of influence it advanced upon Buddhism when, given the opportunity of gradually rising to prominence, it came unexpectedly face to face with the latter. It is, of course, historical chance which brought about Buddhism's importation, acceptance, study, spread, and so on. Looking no farther, it would seem Japanese spirituality only busied itself trying to follow and then to absorb Buddhism. But since spirituality is essentially a living thing it does not always assume a position of passivity. Even in the physical world the existence of a genuinely passive thing has never been possible. If we suppose one thing's existence to be one power, then any power that is added to it will breed many varied responses, according to the force of the original element. This is all the more so concerning spirituality with its apparant passivity that is in reality an active force in great movement. For this reason it is more appropriate to call Japanese Buddhism an expression of Japanese spirituality than to say it is a Japanized Buddhism. When the time came ripe for this expression Japanese spirituality lent itself to the shape of Buddhism. Such, in my opinion, is the best way to understand the words "Japanese Buddhism."

Still were it not for Buddhism I imagine we should have nothing much to say about Japanese spirituality. Yet to call it a Japanized Buddhism would be to confuse cause and effect, like saying that because grass will not grow without rain, therefore rain is grass.

The growth of plants and trees is brought about thanks to rain, sun, wind, and soil, but they do not themselves produce plants and trees. They have their own primary essence. I should like to take up Japanese spirituality as one such primary essence.

One thing I wish to have clearly understood is that there are no political connotations whatsoever attached to the Japanese spirituality of which I speak. It just happens that Japanese spirituality is Japanese. It has no wish to excel, politically or in any other way, or to rise above any other spirituality with its particular characteristics. It does not want to subjugate other elements of any kind. Moreover, it is not something to be brandished by any group or faction as its own exclusive possession. Nor is it connected in any fashion with such things as ancestral honor.

Plum trees are not cherry trees. Cherry trees and tree peonies likewise have their own special characteristics, endowed with their own respective merits. To support only one individual self and suppress all others is a shortcut to the self's destruction. That is why I do not wish any political coloring at all to be attributed to Japanese spirituality, for really it is something to which such values should not be attached.

The idea of the existence of a distinct phenomenon called Japanese spirituality might be considered audacious. It might further seem that spirituality is spirituality because it is universal, that particularized it would cease to be spirituality and become nothing more than a psychological characteristic or idea. That would be true only when spirituailty is treated scientifically or philosophically. When we discover, as I believe we do, individual instances that are historically distinct, I believe is it all right to posit the existence of Japanese elements in spirituality. Just as there are Japanese qualities in both the sensory and emotional natures, Japanese elements are present in spirituality as well. When we closely investigate the sensory nature, we find that various quantitative and qualitative differences exist between individual as well as racial groups. But the easiest for most people to understand is emotional individuality. To illustrate this, here is an example from a work entitled *Lectures on National Morality* (*Kokumin Dōtoku ni kansuru Kōwa*, Hori Koretake, 1913):

> *The indefinable essential of the refreshing, manly spirit of the Kamakura samurai is finally the feeling of* aware *bequeathed to them from Heian times. The lives of Heian men and women differed from those of the Kamakura samurai, so naturally this feeling was also manifested in different ways. We find it in the appreciation of natural beauty and the loves, etc., in the former, and in the latter's battlefield concerns; loyalty, filial piety, and so forth. But when we leave externals aside and look at their true existence, we see them submerged in the same emotional tone. There is Taira Tadanori who, wanting his poems included in the Imperial*

*Collection, returned in the night from a battlefield path at the risk
of death to knock at the gate of his poetry teacher. Shinra Saburō transmitting the secret of the reed flute in the moonlight
of Mount Ashigara; Minamoto Yoshiie regretting the wind blow-
ing against the falling cherry blossoms; Hatakeyama Kagesue
rushing on the enemy with a spray of plum blossoms inserted in
his quiver; Kumagai Jirō Naozane wanting to spare his captive
Taira Atsumori. These figures exhibit clearly the style of the
Kamakura samurai. The clarity is indeed perhaps too intense,
throwing the examples into a superficial light.*

*The Kamakura samurai were brave and strong. Their feeling
of loyalty to their master was very deep. But it was their spirit of
aware that imparted a refined elegance to their bravery and loyalty, rendering them more beautiful than flowers. The way of the
samurai will never be known by literary exposition, nor can it ever
be organized into theories or creeds. Rules and theories could
show only the appearances. There is no way to grasp its genuine
spiritual marrow, which could only be known by bodily experience. Herein is the reason Zen lived in the Kamakura warrior.
There are various interpretations of this: some say the samurai
depended on religion because they did not know at what moment
they would die; others say Zen was accepted because of the decay
of existing Buddhist traditions. But I believe the intuitive realization of Zen and mono no aware, which constituted the essence of
the way of the samurai, are one and the same thing.*

I hope to return to spend more time on this relation between the samurai and Zen. Regardless, one cannot imagine the spiritual breadth the
appreciation of refined and elegant matters added to the life of the samurai, who are generally regarded as bonded to military affairs alone. This
traditional insight—what must be termed the Japanese emotional insight
—flowing not only within the warrior classes but within the townspeople
as well is a historical shape which must be accorded great consideration.
Even in other areas the Japanese have this wealth of emotion and seem
in some cases unable to shed their primitive nature. When manifested
in the right direction, with suppression of self and in benevolent accord,
it is really quite beautiful. But when it is an expression of something

guided by mere narrow-minded reason it comes to breed difficulties in no small measure, in international politics and scholarly research to name just two areas.

The emotional insight in which a special Japanese character can be found not only appears in the so-called elegant artistic pursuits or ethical concerns, but is frequently seen emphasized in the political structure as well. However, since all of these fail to leave the realm of the emotions no spirituality is visible. The unusual contacts with foreign countries that started during Kamakura times, teachings such as the *taigi-meibun* ('true sovereign-subject relation') that were transmitted by Zen monks from the Southern Sung, stimulated and largely influenced the author of the *Jinnō Shōtōki*.[19] Due to such stimuli there occurred a greater and greater elevation of the Japanese *seishin* along political and emotional lines. This was limited to the rise and emphasis of the Japanese emotional nature alone, however, and had no relation to Japanese spirituality. Spirituality has a sphere to itself, independent of its Japanese character, its movement different from those of the emotional sphere. If these spheres are confused, unsavory complications arise in human life, which will work even to hinder advancement on a national level as well. Emotional insight has to secure its balance on the one hand by means of the intellect, but on the other, its characteristic narrowness must be corrected through its convergence into spirituality.

2. The Manner of Spirituality's Operation

Now we must shift our concern to spirituality's role in human life. "Spirituality" is not something that has an existence somewhere, but since its operation can be felt we call it spirituality for the sake of convenience. Although I said its operation can be felt, it is nothing like the cosmic rays one hears about these days that are detectable by man-made devices. In trying to think about and give meaning to human life it is easier to communicate if we posit something like spirituality. Under no condition should we acquire a fixed idea regarding it. Although human life is a harmonious whole the intellect longs to analyze it—indeed, analyzing is the intellect, or perhaps, the analyzing faculty is called the intellect. The intellect tries to distinguish spirituality apart from the senses and emotions.

In talking with one another human beings call this is a plum tree and that a pine tree, say that this is rain, this is water, that ice, this steam, and on and on; this is wisdom, this virtue, that is courage and that is science, philosophy, law—we make various distinctions and want to establish spheres for each idea or concept. This is done for convenience; they are not rigid divisions with inviolable boundaries, and to think they were would breed unforeseeable confusion in everyday life. Human beings expect that through such precise delineations their thought will be clear, precise, and decisive; instead they often attain the opposite result. Like the entomologist discovering a new insect, or the researcher detecting an unknown microbe, the thinker contrives new concepts from things hitherto unperceived within the existing confusion of thought. However, newly contrived concepts do not have the isolated existence of newly found microbes. They are what men of genius have developed in order to put the existing entanglements of thought into some kind of order. I would like to interpret the concept of spirituality in this manner as well. Therefore I would like to sketch in a rough manner the way spirituality's role is manifested in the operation of the human psyche.

We see flowers as red, willows as green, feel cool water as cool and warm water as warm. This is the function of our senses. Human beings do not stop there, they say red flowers are beautiful, cool water is refreshing. This is man's emotional nature. The sensory world is given various values, on top of that beautiful things are desired, the feeling of refreshing coolness is yearned for. Instead of separating oneself from these things objectively and attaching values to them, we want to take possession of them. This is the work of the will. It is also possible to say that the previous value-attaching derives from the will, but in any case it is convenient to place some distinction between emotion and will. And to make such distinctions in these various functions is the work of the intellect. It is for the psychologist to study their every side, yet there are points I should like to give much more detailed discussion. But now I must turn to the subject of spirituality.

Spirituality is the name applied to the operations that cannot be clearly explained by the mental functions of the above mentioned varieties. It is spirituality's operation that makes the refreshing quality of water or the redness of flowers felt in their unalloyed truth. In other words, spirituality's operation enables man to perceive the genuine value of the truth that redness is beautiful or that coolness is refreshing. Spirituality does

98

not move the individual's will to desire beautiful objects or to seek refreshment; rather, it causes the will to turn to the supra-individual Person. Although this function may be thought to be one performed by the intellect, the intellect does not possess the power to influence the will. It remains slave to the will. Although many recent philosophers have spoken of the powerlessness of the intellect, in the Orient the great power of the will has long been recognized, and all effort has been focused upon its subjugation. The intellect can never equal the power of the will solely through its own efforts. In a sense it is by means of the will that the intellect can be said to sustain its capabilities. In other words, the intellect is the product of the will. It could even be said that the will moves the intellect in order to render its own capabilities stronger and more efficacious. In any case, the intellect is incapable of ridding itself of the will's yoke by itself. That is possible through the operation of spirituality, thanks to which the intellect is able to transcend the individual self. The discrimination of non-discrimination works in a similar manner.

But spirituality's operation does not simply end there. If it did, Japanese spirituality would not be possible, and spirituality would end at the Great Mirror Wisdom and the Wisdom of Exquisite Observation. Things general or universal prepare only black or white ground, and become both things of the sea and things of the mountain. They are, as a consequence, neither things of the sea nor things of the mountain. In Buddhist terminology, spirituality also possesses the Wisdom of Action.[20] Here the special characteristic of *Japanese* spirituality is revealed; that is, here spirituality begins to operate in its Japanese manner. To find the "where" of this operation's appearance this discussion would have to turn in a different direction. If we call the Great Mirror Wisdom the intellectual insight of spirituality, then the Wisdom of Action would be its volitional insight. Although this is an extremely awkward use of words, I will use it for the time being.

3. *Japanese Spiritual Insight*

Intellectual and volitional insight are the two modes of spirituality's operation. The former moves in the sensory and emotional natures, the latter in the will. The volitional aspect of human life is found in man's acts and conduct. Here we could include karmic retribution and ideas such as sin, death, and future existence, all of which are associated with Buddhist thought. But though the vocabulary is Buddhist, the thought is the product of religious consciousness generally.

How did the Japanese of times past foster their own characteristics with regard to these ideas? It is my belief these characteristics were first clearly evident in Kamakura times, and that this was owing to Shinran. He does not speak of salvation from sin, he does not preach freedom from the shackles of karma. He wants this existence—this worldly, relative existence of karmic suffering as it is—to give itself up completely to the working of the power of Amida's absolute Prayer. Here lies the existential experience relating Amida (the Absolute One) and Shinran himself. Since the Great Compassion of the Absolute One transcends good and evil and right and wrong, one can never reach it through one's own insignificant intellection or acts of goodness. Man simply receives the Infinite Light of Great Compassion and delivers himself into the working of naturalness without any intention of discarding or retaining anything he might consider his possession. This is none other than the consciousness in Japanese spirituality of *kannagara*, the "Way of the Gods."

Chinese Buddhism was incapable of passing beyond cause and effect; Indian Buddhism sunk into the depths of emptiness. Japanese spirituality alone, in not destroying cause and effect, nor the existence of this world, succeeded in including all things as they are completely within Amida's Light. This was possible with Japanese spirituality alone, and it was the Kamakura period that produced the opportunity for it. It is a strange thing indeed, that while Pure Land thought has had a continuous existence of over fifteen hundred years in China, it still has not arrived at a Shinran-like spiritual insight. In Japan it progressed from Genshin to Hōnen and then came directly to the fore in the thought of the Shinran school. It is a thought that existed neither in India nor China, nor in the Judaism or Christianity of the Western world. Therefore it is often justifiably said that Shinran's teaching is not Buddhist, inasmuch as it is something that emerged from the insight of Japanese spirituality meeting the stimulus of Buddhist Amidist thought which uprose suddenly in Kamakura times.

Life in this world is felt to be sinful. When we see from the standpoint of our present existence that with a single thought of resolute faith this sinfulness can be received absolutely and unconditionally into Amida's compassionate hands, then this standpoint as it is is affirmed as good. This is *jinen hōni* (naturalness), the *shimo* (thusness) of Zen. It is Shinran's 'meaningless meaning,' the Way of *kannagara*, the heart that dwells in suchness through and through (*jikishin*).[21] It is the consciousness of unconsciousness that does not admit of the discriminations of man. It is the presentation of the true heart in all its nakedness, without calculation, severed from all inclination to gauge or measure. There is one thing not be forgotten—Absolute Compassion. When a heart is embraced by Great Compassion it achieves truth and purity, and non-dependence upon words or letters is possible.

Kannagara is "The Way of the Gods." With one more leap (in Shinran's terminology, *ōchō*), Japanese spirituality is revealed in the purity of its suchness. One by one each individual touches the person of the supra-individual self, and one by one each becomes the person of "this one individual person, Shinran." It is faith that grasps this wonderful change. The person of the individual self does not grasp faith by placing an object opposite and confronting it. The person of the individual self is 'one by one,' yet at the same time it is, as it is, the supra-individual Person. Since this spiritual insight first appeared in the Japanese people we are obliged to call it Japanese spirituality. Abstractly, it was present in India and China, but concretely, as personal experiential reality, it was realized in one Japanese man. Since its realization, Japanese all have possessed the opportunity whereby they too might experience it. (In this fundamental area those of the present-day Shin sect do not fully grasp their own faith. They attempt to view it in terms of historical relationships to other groups, traditional creeds, outward behavior, ritual manners, etc. I think these attempts are mistaken. At another time I intend to deal with this problem separately.)

4. The Background of Shinran's Japanese Spirituality

To discover how Shinran's Pure Land thought got the backing of the religious consciousness that arose during the Kamakura period, the following historical facts must be appraised.

Historians tell us that during the final years of the Heian period a *mappō* (Latter-day) thought took hold and people began to feel an aversion to the world, and that seizing upon this opportunity, Pure Land teaching was able to prosper and spread. Among Buddhists some had even calculated

101

think, study much more deeply the question of whether human thought is influenced by such conceptual propaganda. Regarding *mappō* thought in particular, it was those Buddhists possessed of some measure of intellectual attainment who began to speak of *mappō*. Unless their declarations were rooted firmly in a life of reality they would be useless, incapable of producing anything of a positive nature. In my opinion, the average Japanese of that time did not care one way or another about *mappō*. Still, there was an indefinable uneasiness abroad, and it was felt that the world was on the brink of an onslaught of political, social, and intellectual change. Later in Heian times changes came in life conditions, there was a collapse of economic structures, changes in political power, in ideological transformations, and in Japanese life as a whole, probably generated a vaguely unconscious feeling that things could not continue as they were. I do not think this was taken as *mappō* in any specific sense. The upper classes of society—the intelligentsia—gave the name *mappō* to the general feeling of uneasiness in society, and thought to devise some plan to counter it. Among Buddhists this was probably particularly true, and it was no doubt they who evolved countermeasures. But for those whose lives were passed in proximity to the earth, without concern or relation whatever to the politics, religion, or current abstract culture, for those of the soil whose lives were lived within reality, there was probably no undue concern with this feeling. Their spirituality tried to grasp something fundamental outside the existing emotional life and insight and there to seek composure of mind. They were unable to sustain an interest in complicated argument, science, class structure, and the like. They were unceasing in their search for something capable of working much more directly and strongly on their daily lives. They might not have felt such a need consciously, but there seems little doubt they felt anxiety. A sensitive religious spirit could not help but notice this kind of uneasiness and anxiety rippling through the social consciousness. A heart spiritually pure and lucid and filled with love would have to be extremely sensitive to such a mood. It is said that if there is a call Kannon is sure to answer. The possessor of a deep and keen spirituality will likewise grasp directly and immediately those occasional shifts in the heart and mind of man. Or perhaps it should be put this way: the great spirit of the universe, the supra-individual Person, reflects itself in those persons endowed with the greatest receptivity of all who live and die at each

102

that *mappō* started the seventh year of Eishō (1052). Yet we must, I respective juncture of changing history. Therefore a great individual spirit may be said to be a mirror in which the universal spirit, the transcendent spirit, is reflected. We may say that by viewing the working of the superior individual spirit it is possible to see the working of the transcendent spirit. Shinran's individual spirit was able to attain to this and was able to touch Japanese spirituality which then was functioning in accord with the earth.

Whatever is said of *mappō*, surely such an abstract concept cannot be called the source of the Pure Land Shin sect. Scholars in attempting to discover religion in written matter or in institutions or systems of one kind or other, are unable to touch the breath of religious life itself. They even try to derive Amida's Absolute Love from their speculations. Speculations and logic come afterwards, the first experience must be Absolute Love itself. Therefore, I wish to view Shinran in the realization of his spirituality, and not as the great majority of historians and Buddhist scholars do, in reference to the tradition or history of Pure Land thought.

5. Ise Shinto

Doubtless there are various causes for the awakening of the spirituality of the Japanese during the Kamakura period; the actual fact that it did occur alone is certain. It is something that can also be seen in the contemporaneous promulgation of Ise Shinto.[22] Although the opportunities that appeared to produce Ise Shinto have no direct connection to spirituality, such a connection is manifest in what was produced. It is generally believed Shinto is totally lacking in thought content, and that even if there may be some Shinto thought, it has merely been borrowed from Buddhism, Taoism, or Confucianism. This is not altogether an unreasonable assertion, yet even were something borrowed, there have to have been some constituents present to begin with to do the borrowing. It has been said that since what content Shinto may have is of a simple and primitive character and without any essence of its own, it is therefore incapable of resisting so-called foreign elements. I do not think the picture can be drawn with so broad a brushstroke. That is because Shinto always emphasizes its independence by going under its own name in opposition to these foreign elements. Of course that this contains strong political overtones is beyond question, still if there were nothing there at all, it would not be able to affirm itself in this manner. What then are the "it" and "itself" of the preceding sentence?

I personally feel that Shinto first realized itself in Ise Shinto—that is, that Ise Shinto was the awakening of Shinto—and consequently that Ise Shinto has come to be the essence of all Shinto. When this essence appears via the discriminatory nature of the individual self, it becomes Laotzean, Chuangtzean, Buddhistic or Confucianistic. It assumes these varied modes of expression according to the person and time in which it happens to appear. In most cases its appearance is thickly coated with political colorations that depict Shinto in a utilitarian light; that is certainly a deviation from the essence of Shinto.

Although one aspect of Japanese spirituality certainly is manifested in Shinto, there is another aspect not in evidence; the Absolute Compassion of the Absolute One (Boundless Great Compassion) found only in the Shinran tradition. The sin and retribution of each and every person can be completely absorbed within the Great Compassion of the Absolute One —such is Shinran's view of the supra-individual spirit. I believe it would thus be appropriate to state that the Person of Shinran that had experienced the supra-individual spirituality is the incarnation of Japanese spirituality. Neither Ise Shinto nor any of the other forms of Shinto were awakened to the supra-individual Great Compassionate One. But Japanese spirituality caused the Great Compassionate One to be reflected in the individual spirit of Shinran. Spirituality that does not know the Great Compassionate One has not yet awakened to the true essence of spirituality. And there is in the manner of this awakening something possible for the Japanese people alone. It is in the possible world-wide application of this we must find Japanese spirituality's meaning. What works only in the Japanese pattern with no world-wide nature—and which is incompatible with such a nature—cannot be said to have attained true Japaneseness. This would be especially true with the question of spirituality.

6. The Way to the Fundamental Source

The insights by which Shinto in its basic nature attempts to maintain its independence are not spiritual but emotional. In trying to maintain, in addition to such insights, a conceptual system based on spiritual awakening with which to consolidate these insights, the Shinto of the Kamakura period can be said to have moved a step, albeit unconscious, in the direction of spirituality. Shinto virtues such as sincerity, honesty, purity, and cheerfulness of heart are emotional in nature, and do not enter the domain of spirituality. When abstinence and purification are not accompanied by an added depth they do not exceed the mentality of a primitive people. Although Ise Shinto made attempts to build metaphysical and religious foundations with these insights, they could not be termed successful because they were not spiritual insights. Because things belonging to the emotional aspect cannot maintain a metaphysical base, these attempts were nothing more than psychological characteristics. Hence those who wished to establish a Shinto philosophy tended to rely upon Buddhist, Confucian, or other thought systems, which meant a resultant loss in Shinto's independence. Though insights such as Shinto possesses have the Japanese emotional nature; they do not have Japanese spirituality.

Shinto's insights are emotional because they have yet to pass through the stage of denial. This is true of sensory insight as well. Insight of a simple and primal character will not attain spirituality unless it undergoes denial. And metaphysical systems cannot be erected upon insight or affirmation that has not gone through this denial. Japanese do feel in Shinto that which is indefinably Japanese. At this point Japanese—all Japanese—are Shintoist. But somehow or other an unsatisfactory feeling remains that cannot be repressed, that derives from the lack of Japanese spirituality in the insights of Shinto. There is an undeniable charm attached to the primitive and child-like that attracts all men. But this is as adults, as mature or elderly people. When one is a child, consciousness of a child-like nature is of course impossible. When one does become conscious of it, is the time of denial. In proportion to the strength and profundity of this denial there will also be a yearning for and consequent appreciation of the primitive nature; and this will result in an accordingly increasing purification of spirituality. What is produced is no longer emotional insight but spirituality.

"*Aru ga mama no aru*" means "to exist in suchness." Plants and trees exist in suchness, as do dogs and cats and mountains and rivers and streams. When existence in suchness undergoes negation and returns to *aru ga mama* (to suchness), it then becomes the original, primary "existing in suchness." Human consciousness passes through such a process.

105

If someone argues this away, calling it unnecessarily complicated, or saying that it is morbid or unhealthy, then that will be the end of it, for nothing would persuade such a person. He is like the golden carp that is without the experience of breaking through the net of the fish-enclosure. Even if it is told what to feed upon in the outer pond, it will have no reason to understand.

It is not a case of either right or wrong, but of the existence of such a reality in the world of insight. From a higher insight, what is beneath can be seen, since it is a prior stage that has already been passed through. But from beneath, what is above is not visible. It depends upon spatial conditions. Be this as it may, 'existing in suchness' must once have been strongly denied, existence must once have been non-existence. There is only one way for sensory or emotional insight to enter the realm of spiritual insight, and that is through denial. If red flowers are not at one time not-red, if beauty has not once been not-beautiful, then red flowers are not really red and beauty is not really beauty. Some may think this strange, and for them it will never be otherwise.

In the realization of spiritual insight, therefore, impurity is not simply impurity, it must be a sin the weight of which will cause a fall to certain hell. The true and honest heart of Shinto must become black as blackest soot, until both Heaven and Earth are hidden by its dark clouds, and man has no place to lay his head.

In itself it is not enough that "the *kami* dwell in an honest man's heart."[23] The *kami*, the honest man's heart, the heart pure and upright—these must be renounced completely, and all must sink into the bottomless abyss. When one returns and is revivified, the doors of heaven will open and spring will come to Heaven and Earth for the first time. Such an experience of spiritual awakening is lacking in Shinto. Attempts to complete this conceptually are like making clothing from borrowed materials. The process in which existing in suchness follows the path of denial and then returns to the place of origin, bears a Japanese character. It is the direct passing to Japanese spirituality, and the discovery of the Absolute Love of the Absolute One, which attaches no relative conditions of any kind on its objects. Its acceptance just as it is, in the form of its suchness, is the insight of Japanese spirituality. The usual ethic is the affirmation of good and the negation of evil, but in this case good is negated as well as evil, and afterwards, good is Good and evil is Evil.

Moreover, from the standpoint of Absolute Love good and evil are not abandoned, but are taken in within the Love itself. Seeing impurities and driving them out does not transcend the region of objective logic either. Impurities once driven out are certain to return. This is inevitable in the objective world. Impurity can be said to recur as soon as the purification has been performed. The moment we speak of a region of purity which must not be touched by the dust of the world, has not the first speck of dust already drifted in? Purification belongs to the world of the senses and emotions. With the world of spiritual insight there is no dust to be cleansed, the very act of cleansing becomes needless. This is *"aru ga mama no aru,"* existing in suchness, where the impurities are being swept away at every moment. This must be the actual fact intuitively experienced when one comes to the "primary, ultimate, and original nature" in its true meaning. Shinto while in the world of the emotions tries to realize the spiritual world conceptually, and it is in this we feel something unsatisfactory, that something is somehow missing. What is missing is the existential reality in which Absolute Love is experienced through Japanese spirituality.

7. The Buddhist Manifestion of Spirituality

One might assume that because Shinran was a Buddhist his experience and statements were Buddhistic. Such a view of him is incomplete, however, for he was a Japanese as well, and therein lies his essence; that he was a Buddhist is somewhat secondary. We can be parents and children at the same time, and both aspects must be taken into account. There is a certain inevitability in Shinran's becoming a Pure Land Buddhist, that lies in the fact he was born in the Kamakura period and became Hōnen's disciple. Yet his Japanese character can be seen in his substantiating the thought inherited from his master by means of Japanese spirituality. Although spirituality is fundamentally supra-individual, it does not express itself unless it passes through the individual. That is, it had to be "for the sake of this one individual person, Shinran." Absolute Love is basically supra-individual, but only when it is known intuitively in the individual does it become a genuinely Absolute Love. This contradiction is Shinran's religious experience, and finally it has to be our religious experience as well.

This experience was encountered by a Japanese in Kamakura times, and not by any other religious person in any other place in the world, not even by Chinese Buddhists with a nearly two thousand year Pure Land tradition. Consequently, I call it the insight of Japanese spirituality. There seems to be something within Japanese spirituality that is essential for producing the possibility of insight or intuition of this kind.

Why was this not experienced by someone of Shinto, that most typically of all Japanese things? Some even assert one is not truly Japanese unless one subscribes to Shinto. Regardless, why did a man of Shinto not possess something like this spiritual insight? It is because, as has been indicated above, Shinto experience is sensory and emotional, not spiritual. Spiritual insight—the insight of the Person—is not possible except in the spirit of the individual. Shinto, though amply blessed with elements of the group and with a political character, has nothing like this Person. The emotions and senses like the collective or group situation. It is when reflected on the group that one's existence is most clearly recognized.

Spiritual insight has a solitary element that is not found in Shinto. For that reason there is in Shinto no one who could be called a founder. Since a founder is inevitably the Person that has expressed the supra-individual in the individual, he is not able to have or to maintain a group or collective character. The group is what comes to gather around the Person of the founder. Something spread throughout the group has no center. In a sense it covers the whole, but it is a wholeness with a multitude and no center. There is nothing but the multitude, among whom uncertain actions are common, actions at the mercy of the prevailing movement of the emotional or sensory nature. They must be guided by spiritual insight, for a metaphysical system can be added only to spiritual awakening. Moreover, if this system is not present, the various sensory and emotionally based insights alone will have no constancy. It is here Shrine Shinto and Sectarian Shinto are differentiated. (Although I feel these terms [Shrine Shinto and Sectarian Shinto] lack preciseness as well as appropriateness.) The former, without the Person of spiritual insight to act as its axis, tends to launch into political action. The confusing of the world of emotion with the world of spirituality is not only logically inconsistent, it breeds considerable risk in everyday life and for the actions of the group.

108

8. Shinto and Buddhism

When I envisage Shinto, the following images begin to appear, which evoke an indefinable fondness in me as a Japanese. A small, quiet clearing, not infinitely expansive, surrounded by deep woods. Within, a structure of plain white wood stands alone, open on all sides. It is not large. Surrounding it is an open area covered with white pebbles. All is very neat and tidy, not a speck of dust to be seen. A small stream wends its way onto the scene, with fresh water running clear enough to reveal its stony bottom. At dawn, the morning sun, from nowhere, starts its rise. Through the trees its light begins to filter in, shining on the whiteness of the small pebbles that encircle the solitary structure, then hitting the structure itself. A refreshing mist drifts all around. There is a feeling of inexpressible serenity and freshness. If you listen a voice may be heard from within the building, where a solitary figure dressed in white is seated reverently reading something aloud. How humble and modest is the clear sound of his voice—a quality probably produced by his awe and reverence before the majestic. He is filled with a tense and serious bearing. Yet from this a restful feeling does not emerge. What is discernible is a brightness, a feeling of infinite clarity and elation, like the New Year's Day morning spoken of by the poet Kyorai in the following haiku:

> *New Year's Day;*
> *I will gird on this sword,*
> *Heirloom of my house.*
>
> (trans. Blyth)

In contrast to this, what kinds of images are produced from the spiritual insight of Absolute Love. We might imagine the figure of the exiled Shinran, bending down like a peasant over the soil. Shinran is said to have admired Kyōshin, a Nembutsu follower of the Heian period. Some idea of Kyōshin's manner of life may be gained from the following.

> *Kyōshin mastered the teachings of Buddhist psychology and logic as a scholar at Kōfukuji Temple, where food, clothing, and servants were in abundant supply. Yet there quickened in him a deep dislike of and urge to renounce the world of impurity, and*

109

a desire to seek the Pure Land arose. He finally resolved to leave the temple. Smearing his body with ashes and leaving no trace behind him, he proceeded to the west until he reached a place called Nishinoguchi, Kakogun, in Banshū province. From there, far to the west, it looked so clear; it was an ideal place for seeking Paradise. He built a hermitage and left his own appearance to nature, no longer wearing priestly clothing. To the west he built no fences, and he did not enshrine any images. He raised a family and worked under the villagers, toiling in the paddies, or acting as a porter for occasional travelers, always repeating the Nembutsu day and night without ceasing. People gave him the name 'Amida Maru.' He seemed to have forgotten everything save the Nembutsu. Thirty years were spent in this way. He passed away quietly the 7th year of Jōgan (865), the 15th day of the eighth month.[24]

He is flecked with mud all over, a farmer with only thin one-layer cotton clothing. He does not even bother to wipe off his sweat-covered face. He knows nothing but strenuous labor. The Nembutsu comes with each up-and-down sweep of his hoe. One cannot tell whether his hands pound the hoe into the earth or the Nembutsu becomes the hoe and allows itself to be swallowed into the soil, yet his hoe swings through the air. When he becomes tired he throws himself back onto the earth with his arms outstretched, his face to the sky. Warm spring sunlight flickers through the leaves overhead. Tasting this to his heart's content, not a sound is heard except his deep snoring. Someone brings tea in a plain earthen pot. Awakened, he drinks a few cups; there might be some amusing exchange between the two, followed by laughter. They might conjecture about the fall harvest, or perhaps the soft light of spring brings about a natural relaxation. All the while there comes from their mouths the strain of Nembutsu. Their mud-covered hands and feet passing through the fields of grasses and leaves—this is the genuine scenery of the Way of the Gods. Shinto's 'pure heart,' or 'honest heart,' or 'upright heart' does not appear here, just the great stark sweat-dripping faces in full smile. Devoid of "heart," possessed of bare skin—such is the distinctive feature of this landscape.

Are we to say the man sitting erect in white in the small plain wooden structure in the sun's first rays is Japanese, and that the laborer, his hands dirtied with night-soil, his body covered by sweat, is not? One is a rice-eater, the other a rice-grower. Rice-eaters tend to abstraction; rice-growers live in constant conformity with reality. Spirituality wants its food within this reality. Clean white robes do not go together with the hoe. Traditional ceremonial dress is not suited to daily life on the earth. Those who do not grasp the hoe and live close to the earth are totally without knowledge of the earth, and are incapable of experiencing the earth in a concrete manner. They may say that they do, and even feel that they do in their hearts, but it can only be conceptual and abstract. Those who know the earth only through the fruits or blessings it imparts to them really do not know the earth. To be familiar with the earth is to taste its sufferings. It does not reveal its secrets merely by the raising and lowering of the hoe. It does not make any criticism, yet it will take to itself those who work upon it, if they are sincere and become one with it, leaving their self-centeredness behind. The earth hates deception. The farmer's simplicity and honesty derive from his receiving the spirit of the earth. Those absorbed in the explanations of old books know of the earth's blessings and the taste of rice only conceptually. The experience of Absolute Love through spiritual insight cannot spring from such conceptual foundations. Japanese spirituality has been nourished in an especially tangible reality. Where this reality is not at work spirituality will not begin to function. Japanese spiritual insight has nothing to do with the searching of documents or other writings, for anything produced from them is necessarily intellectual.

Of course, the intellect's importance cannot be denied, but it is necessary that its working come from within spiritual insight. There must not be, in reverse of this, intellectual polemics and then attempts to bring about insight, for that would be impossible. Those who preach the virtues of emotional insight abhor the polemics of the intellect too, but it must be well remembered that this aversion does not belong to the same category as that which issues from spirituality.

9. *The Temporal Nature of Spiritual Insight*

It would seem Shinto seeks to lay its total significance in cosmogony, and that it considers the attaching of political, historical, and ethical

111

values to this the culmination of its work. Such a course is certainly not unwarranted, but it produces a tendency, which leaves much to be desired, to overlook the existence of the Japanese spirituality. If the continued existence of the Japanese holds any world-wide meaning, if they have something to contribute to the formation of world history (it is my conviction that they do: this book was written with that idea in mind), then the Japanese must not neglect to promote the special characteristics of Japanese spirituality.

Though Shintoists have a cosmogonic theory, it bears a straight line, temporal nature that does not entitle it truly to be called creation. When attempts are made to interpret history by means of this rectilinearity it is impossible to include either present or future, and even the past is limited Lacking creativity, history hardens up completely and any capacity for spirituality to function disappears as well. With the straight line view, everything is a geometrical diagram, and the generative and transforming nature of the universe vanishes. Living is not something signified by drawing a long line. A thousand, ten thousand, one hundred thousand years notwithstanding, every form of life that has a beginning has an end. Eternity must apply to the directions of both past and future. It cannot be a finite straight line. Actually all straight lines are finite; because they are finite they are straight lines. When we try to cut off eternity at some point, that interval alone is a straight line. Eternity cannot be a straight line, the very moment a beginning is indicated an end is already decided. Something thus limited is not living, for life must be without limits; it cannot be a straight line. It is a circle that has no center, or rather, it is a circle with its center everywhere. This infinite circularity of life can be intuited only by spirituality. All other insights are certain to have some limitation somewhere.

There are many who will say that things such as this infinite 'great circle nature' are incomprehensible, that they are mere conceptual abstractions, that they are the ultimate in nonsense; those without spiritual insight will all say this. Those without the experience that has attained the world of spirituality will inevitably come around to such an opposition.

In fact, people who view life or history or the world in terms of a straight line hold a view in which their time—their straight line—limits the infinite circle. They do not realize that things thus limited are all the more abstract and conceptual. With spiritual insight, life that seems to be functioning

112

through time and space is seen really to have infinite circularity. We must not use the discriminatory intellect to conjecture upon, gauge, or criticize this insight, for the intellect must be based on spiritual insight, spiritual insight cannot be extracted from it. If the order is reversed, the most concrete reality becomes abstract and conceptual, as in a dream.

What comes to mind here is the story of the Zen master Nansen (Nan-ch'uan 南泉: 748–834) and the flowering plant:

> *Once a high official named Rikkō (Lu Kêng) visited Nansen.*
>
> *He quoted the words of the noted scholar monk of an earlier dynasty, Sōjō (Sêng-chao 僧肇), to the effect that,*
>
> *"Heaven and earth and I are of the same root,*
> *The ten-housand things and I are of one substance."*
> *and continued, "Is this not a most remarkable statement?"*
>
> *Nansen did not give any direct answer to this question, but called the attention of his visitor to a flowering plant in the garden and said, "People of the world look at these flowers as if they were in a dream."*

The chrysanthemums flowering fragrantly before one might seem the ultimate in concreteness, but one who is really able to see them so is one who is spiritually awakened. He who views all Creation as one substance cannot separate himself from between philosophical concepts, he cannot see the flowers as flowers. Even flowers become a kind of dream, their form fades away, and they become completely abstract. Though the sensory world may be real, if it is not supported by spiritual insight, it becomes a floating thing. And one who wanders in the regions of intellectual discrimination will be all the more unable to strike home to the true concreteness.

If we believe it sufficient to interpret cosmogonic theory by means of a rectilinear temporality, the Creative Spirit becomes a piece of biological life and loses its spirituality. Then the interpretation of the *kontai ryō mandara*[25] as taught by the Shingon sect could be adopted, with its duality and emotional nature. It was in this area Shinto came naturally to merge with Shingon. The Buddhist *hokkai-engi*, the interdependence of all

113

things, is based on Kegon teachings, but whether it ever exerted any influence on Shinto, I do not know. Inasmuch as Shinto interprets time as a straight line, it is doubtful it ever had any relation to the Kegon world-view.

Being surrounded by the sea, it is strange Japan did not conceive an oceanic (circular) world or historical view, instead of one with the flowing straight line nature of a river. This probably did not happen because the Japanese did not attain spiritual realization until Kamakura times. When cosmogony cannot go beyond the level of sensory or emotional life it inevitably is established upon a rectilinear aspect of time. Spiritual insight does not destroy this, rather deepens and elevates it, gives it a foundation and makes it real. Where it can be erected upon spiritual insight it settles right into place, assuming a stability and catholicity. When cosmogony is not seen as a straight-line and is regarded intuitively as having an infinite circularity, the straight line view as well naturally assumes its proper place. If ethics, politics, history, science, philosophy, or logic takes rectilinearity alone as ultimate, the consciousness of Japanese spirituality, without any other background, will become not only meaningless, but its relation to the universal spirit, the supra-individual Person, will be severed as well. That would probably mean the destruction of all things, nothing less than a suicidal negation of life itself.

Because spiritual insight has this infinite circularity, its center can exist everywhere. In this light it should become possible to realize the meaning of Shinran's Person in his words, "for the sake of this one individual person."

Perhaps it bears repeating once again that this Person is not the individual self, for to think so would be a great error. It is the supra-individual Person, and it forms the center of a centerless infinite circle. When this centerless center is gained, spiritual awakening is accomplished. At that moment one becomes the I of the Buddha's assertion, "Heaven above, earth below, I alone am the honored one." This is the real individual person—the self-realization of the supra-individual Person. The contradiction of a self that is not a self is then perceived as the most concrete fact, and its existence assumes ultimate reality. While on the one hand the Japanese spirituality of Shinran was stimulated along traditional lines by Hōnen, it gained on the other hand the materialization of an insight that was brought about through a vital contact with the earth as a truly

114

living thing.

Being a supra-individual individual, the Person possesses a solitariness that must be said to be absolutely solitary. It is "a figure, solitariness itself, between Heaven and Earth, standing alone before an infinitely expanding vista." The meaning of experiencing the I, the center, within the infinite centerless circle has such a contradictory quality. Therefore, aloneness is absolute aloneness, and at the same time

> The spring mountain is seen piling up one layer of green over another;
> The spring stream is reflecting, as it flows, wavy shadows of green.

The I of absolute aloneness is none other than the infinite variety of individuals. Such a contradiction is possible because there exists a stern reality, a most concrete fact, that each of us is living out his daily life in the centerless center within the infinite circle. This is spiritual insight.

Since spiritual awakening is the ultimate experience of the individual, it has the nature of the Person. Solely from the standpoint of ordinary logic this could be called solipsistic. In those terms that is what it is. But since to call it solipsistic already implies the working of something not solipsistic, a solipsism would not really obtain even in ordinary logic.

Be that as it may, in the world of spiritual insight everything else is wholly secondary to the insight itself. Those things not possessed of an individual-type directness are all treated as stale and aged. It is not a world in which one worries oneself miserable interpreting the documents of others. Being old books, left-overs, hearsay, second-hand information, etc., they are as such valueless. Because spirituality is always the Person, always immediately open and unbared, it dislikes to live in the world of old books. The individual spirit begins a relation straightforward to the supra-individual spirit. In no case does it allow intermediaries. In this insight the supra-individual spirit is transformed into the individual. The spirituality of the individual is the spirituality of the individual and yet it is not the spirituality of the individual. Therefore it must be that the individual is the supra-individual, the supra-individual is the individual. For this reason as well it is said that "the mind is the Buddha" is "no mind, no Buddha"; that "no mind, no Buddha" is "the mind is the Buddha."

115

Because spiritual awakening is ultimate concreteness, it is individual in the utmost. And because of this it is utterly general and universal. It is the insight of the Person, the realization of occupying the centerless center of a circumferenceless circle. Presented in terms of Shinran's Japanese spirituality, it is his words, "Amida's Original Prayer is . . . for the sake of this one individual person, Shinran." Good and evil are received within Absolute Love just as they are. Dualistic, historical, rectilinear life remains as it is, and need not be denied. The contradictory logic that states that negation is affirmation and affirmation is negation can also be applied appropriately to Absolute Love or Boundless Compassion. Only we must not forget that Japanese spirituality sees this not as logic, it sees it as the intuition or direct apprehension of reality.

10. The "Popularization" of Buddhism

It is often said that Pure Land thought popularized Buddhism. I cannot agree with such a statement, inasmuch as religion essentially is based upon spiritual consciousness, and its foundation is not deduced from some definite conceptual system or built up in an arbitrary manner. The popularization of Buddhism seems to imply something of artificial, man-made manufacture, an exercise of an intellect making something suited to fit a preconceived objective. Intellectually manufactured elements can be added provided spirituality is once attained; no, elements of this kind must be added to it. Insight cannot simply end with insight, human consciousness wants to give it some form of expression. Therefore, in the materialization of religious consciousness as well, there must be some metaphysical system. Nevertheless, to draw spiritual experience from within the system itself is to hit the cart and not the horse, because it tries to place first what properly comes afterward.

To say Hōnen extracted Pure Land thought from Tendai doctrine and adapted it for the populace fails to grasp the essence of his religious experience. It also reveals an insufficient understanding of the spiritual life of the very common people that became the object of this popularization. I would like to discover the reasons why this so-called popularization had to come about. There are such things as right opportunity and proper timing, but I believe even when they are present there must also be mutual response on the part of subject and object. There must be a simultaneous

116

pecking from the inside and from the outside of the egg and a box-and-cover suitability. Though one side may be passive and the other active, if there is no activity on the side of passivity as well there will be no possibility for any sort of response between the two. This is likewise true of Buddhism's popularization. If we say the Buddhism that prevailed among the upper classes was unacceptable to the common people, and therefore had to be popularized by a watering-down or sugar-coating process so as to be swallowed by the latter as children swallow candied pills, it would follow that a good many other things alien to the essence of Buddhism—harmless though they may have been—were also taken in. I wonder if this "popularization" was generally such a process. It should have a clearer and more distinct meaning. In any case, I think we should expect there was something positive and spontaneous in the minds of the masses who were the recipients of this popularized Buddhism.

To my mind, the reason the popularization became possible in the Kamakura period in particular developed within the populace, and that this same reason gave rise to a movement in the spiritual life of the ordinary people. Because this movement appeared, an intellectual structure in response to it projected or else exuded from the existing systems of religious thought. Hands were held out from both sides and for the first time they were in accord. Most scholars tend to think if only the structure of the external world is changed through some artificial maneuvering, the inner life will adapt itself to it. The influences of environment are of course strong, but heredity is not to be disregarded in this respect. Above all, the relationship between causes and conditions must be opportune. I feel that scholars should give full attention to cause, which is easily overlooked, to heredity, and to spirituality as well.

Now I would like to dwell for a moment on the thought of the so-called Dual-Aspect Shinto and the Shinto-Buddhist "amalgamation" that first came into being as the theory of *honji suijaku*.[26] Though scholars usually attribute this theory to Buddhists conforming their teaching to Shinto, or to a Buddhist cunning that attempted to develop and amplify Buddhism among the people, or some similar theory, such explanations seem to me extremely strange. I do not think the Buddhists, who are generally regarded as the originators of *upāya* (ways or means of leading sentient beings to the truth), would have thought to indiscriminately twist their teaching in order to capture the Shinto *kami*. I feel that a Shinto-

117

Buddhist accommodation could be accomplished in a more natural way. In the aspect of mental training, the Buddhists had undergone many trials and difficulties, so from the beginning they were not rival to the simple and artless Shintoists. Shinto never had an identity that could contend with the Buddhist, therefore it was silent. But that did not mean a Buddhist silence regarding Shinto, for although Buddhism was an import that became an organic body after a period of time, it could not have built itself up without assimilating what was already there, i.e., Shinto. Buddhism could not have lasted as an organic body in Japanese soil without giving some consideration to it. I feel the combination and co-existence of Shinto and Buddhism were produced without anything artificial or unnatural whatever, by a natural process under natural conditions, by which I mean that no artificial means were added to the process of amalgamation.

Such a description would apply as well to the popularization of Buddism. Hōnen, for example, did not use traditional means of thought to attempt to effect the popularization of Pure Land teaching, setting about this work intellectually. Even *masse* thought is a mixture containing conceptual elements, so that it would not describe correctly in itself the prevailing spiritual life of the Japanese people. What I wish this section to emphasize is that in the establishing of religious consciousness, spiritual awakening must be first, and intellectual or thought structures must be erected on it. In what manner, then, is this spiritual insight produced? All we can say is that it is naturally produced in the process in which human spirituality makes its historical development. Contained within this historical development is a rather complicated factor, which I will not get into now: briefly, it is that the human *seishin* will develop, historically and temporally, the possibilities contained within it in a one-after-another sequence. The spiritual life of the Japanese was not experienced in its essential meaning until the Kamakura period.

11. Tradition—Following Another's Teaching—Faith

I would next like to examine the relation between teaching and self-awakening. It is an age-old question that has been explained in many ways; from political, ethical, religious, and educational standpoints among others. They all finally boil down to the subject-object relation that ex-

118

ists between oneself and others. It should perhaps be added that this is a mutual reliance between the two. In religious terms, it is a relation between *Jiriki,* "Self-power" and *Tariki,* "Other-power," between *hō* (法), the dharma, and *ki* (機), the recipient of the dharma. It is a problem that exists in Christian theology as well. It should not be put off as long as there is the notion of an individual self. In human terms it is the relation between the teacher and the taught, concerned with the question: Is that which is taught everything, or is there something that must come from the taught as well? Here, by way of example, is a well-known passage from *Shōbōgenzō Zuimonki.*[27]

> *We know of Shakya and Amida with the thirty-two bodily characteristics, crowned with light, preaching for the benefit of all beings. Yet if the master should say that frogs and earthworms are Buddha, then the disciple would have to surrender his previous conceptions and believe that frogs and earthworms are Buddha. . . .*

Here, on the surface, it would appear everything is to be passed down from master to disciple, believed just as it has been taught by the master. If mountains are called rivers, the response should be a resounding, *"Hai"* (yes). Were the master to point to a horse and call it a deer, if the disciple does not reply "splendid!" he will be reproached as a fool for relying upon his own judgement and not trusting in his master. If it is true that reliance in the master—the supra-individual self—is the road of the disciple, then the disciple would be incapable of any creativity whatever. Even the changes in the external world would gradually assume the dreary changelessness of a cemetery. Is this really what Dōgen meant to say? From one angle we might say yes, but from another it becomes manifestly not so. Religious tradition may be said to be produced from just such a contradiction.

In the *Tannishō,* Shinran makes the following confession: "As for me, Shinran, I but trust in the word of my good master, by whom I was told that only through the Nembutsu are we embraced by Amida Buddha. There is no other thought." This is the other side of Dōgen's statement, the acknowledgement from the side of the disciple. But there is no difference in their view that the relation of both individuals is based upon faith. In other words, the problem here is never concerned with an ethical category of "obedience," but with the realm of spiritual realization. If this is not clearly understood, Dōgen and Shinran are both incomprehensible, and their Japanese character is not grasped. Spiritual awakening, if expressed in terms of a human relation, is *faith*. In the reply '*Hai*' that comes on hearing the word '*Oi*' called out from the master,[28] we should not see simply sensory or emotional insight, but beyond that, we must experience something of much greater profoundity. The realm of spiritual response is said to lie in immediate obedience, but if one fails to see the *faith* within this, one sees only the superficial appearance of things.

The Confucians would ask, "What does Heaven say?"; yet "the seasons come and go and all creation grows"—that is *faith*. The Confucian dictim, "without the people's faith nothing is possible, is a political principle, but only when this belief is well rooted in spiritual awakening is it unshakable. Standing within this insight, Dōgen demands a disciple's obedience and Shinran confesses his own devotion. In this light Dōgen's "frog-and-earthworm view" continues: "If you seek Buddha's shining countenance and his many virtues in an earthworm, your mind remains deluded as before."

Dōgen is merely telling the disciple to see earthworms as earthworms and frogs as frogs. Trying to find the thirty-two physical marks of a Buddha in an earthworm is merely an example of view-attachment. He continues: "Simply know what you are seeing is, as it is, Buddha." When we see earthworms as earthworms we then know earthworms are Buddha. "Throw aside this persistent illusion and attachment, follow these teachings, and you will come to natural accordance with the Way." "Natural accordance with the Way" is the gist of the whole passage. It means nothing less than spiritual insight. When this insight is achieved one discovers the true meaning of obedience to one's master. When ordered to the top of a hundred-foot pole and then told to let go with hands and feet and kep on going, the disciple answers "Hai," and does just that; then and only then natural accordance with the Way is attained and frogs and earthworms are Buddha. This 'Hai' does not emerge simply from following another's teaching, it does not appear until after many repeated doubts and hesitations. If obedience does not first pass through negation or denial it is not obedience in the profound sense of that word. But when it does pass through denial, obedience is an act of spirituality, and natural accordance with the Way. It is something that has passed through denial. In short, obedience is obedience because it is not obedience. Where this is not so, earthworms are not Buddhas, or perhaps we should say, earthworms are not earthworms.

Shinran's case is similar. First it is "receive the word," then, he said, "there is nothing but faith." Still the ultimate reality of his mental experience has faith, and then he hears "the word of my good master." He said he realized spiritual insight thanks to Hōnen's indications. But insight and indications regarding it are two manifestly different things. Hōnen's instructions were imparted to all his disciples, but all did not attain insight. Shinran alone possessed an immediate "Hai" that conformed to Hōnen's "Oi." If the sequence of "Oi" and "Hai" is not observed, then continuing on, "Oi" cannot be "Hai" and "Hai" cannot be "Oi." This contradiction characterizes spiritual insight.

Faith materializes because there is this contradiction. It can even be said there is no faith without the contradiction. In the same way, a Christian theologian once said, *"Credo quia absurdum est,"* I believe because it is irrational. Shinran's obedience to his master comes into being through faith; his faith comes into being through non-obedience. Nothing could be as "absurd" as this. It means spiritual awakening cannot be gauged by the discriminatory standards of the intellect. Shinran's Nembutsu develops from his words, "Nembutsu has meaningless meaning," where for the first time the "words of my good master" materialize. Do we not know at all whether the Nembutsu is a guide to Heaven or a passport of Hell? (Of this I will have more to say later.)

Dōgen's required absolute obedience is impossible to realize unless conditions for it are ripe. 'Ripeness' means the conditions are ready for the follower's spiritual insight to work. Spirituality is endowed with something active; touch it and the effect is like the tremendous explosion of gunpowder from a single match. Through intellectual discrimination alone, man cannot advance even though ordered to go beyond the end of a hundred-foot pole. When something impelling comes to stir within him, then, indifferent to discrimination, he will advance. Looking back there is obedience on the part of the disciple; but seen by one who has experienced the reality of natural accordance with the Way, obedient following can be none other than accordance with the Way. It is like

121

the simultaneous pecking within and without the egg, or like drops of water that freeze the instant they strike the ground. Obedience never comes about fortuitously, and it is not mere passivity. The subtle moment of spiritual intercommunion can only be grasped when one has spiritual insight. The relation that existed between Hōnen and Shinran must also be seen with this insight at center. The insight is none other than faith. With the attainment of faith's essence the term "obedience" becomes an appropriate one.

Generally speaking, a realm that speaks of isolating object from subject cannot attain a genuine passivity. When we speak of a popularization of Buddhism, or of the combining of Shinto and Buddhism, it will not do to think of them solely from a singly-directed viewpoint. A world in which two things confront one another is only possible when one fully understands the nature of their reciprocal relation. It is not that one is always passive and the other active, or that one is life and the other death. Obedience is, after all, the mutual influence of one upon the other, a reciprocal activity. It is the emergence of the true essence of life.

Absolute obedience, a submissive spirit, is a requirement in some of the priestly orders of Catholicism, where the command of one's superior is absolute. As a magistrate of God his word is supreme command, and the slightest transgression from it is unallowable. Although first hearing of their extreme arbitrariness and dogmatism, one wonder how someone could spend a whole lifetime under such conditions, in reality, such a life in fact is viewed as being a happy one. When a sheet of paper is desired one does not just go and pick it up; first permission must be obtained from the superior—something that would appear difficult for an adult to tolerate. Further, if commanded to jump from a cliff and sink into the sea, the answer is simply "yes," jump, and no objection. Saint Francis likens one who obeys to a corpse; pushed to the left you fall to the left, pushed to the right you fall to the right, stand up, sit down, all is done exactly as ordered by another. This is taught as being the absolutely necessary state for a servant of God. The absolute obedience of Dōgen is intellectual, but the above-mentioned obedience of the Catholic orders permeates even to the center of the will. Though I speak of the intellect the root is probably the will. Still Dōgen's, that is, the Zen man's requirement lies in casting aside the discriminatory intellect at one stroke. Thanks to this, natural accordance with the Way is attained, and the absolute,

122

incomparable affirmation of being "the only one in Heaven and Earth" is realized.

However, there is nothing like this in the case of Christianity. God is absolute power, not absolute wisdom or compassion; no, God is compassion and wisdom, but since on the part of those who accept Him the power or authority aspect is emphasized over these, it is only submission or obedience that becomes prominent.

Here an interesting mental situation appears. Although there is a certain sense of *mushin* (no-mind) or *muga* (no-self) in the Christian orders, it differs greatly from that of their Buddhist counterparts. The idea of power is strong in Christianity, where one entrusts one's own will to something more powerful. It is not that one does not have one's own will, but that the will becomes enfeebled to the point it does not come into play of its own accord. Since the *muga* of Buddhism is natural accordance with the Way (realization, enlightenment) that materializes in spiritual insight, one is utterly free and unrestrained in moving and in being moved, and therein the world of naturalness unfolds itself. The *muga* of Christianity is wholly *Tariki*, placing the self opposite the Other and then setting Him up as the sole Other-power. In Buddhism, the opposition of self and other is an opposition, but the operation of something beyond opposition is intuitively known (call this something spiritual insight), and from this insight another look is taken at the world of opposition. Which is to say that through the working of this insight the world of the opposition of oneself and others—the infinite variation of each of the myriad individuals —comes to have no room for the problems of obedience or submission, helpless servitude, or the oppression of absolute power.

That does not mean to suggest all comes from a single distinct cause. All things in the world are subject to the so-called Law of Dependent Origination. All the myriad variety of individuals are, just as they are, individualistic and independent; they do not hinder one another and are completely free. Here the circumference-less circle defines itself and establishes its center everywher. Here Shinran's I is realized, here the Great Way with Obstacles passes straightway to eternity. This differs vastly from the absolute submission or absolute reliance of Christianity.

However, Christianity's absolute obedience has a psychological foundation. Postulate an individual self and it will come about that it must carry the responsibility for its actions. This causes all sorts of difficulties. Man,

123

who must carry on in the group life, must also be ethical. If each individual self is not responsible for its acts, then the group cannot maintain its combined resources. On the other hand, human beings, besides being like colonies of ants or bees, exist like lions and tigers, attempting to live and act alone. In a word, human beings have on one hand an ethical feeling or responsibility, but on the other hand have an independant, self-indulgent nature that likes to operate in its own way without responsibility, on the principle of the self. Man desires the latter, but life's reality does not permit this, and he must follow the dictates of the former. Since he finds this irksome, his mental configuration is divided, one aspect tries to be as wilful as it can and weaken as much as possible the feeling of ethical responsibility, and the other is passive. Even though the will—which wishes to be wilful—is strong, the powers of criticism and self-examination are yet stronger. The feeling of responsibility is great. Hence, self-suffering is great. The first is abundant in the so-called great man, the second is found in the figure of the saint. The type of man who troubles himself with self-examination, because he will probably try to escape his worry and suffering, will try to debilitate his will as far as possible. To accomplish this he searches for something much stronger than himself and casts everything to it. To it all the responsibility for his conduct thereupon reverts. Since with the functioning of the Other-power one's own actions do not come from one's own will, whatever occurs is not one's own responsibility. Living or dying, killing others or oneself, good or evil, are all due to outside forces. It is a feeling of extreme relief. This is the mentality of the Catholic priesthoods. Although it is a military mode the inner motive force might even be termed passive. Still, it is based on the idea of power.

Either way, when considering the disciple's obedience to his master, attention must be given to the fact that we must under certain conditions view it ethically and emotionally, and under other conditions view it spiritually. If a Dōgen-type obedience is understood without spirituality, it risks falling into the mentality of the Catholic-type priesthoods. Actually the latter possess spirituality as well, but their way of viewing it is different from that of Japanese spirituality.

NOTES

1 In the popular story of Urashima Taro, a fisherman named Urashima is taken to the Dragon Palace at the bottom of the sea by the sea-god's daughter. After three years of happiness he becomes homesick and returns to his parents' home, to find that seven hundred years have passed. Trans.

2 Fa-tsang 法藏 643–712 (J. Hōzō). Patriarch and systematizer of the Chinese Hua-yen (Kegon) sect. Chih-i 智顗 538–597 (J. Chigi). The Chinese Buddhist patriarch regarded as the founder of the T'ien-t'ai Sect.

3 *Chūron* 中論: Nagarjuna's *Mūlamādhyamikakarikā*. *Yuishikiron* 唯識論: Vasubandhu's *Vijñaptimātratāsiddhi*.

4 The Four Books of Confucianism: *Analects, Mencius, Great Learning*, and *Doctrine of the Mean*. The Five Classics are the *Book of Poetry, Book of History, Book of Changes, Spring and Autumn Annals*, and the *Book of Rites*.

5 A good discussion of *Shugendō* in a western language is Gaston Renondeau's *Le Shugendō. Histoire, doctrine et rites des anachorètes dits Yamabushi,* Cahiers de la Société Asiatique, 18, Imprimerie Nationale, Paris, 1965. Trans.

6 Murasaki Shikibu, Izumi Shikibu, and Sei Shōnagon, active around the year 1000, are the three famous literary ladies of the Heian period.

7 "National Learning" (Kokugaku), a movement of nationalistic thought that arose in the Tokugawa Period in response to the Japanese Confucianism of the time; represented by such men as Kamo Mabuchi (1697–1769) and Motoori Norinaga. Trans.

8 *Manyō-gana*. In the original text of the *Manyōshū*, the poems are transcribed in Chinese characters that are generally used phonetically and for meaning as well to represent the individual syllables in Japanese. This *manyō-gana* ("manyō syllabary") gave rise later to the purely phonetic kana syllabaries, hiragana and *katakana*. Trans.

9 *Hekiganroku*, "Blue-Cliff Records" (C. *Pi-yen-lu:* 碧巌録). A collection of 100 koan with commentary much used by the Rinzai Zen sect. Trans.

10 *Shindō* (April, 1944).

11 *Hosshin seppō* 法身説法; the Shingon teaching that the *Hosshin*, the dharma-kāya or dharma-body, also preaches the Law.

12 *Sokushin sokubutsu*; 即身即佛.

13 *Kyōgyōshinshō* ("Teaching, Practice. Faith, Realization" 教行信証); a six fascicle work by Shinran.
   Tannishō ("Tract Deploring the Heterodoxies" 歎異鈔) written by Yuiembō, one of Shinran's disciples.

14 The "scholars of Nara and Hiei" refers to the priests of the old pre-Kamakura temples at Nara, and on Mt. Hiei, adjacent to Kyoto, who were inclined to an aristocratic, ritualized, philosophic Buddhism, contrasted with the opposite tendency of the practical Pure Land schools.

15 The original Hongan-ji Temple, the head temple of the largest branch of the

125

Shin sect, was divided in the early seventeenth century into Nishi (Western) Hongan-ji and Higashi (Eastern) Hongan-ji. Since then both of their huge-structured temples have been located in Kyoto. Trans.

16 *Ōgen-nisō-ekō* (往還二相廻向), the two aspects of merit-transference: going to the Pure Land (*ōsō ekō*), and returning to this world (*gensō ekō*) to help sentient beings. Shin teaching makes Amida the source of all the activities belonging to merit-transference, going and returning aspects alike, and individual beings are made passive recipients (ki) owing all to the Other-power (Amida).

17 Genshin 源信 (942–1017), is the first Japanese patriarch of the Pure Land school. His influential work, *Ōjōyōshū* ("The Essentials of Salvation" 往生要集), is a collection concerned with birth in the Pure Land.

18 "One Page Testament" 一枚起請文. Written in 1212, two days prior to Honen's death.

19 *Jinnō Shōtōki* 神皇正統記 ("Succession of the Imperial Rulers in Japan"), by Kitabatake Chikafusa, 1292–1354.

20 Great Mirror Wisdom, *Daienkyōchi* 大圓鏡智; Mirror of Exquisite Wisdom, *Myō-kanzatchi* 妙観察智; Wisdom of Action, *Jōshosachi* 成所作智.

21 *Jinen-hōni* 自然法爾; *Shimo* 只麼; *Jikishin* 直心.

22 Ise Shinto, generally speaking, is a school of Shinto established at the Ise Shrine, containing Buddhist, and later, Confucian elements. Trans.

23 A Shinto saying. Trans.

24 *Bukkyō Daiji-i.*

25 *Kontai ryō mandara* 金胎両曼茶羅—the two mandalas of esoteric Buddhism, representing the two aspects of cosmic life: the Diamond World 金剛界 (Kongō-kai) and the Womb-store World 胎蔵界 (Taizōkai).

26 *Honji suijaku* 本地垂迹, "traces of descent from the original soil." An explana-tion that regards Shinto *kami* as manifestations or reincarnations of Buddhas and Bodhisattvas. Trans.

27 *Shōbōgenzō zuimonki*, a collection of Dōgen Zenji's teaching compiled by his disciple Ejō. Trans.

28 "Oi!" is a call (Hey!); "Hai!" is the answer to it (Yes!). Trans.

CHAPTER 3   HONEN AND NEMBUTSU
SHŌMYŌ

I think it reasonable to regard Hōnen and Shinran as one when viewing them as individual manifestations of Japanese spirituality. Of course it will be necessary to see them separately in some instances, but when we try to consider the Japanese character in the manifested forms of spirituality, they are most easily understood as one. Thanks to them the true significance in Nembutsu shōmyō[1] was developed. Without either of them it probably would not have evolved completely. Thus we may view them as one character. This is corroborated by Shinran's own statements professing only to obey the teachings of Hōnen. Yet there was not only this subjective side to Shinran's faith, for it is certain there was an objective element supporting it. It seems that in trying to endorse him alone, thus separating him from Hōnen, his followers were overly zealous. He rather should be seen together with Hōnen, and it should be said that in them Japanese spirituality reveals its characteristics.

I. THE FALL OF THE HEIKE

1. The Heike Monogatari—The Significance of Hōnen's Appearance

To my mind, nothing in the political history of Japan is as tragic as the downfall of the Heike clan. Taira Kiyomori (1118–81) was an extremely suitable figure to decorate the close of the Heian era. Kiyomori, who through military might swept away four hundred years and more of deepseated political evil, because he became thoroughly aristocratized as well, had no alternative but to taste the bitterness of defeat himself.

He became the Chancellor of the Realm (Dajō Daijin) in 1167, and in 1171 his daughter entered the imperial court as Kenreimon-in, the consort of the Emperor Takakura. This was the pinnacle of the Heike's prosperity; nineteen years after Kiyomori became Chancellor they were delivered their final stroke on the seacoast of Dannoura. The swiftness of the complete reversal accompanying this rise and fall, and the extreme misery of the Heike's last moments, can all be known in full by reading the *Heike Monogatari*,[2] the supreme masterpiece of its kind. Not only is it an epic story of political tragedy, it is also an outstanding example of poetic literature describing life in this fleeting, unpredictable world.

That the *Heike Monogatari* was written in Kamakura times must be given deep significance. During the long duration of the Heian, literary production was considerable and varied, yet nothing like the *Heike* appeared. It is not so much there were no battles during the Heian period, just that no 'Battle Literature' evolved. Constant karmic vicissitudes obtain naturally in all worlds, but in the world of the Heian they were treated in an intellectual, literary manner, and did not appear as a raw experience of human life. The following could be said anywhere by anyone, yet when we open the *Heike Monogatari* and begin to read, we do not feel that the words are merely abstract and conceptual: "The tolling of the bell of Gion Temple echoes the transience of all things." "The color of the flowers of the Sāla trees reveals the truth that all who rise must fall." "Prosperity is not long, it is but like a dream on a spring night." "Brave men in the end must vanish too, as dust before the wind." Had these appeared in Heian literature, the words would carry an empty ring. When we come upon them in the *Heike Monogatari*, we receive the profound impression that the author is directly conversant with the reality of human life. Coming to the Kamakura period, the Japanese first underwent a keen introspection regarding human existence.

There is still in the *Heike Monogatari* quite a bit of the residue of the Heian's feminine culture. What perhaps ought to be called the sentimentality of the Japanese people is quite apparent, but behind the sentimentality an introspection was added. It is here the awakening of Japanese spirituality is to be perceived. Spiritual life begins from introspection; without it there can be no spiritual life. Introspection is denial. It occurs when a person who has gone wholeheartedly and directly straightforward without looking to the rear or to the right or left, questions, stops, holds his ground, and looks to himself and to his situation. It is the denial of a prior reckless attitude. It is a privilege limited to man, and is not found in the other animals, even celestial beings do not possess it.

128

If we say animals move solely by means of instinctive affirmation, we would have to say that celestial beings do as well. We may imagine this to be bad in the former and good in the latter. But without introspection and denial there is no good or bad; accordingly, there is neither freedom nor creativity, which become possible only through the experience of denial. Spiritual existence springs from this. In the *Heike Monogatari* we are able to see the situation of the Japanese of Kamakura times as they were awakening to spirituality. Whoever the author was, he touched the current of spirituality running at that time. This current or movement has at its hub Pure Land thought, which makes its starting point the denial of this life. Although denial of this life does not necessarily imply birth in the Pure Land, still it shows serious criticism of present existence.

Though Pure Land thought existed even in Heian times, it was then conceived of as an extension of the present world. People of that age lacked denial, criticism, and introspection of the present world. Even had these been present, they would have been conceptual or else of a merely imitative or educative nature without firm roots in profound human experience. The spiritual life of the Japanese had not yet come to the fore.

The differences between Heian and Kamakura Pure Land thought are really differences between that which was added from without and that which emerged from within. Therefore, though people of Kamakura times spoke of doing Nembutsu *shōmyō* and gaining rebirth in Paradise, that which moved at the ground of their consciousness was not rooted in mere convention or tradition. It is there we must seek the meaning of Hōnen's appearance.

If we except those with an especially rich inborn genius, the movement of spiritual life is not visible among the courtiers who lived between Heian and Kamakura times. Many Buddhist scriptures were read and recited, lectured upon, and studied; Buddhist images were worshipped, and ceremonial rites of various sorts were conducted, yet it would be very difficult to regard them as anything but cultural pastimes. There were few indeed even in monastic circles on a truly spiritual footing. Even after entering the priesthood and donning black robes, it is necessary to "enter the priesthood" once again, and the black robes have to be "re-dyed" occasionally as well. Thus, no matter how many times the Nembutsu was voiced, the minds of the so-called men of culture, the intelligentsia, or even the priests of the time, probably did not move in accord with it. As they came to

129

confront the reality of war's ruthlessness and sorrow, and the vicissitudes of human life that accompanied the downfall of the Heike, both the courtiers and the priests were compelled to be in earnest. Here is the example of Taira Shigehira, from Chapter Ten of the *Heike Monogatari*. [Shigehira, of the Heike, is captive of the Genji, who had offered to ransom him in return for the Three Sacred Treasures. The Heike refused.]

When the answer was received, the Genji decided to send him to the Eastern Provinces. The prospect of leaving the capital filled him with regret. He asked Doi Jirō whether he might be permitted to become a monk. His request was communicated to Yoshitsune who reported it to his Majesty, who decided to refer the matter to Yoritomo. Informed of this Shigehira said, "May I not then see a priest and old friend of mine in order to speak with him about future existence?" "Who is this priest?" asked Doi. "His name," replied Shigehira, "is Hōnen of Kurodani." "In that case permission is given."

Very pleased, Shigehira soon met with the priest and said to him, weeping: "I was captured alive and brought here to the capital. Yet what will be my fate in my future existence? When I had rank and high position in the world I was distracted by many things and grasped tightly the bonds of this life. My heart was totally given up to pride, without a thought for what might befall me. Then when misfortune came to our house and we fled the capital, fighting and struggling here and there, my mind was obstructed with the evil desire of killing others and saving my own life, so that no good thoughts could dwell in me. As to the burning of Nara, whether it was an imperial order or a military order, since the way of this world is difficult to escape, on account of the evil deeds of the monks we marched against them, and the chance burning of the temples that followed was beyond my power to prevent. Still, as I was the Commander at that time, if punishment is to fall on one person, it must be on my head that it will fall. So whatever shame may overwhelm me I know that it is but retribution for this deed. Therefore I would like to shave my head and go as a mendicant priest, keeping precepts and seeking only the Way of the Buddha. But such being my situation, I can-

not do as I would like. Since my own lot is unforeseeable for today or tomorrow, I feel it regrettable that it appears most unlikely that my past karmic life will be resolved, whatever discipline I may practice. Alas! When I think over the conduct of my past life, my guilt is greater than Mount Sumeru, while all my righteousness is less than a speck of dust; and if thus in vain I end my life, without doubt I shall be reborn in the three ways of torment. And so I beseech you, Hōnen, of your kindness and compassion to help even such a worthless one as myself, and to show me how to achieve salvation."

At this Hōnen, choked by tears, could answer nothing for a while. Finally, however, he raised himself and spoke as follows: "After having the rare opportunity of being born as man, to fall again into the three ways of torment is too grievous a lot. But if in disgust at this sinful world you seek rebirth in the Pure Land, cleansing your mind of evil and turning to good, all the Buddhas of the three worlds will certainly rejoice and be glad. There are different ways to salvation, but in the degeneracy of the Latter-day, Nembutsu is the best. Thus fixing the whole mind and concentrating all practices into the repetition of the six syllables, none can be so dull or ignorant but his Nembutsu will be heard. Even though your guilt be ever so deep, do not feel despised. Even a man of the ten transgressions and five rebellions will attain Paradise if only he will return to Amida. However small your merit, do not give up your desire. If with earnest mind you repeat the Nembutsu, surely Amida will come to meet you. If with faith that Paradise is to be obtained by the repetition of the Nembutsu, you wholeheartedly repeat it, then Paradise is yours. If you repeat Nembutsu with repentance, you do indeed repent. If you trust Nembutsu as the all powerful sword, no evil karma can approach, and if you have faith in the Nembutsu to cleanse from sin, all your sins will be washed away. The essence of the Pure Land teaching lies in this, and can be summed up as above. The attainment of Paradise depends on faith. If you deeply believe this teaching, and have faith in your mind and repeat Nembutsu with your mouth in all your actions of body, speech, and mind, and in your four modes of life (going, standing, sitting, and lying), the

131

instant your life ends, departing from this world of trouble, you shall without doubt be reborn into the Land of No-Return, the Western Paradise." At this exposition Shigehira was greatly overjoyed, and replied, "I would now like to receive the precepts. But is it possible that I can do this without becoming a monk? "Indeed," said Hōnen, "it is quite usual to observe the precepts without becoming a monk." And taking a razor he laid it on his forehead and made the motions of shaving his head, after which he instructed him in the ten precepts. Shigehira received his instruction with tears of gladness, and Hōnen as well, filled with extreme sympathy, taught him the ordinances in a voice broken by sobs.

Although we do not know when Shigehira first met Hōnen, there is little doubt that his mental attitude at that time was a sky-breadth different from his state at the time he was a captive being taken to the Eastern Provinces. His seemingly reverent echoing of "What will be my fate after death?" was a mannerism of the people of the time—seen even today—and does not necessarily mean he desired birth in the Pure Land. He does not, in saying that a mind obstructed with evil desire has no room for good thoughts, that it is unlikely for him to be saved no matter what discipline he might undertake, seem to be a man afraid of falling into Hell. It would be better to see him as one invoking stern criticism of human life. When he says that "My heart was totally given up to pride without a thought for what might befall me," he is acknowledging his downsliding animal-like existence that lived for the day alone without any introspection whatever. Though such a life is "evil," something spiritual begins to flicker when he says "I desire salvation." This is the earnest confession of Shigehira the "evil man." As a person of high governmental rank he would be unable to make such a confession, or, if he did do so the words would have to be empty ones. Herein is the difference between Heian and Kamakura times.

2. Nembutsu and the Kamakura Bushi

Once again we have a fine example in the religious awakening of Renshōbō Kumagai Naozane. From the Heian to the Sengoku period (794–1558) the number of intellectuals and warriors entering the priest-

132

hood increased considerably. I wonder what meaning shaving the head and donning black robes has with regard to a life of spirituality. Although the accord between them is indeed a mysterious one, numerous historical examples attest to its existence. I am not sure whether this is a good or a bad aspect, but something of the Japanese character can be seen therein. When a man who has led a pleasure-seeking, worldly life, or a life of brutality, shaves his head and fingers a rosary, he appears in a favourable light, assuming a gentle and elegant air. This is all esthetically and emotionally agreeable, but after all is fallacious and totally removed from spiritual existence. Renshōbō, however, was certainly one among other warriors of the Sengoku period, the "period of wars," who had a sober opinion of human life. His alleged encounter with Taira Atsumori[3] aside, what is true beyond doubt is that Naozane cast stern censure on his own life.

Here are two poems ascribed to Naozane, in which the bent of his extreme sincerity is well exhibited:

"This paper clothing [of monkhood] is preferable to my former armor;
Even the arrows of the wind cannot penetrate it."

"I am uttering the Nembutsu I promised Amida;
Whether I am born in the Pure Land or not is in his hands."

The latter can be said to reveal clearly the mental attitude of the samurai. One utters the Nembutsu and gives oneself up to the Prayer, and whether the Pure Land is attained or not is entirely in Amida's hands, not according to one's own calculations—this is the attitude of Renshōbō the *Tariki* believer, an attitude that enables him to remain true to the way of the samurai as well. His lack of concern regarding the result of his Nembutsu-calling—the idea that such is not for him to know—expresses very well the ever so honest and straightforward character of the people of the Kanto area. Once he has exchanged his armor for monk's clothing there is nothing at all to fear, however much the winds of transience bring misfortune's arrows—this describes quite accurately the mental state of the monk Renshōbō.

133

II. ASPECTS OF PURE LAND THOUGHT

1. The Nembutsu—Pure Land Ōjō—Prayer

The heart of Pure Land thought lies in the Nembutsu and not in attaining birth in the Pure Land. Pure Land adherents all believe that Nembutsu is the means and attainment of rebirth in the Pure Land the end. But without Nembutsu there is no *Ōjō*. The succession is Nembutsu→*Ōjō*: *Ōjō*→Nembutsu. This being the case, Nembutsu is *Ōjō*, *Ōjō* is Nembutsu. In accommodation to our everyday consciousness, which contrasts "this world" and "that world," a movement from Nembutsu to *Ōjō* is spoken of. Yet this of course is not reality, only an intellectual contrivance, for were rebirth to exist outside of Nembutsu, the way of *Ōjō* would also have to exist outside of Nembutsu. If one says the Nembutsu, *Ōjō* will be attained: it then follows that Paradise exists, *Ōjō* exists, where there is Nembutsu. This is the life of Nembutsu *samadhi*. Nembutsu uttered with the idea to attain *Ōjō* would not be genuine, would not be an absolute Nembutsu.

Hōnen taught the monk Renshōbō that "The practice of the Nembutsu is the practice of the Original Prayer of the Buddha. There should be only the Nembutsu of the Original Prayer." He continued,

> *To attain Ōjō, just repeat the Nembutsu 30,000, 50,000, or 60,000 times with all your heart. If you still have time left, other practices of good merit may be undertaken. If you say it 60,000 times, you do not have to do anything more. If you will repeat it 30,000 or 50,000 times with singlehearted assiduity, even if precepts cannot be fully observed, it does not matter, for precepts do not determine rebirth in the Pure Land.*

What does he mean? It would take at least ten hours to repeat 30,000 Nembutsu; to do it 60 or 100 thousand times would probably leave little time for sleep at night. To say "Namu-Amida-Butsu" "Namu-Amida-Butsu" with a mindless rapidity 30,000 times a day would require an extremely large amount of time and leave one physically exhausted to boot. There would be no time to do any good deeds, or bad ones either for that matter. One would become a Nembutsu machine. The "mind" of the "singleminded" Nembutsu would have no room to enter.

Why must Pure Land $\bar{O}j\bar{o}$ be so avidly pursued when there is really nothing known of the Pure Land? Since there is a study of the Pure Land in my *Jōdō-kei shisō-ron* [Studies in Pure Land Thought], I will leave detailed treatment of the subject to it, but frankly, I am rather inclined to think of Pure Land $\bar{O}j\bar{o}$ as a kind of symbol.

What is important is Nembutsu itself; singleminded Nembutsu alone is important. Tentatively, we suppose that Pure Land $\bar{O}j\bar{o}$ lies beyond the denial of the present world, but in "Namu-Amida-Butsu" $\bar{O}j\bar{o}$ and the denial are really unified. Therefore, thanks to the repetition of the 6-syllable Name, all bad karma can be eliminated. This elimination is Pure Land $\bar{O}j\bar{o}$. Hōnen and his disciples, in the traditional way, consciously felt that Nembutsu *shōmyō* was the required act to achieve $\bar{O}j\bar{o}$. but their spiritual insight was not necessarily there. Since this insight was not yet completely realized in them, "this land," "that land," abhorrence of and release from the world of impurity, joy at and seeking after the Land of Purity were imagined to be opposite one another. "Singleminded Nembutsu" had not been realized. Moreover, since their aim was always fixed on singlemindedness, they never forgot it even as they spoke of $\bar{O}j\bar{o}$

In one sense, the Nembutsu is also a prayer. Criticism of this life is its denial, and behind the denial hides the affirmation of the Pure Land. Prayer is none other than the inclination toward that hidden affirmation. It is not concerned with consciousness or unconsciousness. Where one attempts to rise above his present existence there is prayer. When Shigehira said that a heart obstructed by evil could not harbor good, he was reflecting upon his own evil heart and attempting to transcend it. Unless one can somehow realize how it will be after transcendence is accomplished, the aspiration to transcend will not arise. This is where prayer and "Namu-Amida-Butsu" come in. Here the Nembutsu of the Original Prayer begins to function. Prayer is eternal, and for that reason Nembutsu is eternal, and the Original Prayer of the Buddha is eternal as well. Thirty, sixty, or one hundred thousand Nembutsu merely suggest the eternity of Nembutsu—of prayer. Rather than saying they suggest it, it would probably be better to say they *concretize* it. If it is not singleminded, the eternal Nembutsu does not appear. Eternity is in the singlemindedness. It is the eternal present. It is the voice of "Namu-Amida-Butsu."

135

2. Continuous Succession of Nembutsu Shōmyō—The Instant of the 'One Thought'[4]

The question of Nembutsu *shōmyō* is not one of numbers. Hōnen's words, "Though an ordinary man practice the Nembutsu twenty or thirty thousand times daily, the number means nothing. Yet numerous repetitions are advised," seem to suggest he felt large numbers of repetitions in themselves were desirable. But he immediately continues, "This is because I would secure the continuity (*sōzoku*) of the calling of the Name. Numbers are not necessarily essential, but there is a need for constant Nembutsu. If a definite number of repetitions is not prescribed it might lead to negligence. Large numbers of repetitions are therefore advised."

The question therefore is one of continual Right Mindfulness, which is none other than singlemindedness. Because it is singleminded all acts are contained within it. Generally speaking, 'all acts' would be in a time-succession; but here they are included in the very thought-instant of the calling of the Name, where the singlemindedness must be unobtainable in the three worlds of past, present, and future. For one's acts, that is, time considered as a progression, to be embraced within the instant of one calling of the Name is beyond the comprehension of the discriminating intellect; it is, in a spatial sense, like Mount Sumeru being held within a mustard grain, which is incomprehensible on the level of discriminatory consciousness. May it not be more easily understandable if we say instead that the instant of the calling of the Name is time-succession itself. Without this understanding it is not possible to understand that Amida's Original Prayer cannot be used up in an eternity, or that the practice of Nembutsu leads one immediately to the Pure Land.

"No matter whether one is learned or not, I solely urge him to the exclusive practice of Nembutsu." "All acts are contained in the calling of the six syllable Name . . . if you are very attentive to the Nembutsu you will surely attain *Ōjō*." In my opinion the only way to properly understand these words is to say that Nembutsu must not be a Nembutsu of discrimination, but one that appears from within non-discriminatory wisdom. If it does not flow naturally from spiritual insight, "continual" attention is not possible, and neither is *senju* Nembutsu, singleminded Nembutsu done to the exclusion of all other practices.

136

"The practice of the Nembutsu does not depend upon one's other modes of action or upon time or place."—such words do not emerge from within the discriminating intellect. Pure Land followers always advocate Nembutsu from a situation of discrimination. Although this is to make it more readily acceptable to people, its true meaning thereby is more difficult to attain. Suzuki Shōsan was a man of Zen and for that reason he is very direct on this point, making it all the more easily understood. "Vomit up all learning, delusory Buddhist teachings, and just become a man of Nembutsu through and through. The 'cutting-off' Nembutsu clears away both good and bad thoughts with the sword of Nembutsu, 'Namu-Amida-Butsu,' 'Namu-Amida-Butsu.' " To a samurai who asked him about the Nembutsu he said, "As a samurai, create the idea of your enemy's defense and jump right into it saying Nembutsu. Practice this 'jumping-in' Nembutsu until you can do it freely."

When, after cutting off all ideas of good and evil, yes and no, all actions at all times become one with the calling of the Name, that is the practice of singleminded Nembutsu. It then becomes a Nembutsu of all acts. Though people of the orthodox groups may explain *senju* (exclusive) Nembutsu in many ways, it is all dogmatic finery. *Senju* Nembutsu is not one act chosen from among others; to say that it signifies absolute Nembutsu would be in more accord with the true intent of both Hōnen and Shinran. It is Nembutsu seen from spiritual insight itself, and it is Japanese. When instead of conceptually following the historical Nembutsu, one sees the Nembutsu of Amida's Original Prayer directly with the awakening of his own individual spirituality, it is felt clearly and intimately. This is Hōnen's "Nembutsu of plain wood." Intellectually-minded priests have an unfortunate habit of discussion and argument for their own sake. Even this would not be bad in some instances, but for one who would confront life's truth the Nembutsu must be spoken with spiritual insight, in "plain wood."[5]

For most of us spirituality cannot send forth its essential light because the intellect stands in the way. That is why Pure Land Nembutsu is the practice of those who "know nothing." In one sense, since spirituality has an immediacy that is emotional or sensory, when we speak of "simple-hearted women" and so on, we are liable to imagine spirituality as something instinctive, completely shorn of intellectuality. But as has been repeated over and over, spiritual insight holds its significance within itself.

137

For those "ignorant and unlettered" this has an all the more incomprehensible charm. That is why the Nembutsu was so readily accepted among the common people.

3. Japanese Spiritual Insight and the Ichimai-Kishōmon (The One Page Testament)

As a document that sets forth the circumstances heretofore dealt with, Hōnen's *One Page Testament*[6] establishes the fundamental truth of Pure Land faith.

> *By Nembutsu I do not mean such practice of meditation on the Buddha as is referred to by the wise men of China and Japan, nor is it the recitation of the Buddha's Name which is practiced as the result of study and understanding as to the meaning of Nembutsu. It is just to recite the Name of Amida, without doubting that this will issue in the rebirth of the believer in the Pure Land. Just this, no other considerations, are needed. Mention is often made of the threefold heart and the four modes of practice, but these are all included in the belief that rebirth in the Pure Land is most conclusively assured by "Namu-Amida-Butsu." If one imagines something more than this, he will be excluded from the blessings of the two holy ones, Amida and Shakyamuni, and left out of the Original Prayer. He who believes in the Nembutsu, however learned he may be in all the teachings of Shakyamuni, should behave like an ignoramus who knows nothing, or like a simple-hearted woman devotee; avoid pedantry, and recite the Buddha's Name with singleness of heart.*

It is in Pure Land *Ōjō* that the thought of the Pure Land sects can be said to have its heart. But Pure Land believers do not speak much of this Pure Land, relying instead upon narrative expositions in the scriptures. It is something that should naturally come into question, but strangely enough it is not dealt with. *Ōjō* alone is vociferously extolled, and Nembutsu is emphasized as the only path to *Ōjō*. The Pure Land is not clearly conceived. Rebirth in the Pure Land and the Nembutsu as the absolute requirement for rebirth are alone given imposing stress.

138

In terms of everyday experience *Ōjō* means denial of this world, and thus Nembutsu clearly signifies the transcending of the world. "Everyday experience" signifies the spiritual life. Were we to criticize or consider this intellectually, there is much literature that might be offered—someone said this, another refuted it, and on and on. One becomes enmeshed in the words and phrases of others, and succumbs in the end to debating and emulating the furrowed brows of the learned Hiei and Nara scholars, the result of which is a lifetime in which nothing beneficial comes, a lifetime that does not throw a single thread of light on the life of spirituality. Since Japanese spirituality always endeavors above all to grasp existential reality it has little interest in the vicissitudes of abstract argument.

Had he limited himself to a scholarly outlook, ensconced himself behind the time-honored teachings of the scriptures, and discussed the *principle* of Nembutsu being essential, Hōnen would have been revered as the foremost scholar and wiseman of his day, and would have averted the wrath and persecution of the Hiei and Nara establishment. At most there might have been something akin to the "Discussion at Ohara."[7] It so happened, however, that there ensued a full-blown persecution, with the issuance of a ban upon the practice of Nembutsu, the requiring of a written pledge, and finally, Hōnen's exile to a remote part of the country. These developments testify that Hōnen's Nembutsu was not just a hollow conceptualization, but had achieved an ultimate contact with the reality of human life. The Hiei and Nara scholars had not touched the genuine experience of spiritual life. Kenshin (1131–1192), a head priest of the Tendai sect, even acknowledged this shortcoming, as well as affirming the validity of Hōnen's teaching, when he said:

> *I have studied the doctrines of the esoteric and exoteric sects alike, yet have been so busy looking to my worldly fame that I have not earnestly been seeking birth in the Pure Land, and have not even looked at the expositions of Dōshaku and Zendō.*[8] *No one but Hōnen could make such a declaration.* (Hōnen's Life)

Since they did not yet know what spiritual insight was, they felt that excellence in scholarship and intellectual matters was the end of all things religious. Yet all the more because of this, even though the priesthoods advanced under the patronage of the Imperial Court and had the respect of all, did they not come to be nothing more than lay communities? We find in such circumstances, I believe, the reason Hōnen stood with the ignorant and simple-hearted, and took no special notice of the commandments, to a degree that may even have seemed excessive.

To the question, "Is there any merit in bringing offerings to a commandment-breaking or ignorant (*guchi*) priest?" Hōnen answered, "In these Latter-days we should honor such priests even as the Buddha." This answer in itself is not altogether clear, and since he immediately continued, "All my answers have been entrusted to the messenger—ask him," there was apparently some additional (oral) information given for purposes of clarification that has not come down to us in Hōnen's records. Yet it seems Hōnen felt if one was able to repeat the Nembutsu with singleness of heart, then precepts kept for their own sake did not really matter.

Once Hōnen pointed to the tatami mats on which he was seated, and said, "It is because these mats exist we are able to say they are either worn out or not. If there were no mats, how could they be worn out or not? In like manner, in the Latter-days (*mappō*) we may say that the commandments are neither kept nor broken, for the priests themselves are such in name only. There should thus be no question of the breaking or keeping of commandments." It is from this standpoint that Hōnen saw the priests and priestly commandments of his time.

I do not now wish to go into a discussion as to the meaning the word *guchi* (愚痴) had in Hōnen's time, but will understand it as meaning "ignorant" or "unlettered." Those described as *guchi* are the very ones Hōnen encouraged and welcomed with such zeal. Really, unless one is a *guchi*, one cannot invoke the Nembutsu. Since a Nembutsu of scholarship and intellectuality does not leave the plane of discrimination, the Pure Land rebirth of such a Nembutsu-caller, that is, his spiritual insight, is impossible, and his practice is in vain.

"I no longer wear the cap of the court. I am only the foolish Hōnen, weighed down by the ten evils. Yet such a man is to gain *Ōjō* by invoking the Nembutsu." Here we see the essence of Hōnen.

He also said, "The Nembutsu of the Original Prayer makes one stand alone, without help. Help means help through wisdom, help through precepts, help through virtue or compassion. A good man says the Nembutsu as a good man, an evil man says it as an evil man: one simply says the Nembutsu as one is innately. That is the 'Nembutsu without help.'"

140

Doesn't this strike to the very heart of the matter! It returns one to essential ignorance, becoming as one was at birth, an ignoramus who knows nothing. It attains to the ultimate ground of *individuum*. It is the Nembutsu of "the only exalted one in all the universe." It is precisely here the cherished desire of *Ōjō* is realized. Other than this there is no *Ōjō*. Pure Land believers are inclined to dwell too much upon *Ōjō* and to forget the Nembutsu itself. When "Namu-Amida-Butsu" is Rinzai's "Real Man of No Title above the man of red flesh," it penetrates to the meaning of the words: "Even though you do something else, do it while reciting Nembutsu. Do not allow it to become secondary to anything else." The Nembutsu is not to be recited *while* doing something. The Nembutsu itself wakes up in the morning, goes to bed at night, responds Yes when called to, feels cold when it touches the mountain stream, feels warmth when immersed in warm water. If the Nembutsu and the caller are separated, a single-hearted Nembutsu will not be possible, nor will the state spoken of by Zendō; "Walking or standing, sitting or lying, never cease the practice of it [Nembutsu] even for a moment...." If the Name and oneself do not become one, one cannot attain the Nembutsu samadhi Zendō describes. The Hōnen who said, "In looking at Zendō's Commentary, to the eyes of Genkū (Hōnen) the threefold heart is Namu-Amida-Butsu, the four modes of practice are Namu-Amida-Butsu, the five kinds of practice are Namu-Amida-Butsu,"[9] was a man who truly had penetrated to spiritual insight. A mere scholar could never speak such words, words which tally with the utterances of the Myōkōnin of the Shin sect. On this point the man of Zen who exists "I alone, in all the universe" is together with Hōnen. But a peculiar characteristic of Hōnen's insight is that he does not cry "Satori!" as the Zen man does.

In the *Roankyō*, Suzuki Shōsan says:

> It says in an old poem, "Satori is satori that is not satori; satori that is satori is an illusion of satori." Truly, satori that is satori is dangerous! I too like satori that is not satori. Hōnen's Nembutsu Ōjō is also satori that is not satori.

4. Hōnen and Suzuki Shōsan

I would now like to turn to Suzuki Shōsan, whose view of Nembutsu is strongly reminiscent of Hōnen's. As manifestations of Japanese spirituality they may be said to have lived in the same ray of light.

Shōsan says: "Have a great desire to use up all karmic hindrance in farming. If you farm with a 'Namu-Amida-Butsu' at each hoe-stroke you will surely attain Buddhahood." Again the raising up and striking down of the hoe by means of Nembutsu is not implied here. "Namu-Amida-Butsu" should move the hoe, stroke by stroke. Hōnen's teaching is similar. Rejecting Nembutsu done while doing something else, he teaches that which utters Nembutsu is that which performs these "other things." When asked, "What should I do when distracting thoughts come into my mind?" Hōnen explained, "Just repeat Nembutsu zealously."

Though this is something that could conceivably be encountered in *kōan* Zen, here Pure Land *Ōjō* is also included in the 'distracting thoughts.' For one who says Nembutsu with singleness of heart, all apart from Nembutsu is distracting ideas, illusions, complications, and ratiocinations. The insignificant routine of merely liking this and disliking that is not involved in 'distracting thoughts.' Joyfully seeking the Pure Land and trying to avert Hell as odious are the great and principal distracting thoughts, and the source of every Nembutsu. Hōnen does not say one should cut these off, simply give them no heed. This, in its positive aspect, is Nembutsu *senju*, "exclusive" Nembutsu.

Shōsan says:

> There are two ways of saying Nembutsu: To think to become Buddha by saying the Nembutsu is an act of karmic transmigration. In reality, the correct way is to recite away all passions by means of Nembutsu. Therefore, one does not generally become Buddha through Nembutsu; if one recites away these passions one knows that one's fundamental self is Buddha. Nevertheless, thoughts that you will become Buddha after death and the like are all post-mortem thirsts ... The only way for you is to case aside all things "Namu-Amida-Butsu" "Namu-Amida-Butsu", regulate your respiration, continually study death, say the Nembutsu for all your worth, and die a peaceful death. You must simply do singleminded Nembutsu. (Roankyō)

In these lines the special characteristics of Shōsan's "Nembutsu Zen" are revealed. We can also see a contrast to Hōnen in Shōsan's bent for rushing on straightforward with Nembutsu. The pedantic air of the Hiei and Nara scholars and the left-over customs of the Heian period appear to some extent in Hōnen, and this has its own peculiar interest. But Shōsan was a samurai of Mikawa province during the beginning years of the Tokugawa era (1615–1866). That his words come alive may be attributed simply to the circumstances of samurai life, striving and dying in physical conflict.

> *You must simply employ the Nembutsu with singleness of purpose, without distractions, until you are detached from self. To be detached from self means to learn death while repeating "Namu-Amida-Butsu" "Namu-Amida-Butsu," and to be enlightened as to the matter of death. I know that you too must cherish your individual self greatly, but it is not a difficult or lengthy matter, just use up the self with Nembutsu.* (Ibid.)

The self Shōsan speaks of—*jihon*, 自本—is the consciousness of the individual self. He teaches to exhaust this through Nembutsu. When one goes straight forward saying "Namu-Amida-Butsu" "Namu-Amida-Butsu," both life and death disappear. At that time the self is naturally uttered away, and the true form of singlemindedness appears. This is the occasion of Pure Land *Ōjō*.

In another place, Shōsan states, "Do not think of the past, do not make judgements about the future, do not just trifle away the present thought-instant in vain. Use it purely." Singlemindedness is none other than "the present thought-instant."

Among Hōnen's writings something similar to the following is found. According to Shōsan who quotes it, it goes like this:

> *One wintry day someone asked Hōnen how to prepare for future existence. He answered that as for desires about the next existence, one must say the Nembutsu in the state of mind of someone about to be instantly beheaded. This is a good teaching. If the Nembutsu is not done in this way, self-attachment cannot be extinguished.* (Ibid.)

143

Unless this state of mind is attained, the "Nembutsu of standing alone," the Nembutsu without crutches, the single-hearted Nembutsu of Amida's Original Prayer cannot be called out. At such a time knowledge is of no help: precepts, morality, good and bad, compassion and non-compassion —none of these will suffice. We may call the state of the mind at this time "plain wood," innate or natural, or a "mind of settled faith." Hōnen said that "the Name of Amida's Original Prayer has the greatest potential when spoken by woodcutters, fuel-gatherers, water-carriers, and the like, who know not a single written word, who continually repeat the Name with deep and genuine desire in the belief they will surely be reborn into the Pure Land."

Hōnen did not establish the meaning of singleminded Nembutsu by means of learning. He and the Zen teacher Suzuki Shōsan are at this point on the same footing, one which breeds spiritual insight. Hōnen's true aspect must be seen in his making 'ignorance' instead of learning the primary factor. He boldly challenged the scholars because they put too much store in knowledge and were devoted to the fame and wealth and greed of the world, conditions least conducive to the awakening of their Japanese spirituality. Hōnen walked firmly on the real earth, unseparated from it even for a moment. "He became," in the words of Shōsan, "one with the earth." It is here we can really appreciate the significance of Hōnen's appearance—the rise of Japanese spiritual awakening—in the Kamakura period.

III. NEMBUTSU AND 'THE UNLETTERED'

1. The Meaning of Hōnen's Persecution

> Hōnen's teaching spread to all parts of the land. However, some of his disciples were guilty of acts of self-indulgence, which they committed under the guise of the exclusive practice of the Nembutsu of the Original Prayer. Using this, the priests of Nara and Hiei worked to have the practice of Nembutsu outlawed and to have Hōnen's influence blocked.

144

The above comes from chapter 31 of *Hōnen's Life*. No doubt there were those among his disciples who went to extremes of conduct, but for that matter I am sure there were numbers of such commandment-breakers among the priests of the established sects as well. Certainly it was not limited just to the followers of Hōnen. The attempt to use this to censure Hōnen and his followers seems to have been a pretext, with the real reason lying elsewhere.

These scholars passed their days in discussion of abstract teachings and writings, and did not even try to proceed along the path of spirituality. Opposed to this, Hōnen steadily moved along such a path, and this stirred the others to envy. Of course, abstract discussion is necessary too, but it must be supported by the reality of firm and concrete experience. This the scholars of Hiei and Nara did not have, and thus their influence could never prevail among the illiterate common people. Nor was it welcomed by the samurai class, engaged in mortal struggle on the battlefield. Although some of the so-called intellectual nobles might have inclined their ears as if to hear, theirs was in any case Buddhism of a shallow, ceremonial nature, and not an expression of spiritual life. What Hōnen was aiming at was entirely different from what they desired. He tried to seize the spirituality of the Japanese in its natural expression. Although he said the Buddhist teaching was not suited to the dull-witted common people of the Latter-Day, such words are probably traditional utterance, mere reiteration of the sect founders. What he was unconsciously doing was attempting to touch the life of spirituality which existed among those very people referred to in the Seven Article Pledge that he signed. They were the ones able to touch its true and living elements. Who were these people? In the following Seven Article Pledge I have indicated them with roman type. These seven articles were written by Hōnen to quiet the resentment of the priests of the traditional sects and to warn his own disciples against excesses.

To my disciples, and to Nembutsu priests, I make the following declaration:

(1) You must not adversely criticize the principles of either Shingon or Tendai without consulting sutras and commentaries, or despise the other Buddhas and bodisattvas.

(2)   The ignorant *must not allow themselves to engage in disputes with men of knowledge, or with those who differ from them in religious theory and practice.*

(3)   You must not foolishly *or narrowly insist that those of different faith and practice give up their distinctive religious practices, and you must never jest at them.*

(4)   You must not encourage people to indulge in meat-eating or wine-drinking, in the name of the Nembutsu which you say requires no precepts. *Never say of those who strictly observe precepts that they are the "miscellaneous practice people," or that those who trust in the Buddha's Original Prayer never need be afraid of evils.*

(5)   Ignorant people, who are not yet clear in their own minds about moral distinctions, *must not wilfully press their own ideas upon others, departing from the sacred teachings of the sutras and opposing the opinions of their teachers. You must not lead the ignorant astray by getting into quarrelsome disputes with them, which can only bring you the derision of the learned.*

(6)   Being dullards, *you must not undertake to preach about the Way, and in ignorance of the right Dharma, expound all sorts of evil doctrines to influence ignorant priests and laymen.*

(7)   You must not set forth distorted teachings contrary to the teaching of the Buddhas, wrongly calling them the views of the patriarchs.

Signed and sealed by the priest Genkū (Hōnen), on the seventeenth day of the eleventh month of the first year of Genkyū (1204).

The people these pledges deal with stood opposite the scholars of the establishment. The latter were intelligent men of different faiths and practices, who observed precepts, who knew right and wrong, followed the scriptural teachings and conformed to the teachings of the saints, and held to the right Dharma; they were not simple or ignorant. Because they were diametrically opposed to Hōnen and his disciples, when they saw Hōnen making great strides in the actual life of the people they were unable to control their indignation—a natural human reaction, I suppose.

146

2. Japanese Spirituality—"the Foolish and Illiterate"

In illustrating how Hōnen reached spiritual circumstances in everyday life, let us first look at the noteworthy case of the diviner Awanosuke. Diviners at that time were, I suppose, something like the street fortune-tellers of today. Hōnen said this diviner, who belonged to the class of the so-called ignorant and unlettered, possessed the same Nembutsu as he himself did. This is identical in meaning with Shinran's words, "Hōnen's faith was given by the Tathāgata; Zenshin's (Shinran) too comes from the Tathāgata. Therefore our faith is the same." Such an acknowledgement could not have come from the scholar-priests of the time. Not only in theory, but to say it right in front of his master as Shinran did would not have been possible unless he had touched the ultimate reality of human life. The following is from Chapter 19 of *Hōnen's Life.*

> *A follower of Hōnen, a diviner named Awanosuke, waited on Hōnen and practiced the Nembutsu. Once Hōnen pointed to him and said, 'Which is better, that diviner's Nembutsu or mine?' The question was directed to one of his disciples, Shōkōbō. Shōkōbō, understanding quite well the meaning of Hōnen's question, yet still wanting to make certain of his own idea, replied 'How can your Nembutsu always be the same as his?' This reply brought a change to Hōnen's countenance. 'Well then, how have you been listening to the teaching of the Pure Land all this time? That diviner calls on the Buddha to save him by saying the Nembutsu, and so do I. There is not a bit of difference between us.' Although that was the understanding Shōkōbō had held from the first, it seemed as if its true and essential meaning had come to him anew, nad tears began to fall from his eyes.*

Nobles who came under Hōnen's influence, such as the ex-Regent Fujiwara Kanezane (Tsukinowa no Zenkō) and his wife, no doubt would have become objects of other Buddhist teaching even without Hōnen, but diviners, fishermen, prostitutes, thieves, women, and the like, probably would not have been saved without him. The episode of the Buddhist novice Zuiren gives us yet another chance to clarify Hōnen's Nembutsu. To see a lotus flower as a lotus flower, and a plum blossom as a plum blossom—that is a Nembutsu "whose peculiarity is the absence of peculiarity," and apart from it there is no room for such things as the threefold mind. The lives of those who become absorbed in the five modes of practice, the four modes of practice, or the threefold mind know nothing but the ascetic environment of the mountains and forests. They have been brought up in limited surroundings.

A novice named Zuiren became a faithful follower of Hōnen, and went with him as his attendant to his place of banishment. Hōnen had a feeling of deep compassion for him, and explained the way to attain Ōjō. He received the teaching with profound faith, and practiced the Nembutsu with undivided heart. After Hōnen's death, in the second year of Kempō (1214), someone said to him that no matter how much one practiced the Nembutsu, unless he studied and understood fully about the so-called threefold mind he could not be born into the Pure Land. At this Zuiren said: "The late Hōnen used to say that the peculiarity of the Nembutsu is the absence of peculiarity, and that the only thing is to believe the Buddha's word and practice the Nembutsu, and one would surely be born into the Pure Land. He said nothing whatever about the threefold mind." Thereupon the person went on to say, "But he was there speaking for the benefit of those who would find such things difficult to understand, to make it easy for them." He then proceeded to give his own interpretation of Hōnen's real meaning. He gave many quotations from the sutras and commentaries, until Zuiren began to wonder whether he might not be right, and began to doubt.

Then one night he had a dream. As he was going through the western gate of Hōshōji Temple, he saw a great variety of lotus plants in the pond, all in full bloom. As he went towards the west veranda of the temple, there were a great many priests sitting in rows, talking together about the Pure Land doctrines. He went up the steps and saw Hōnen sitting on the north side facing south; he bowed reverently towards him. Hōnen perceived this and told him to come over beside him. He went near, and before he had said a word, Hōnen addressed him as follows: "Do not have the least anxiety about the subject that has recently been engaging

148

your mind." Zuiren had never told a single soul anything about it, so he wondered how in the world Hōnen could have known. He proceeded therefore to tell him the whole story as above related. At this Hōnen said, "Suppose there were someone who talked nonsense to you, saying that the lotus flowers over there in the pond were not lotuses but plum or cherry blossoms, would you believe him?" Zuiren replied, "So long as they are really lotuses, how could I believe otherwise no matter what anyone says?" "Then," Hōnen continued, "it is just the same with the Nembutsu. For you to believe the teaching of Genkū, and not doubt the certainty of birth into the Pure Land by the practice of the Nembutsu, is just the same as believing that a lotus flower is a lotus flower. The only thing to do is to firmly believe in the Nembutsu without worrying about the reasons. Do not believe such an absurdity as that a lotus flower is a cherry or plum flower." With this he awoke from his dream, and all his doubts were gone.

It is said that he accumulated merit in the Nembutsu, and when the end came he attained his long cherished desire of birth into the Pure Land with perfect composure. (Hōnen's Life, 20)

3. Hōnen and The Unlettered Samurai

Now a few words concerning Hōnen's relation to the samurai. The Nembutsu conversion of Kumagai Naozane and others has already been related. Here I would like to mention the example of Amakasu Tarō Tadatsuna, characterized by the same extreme pragmatism we found in the story of Taira Shigehira. As Amakasu took up arms and readied himself to rush off to the field of battle, he felt a contradiction between the essential meaning of *Ōjō* and his occupation as a samurai. In order to resolve it he decided to visit Hōnen. On the 15th day of the 11th month, 1192, he called upon him at his residence. He reminds us of Arjuna in the *Bhagavad-Gita*, though Amakasu's case was a personal affair. His problem took on an all the more pressing urgency because he was a samurai, at a time when such men had little affinity with learning. His story is found in *Hōnen's Life*.

In the province of Musashi there lived a samurai of the Inomata

149

clan called *Amakasu Tarō Tadatsuna, who was in the service of the Minamoto family. He became a follower of Hōnen and got to be very assiduous in the practice of Nembutsu.* At this time the soldier-priests of Enryakuji Temple on Mount Hiei, in defiance of the more moderate elements in the priesthood, began to prepare for armed resistance against the authorities. They took their stand at the Hiyoshi Hachioji Shrine, and Tadatsuna was by Imperial Order put in command of a body of troops which the Government dispatched to suppress the rising. On the 15th day in the 11th month of 1192, as he made ready to depart, he paid a visit to Hōnen and said to him, "I have often heard you say that even sinners like us, if they only say the Nembutsu and put their whole trust in Amida's Original Prayer, will undoubtedly attain Ōjō. Though I firmly believe in it, I suppose such is the case only with those who are lying in sickbeds, calmly waiting for the end to come. Being a samurai, I cannot do as I would like, and now in obedience to an Imperial Order I am setting out for the castle at Hachioji to punish some rebellious Sammon priests. I was born into a soldier's family and trained in the use of martial weapons, being on the one hand under obligation not to fail in carrying out at least in some measure the will of my ancestors, and on the other, responsible for handing down something of glory to my posterity. Yet if, as a soldier, I abandon myself to the driving back of the enemy, wicked and furious passions will be stirred within me, and it will be very difficult to awaken any pious feeling in my heart. Yet if I allow myself to keep thinking all the time about the transitoriness of life and about the truth of Nembutsu Ōjō, I will be in danger of being taken captive by my enemies, and thereby be eternally branded a coward and straightaway have all my patrimony confiscated. For a foolish person like me it is very hard to decide which path to choose. Will you tell me how I can accomplish my cherished desire for Ōjō without sacrificing the honor of my family as a samurai?"

To this Hōnen made the following reply: "Amida's Original Prayer says nothing about whether a man is good or bad, nor does it discuss the amount of his religious practice. It makes no distinction between the pure and the impure, and takes no account

150

of time, space, or any other of the diverse circumstances in men's lives. It matters not how a man dies. The wicked man, just as he is, will attain Ōjo if he calls on the Name. This is the wonderful thing about Amida's Prayer. So, though a man born into a samurai family goes to war and loses his life, if only he repeats the Name and relies on Amida's Prayer, there is not the slightest doubt whatever that Amida will come to welcome him to his Paradise." Under these gentle instructions his doubts left him and with a glad heart he exclaimed, "Tadatsuna's Ōjō will take place this very day." Hōnen handed him a sacred scarf which he put on under his armor, and he finally set out for Hachioji, where he abandoned himself to battle with the rebel priests. In the midst of the struggle his sword was broken, and he received a deep wound. Seeing it was hopeless, he flung down his sword, and clasping his hands he called the Name in a loud voice, giving himself over into the hands of the enemy. . . .

4. Spirituality, the 'Ignorant and Unlettered'

Although now would be a good point to speak of Hōnen's role as a catalyst in the rise of Nembutsu among the ignorant and illiterate warriors and common people, that will have to be put aside momentarily, for I wish to concentrate on the idea that the awakening of Japanese spirituality in the Kamakura period came not from the intellectuals, but from the soul of the ignorant and illiterate common man. In this respect, Hōnen may be said to have marked a turning point in Japanese spiritual history.

Though he was not altogether free from vestiges of Heian thought, without him Shinran could not have appeared. It is this that enables us to regard Shinran and Hōnen as a single spiritual personality.

The awakening of spirituality has to pass through a denial of intellectuality. Therefore, it may be said that a person who is completely illiterate cannot, in a real sense, be spiritually awakened. Yet in a more profound sense, awakening can be said to appear naturally from spirituality itself. Even where there is intellectual denial, if spirituality's spontaneity does not appear, only the occasion will be present and the actual materialization will not occur. Shinran and Hōnen came to possess both the occasion and the actualization, and their brilliant spiritual lives thus emerged. But

151

for the "illiterate samurai," the "simple-hearted devotee," and the like, the only course open was to follow faithfully the path laid down by their leaders. Still, in the matter of achieving spiritual insight itself there is no difference in the two cases. One who follows the path of intellectual denial and subsequently attains spiritual awakening, by transiting the vicissitudes incurred in such a passage comes to know not only himself, but others as well. Accordingly, he believes the teaching himself, and can make others believe in it as well. If his belief is possible, it means the belief of others is possible too.

Whereas for those termed unlearned or foolish the road to spirituality is comparatively direct, the spirituality of the intellectually-minded person is not easily awakened because of the obstacle of his intellect. This is like the poet Saigyō's autumn twilight—throughout east and west, now and in times past, everywhere the same. Since the intellectually-minded are of course also the objects of salvation, the saint's concern is with them as well. However, in Japanese spiritual history there was really no opportunity for this to be expressed until Kamakura times. It would do us little good to dwell on those saints who themselves bore the hard thick husk of the intellect. Since Japanese spiritual awakening manifested itself through the individual personalities of Hōnen and Shinran, our attention turns naturally to them—as individuals. However, when we view Japanese spiritual awakening we must see it in the context of the illiterate common people and the preparations these people possessed that enabled them to respond and follow Shinran and Hōnen so readily and obediently. With the onset of the Kamakura period, the spirituality of the general populace that was to become the structural foundation of this awakening, those people termed ignorant, foolish, and illiterate, came to possess the natural fertility of the soil itself. That is why Hōnen and other spiritual leaders were then first able to make their appearance in the spiritual history of Japan.

The initial expression of Japanese spiritual realization is found in the *One Page Testament*. It was Zenshōbō, a monk at Rengeji Temple in Tōtōmi province and a scholar of Tendai teaching, who actually put into practice the purport of this *Testament* of Hōnen's. When he heard from Kumagai Renshōbō about Hōnen and his teaching of Nembutsu as the way for ignorant sinners to gain rebirth in the Pure Land, he obtained an introduction and proceeded to the capital to visit Hōnen at Yoshimizu.

After an exchange of questions and answers he was able to gain a deep understanding of Pure Land thought. Hōnen taught him that Amida's Original Prayer would save all ignorant sinners. Even those without knowledge of such things as the Three Teachings (commandments, meditation, and wisdom) would not be rejected by the Buddha. "Those who call upon the Name should do it with the nature they now have, the wise man as a wise man, the fool as a fool—thus all equally may attain *Ōjō*." "It would be a mistake to think that I, Hōnen, cannot attain *Ōjō* unless I gain high religious rank . . . that *Ōjō* is impossible for me just as I am. Our daily lives should be such that they enable us to say Nembutsu most easily." "Avoid and discard anything that stands in the way of Nembutsu. . . . If you cannot say Nembutsu in celibacy, say it as a husband and householder . . . if you cannot say it as a householder, say it as a hermit . . . in the consummation of Nembutsu all else become secondary. . . ."

Thanks to his detailed teaching, Zenshōbō became deeply devoted to Hōnen's Nembutsu. Hōnen gave him the following message in parting: "According to the doctrine of the Holy Path we must develop our intellectual faculties to the very highest to get free from the fated transmigratory round, whereas the Pure Land practice requires us to return to our native simplicity in order to find birth in the Land of Bliss."

After returning to his native place, elated and deeply convinced of the truth of Hōnen's Nembutsu, Zenshōbō decided not to enter the temple, but earned his livelihood as a carpenter.

Passing nearby on the way to his place of exile, the priest Ryūkan (1148–1227) stopped at Kokubu in Tōtōmi Province to inquire of Zenshōbō. He asked if a priest named Zenshōbō was living in Rengeji Temple. The priests said they knew of no such master, but that there was a carpenter named Zenshō working in the area. Ryūkan immediately sent and asked him to come. It is reported that as Zenshō entered the courtyard Ryūkan came out grasped him by the hand and led him inside. Both were in tears as they spoke of the past. When the samurai, who had looked down upon Zenshō as a lowly carpenter, witnessed this moving scene they were wonderstruck. As the two men parted, Ryūkan's disciples asked Zenshō for some word to keep with them. After a brief silence he said, "Always diligently say the Nembutsu, and attain *Ōjō*." Then he disappeared.

153

IV. NEMBUTSU *SHŌMYŌ*

1. Nembutsu Shōmyō in Hōnen's Nimai-Kishōmon *(Two Page Testament)*

In addition the *One Page Testament,* Hōnen wrote this *Two Page Testament.*

> *Priests and laymen alike should consider that they have not a whit of intelligence. Do they believe that the serious matter of Ōjō of those who are caught in wretchedness will be attained without relying upon the Prayer of the Buddha? You must believe in the Compassionate Prayer of Amida Buddha, call upon the Other Power through the constant invocation of the Name; this is the matter of the Original Prayer. Nothing is more commendable than the voicing of his Name, solely imploring for his salvation. Do not let pride mislead you into thinking 'This act of mine is good.' Generally stated, to rely upon the Buddha does not mean to engage in meditative recollection, but just to invoke the Name; this is none other than relying upon the Original Prayer. The practitioner of the Nembutsu should not stop at mere meditative recollection of the Buddha, but should audibly pronounce the Name. For besides this shōmyō [pronouncing the Name] there is no right cause that will definitely determine our rebirth; besides* shōmyō *there is no right act that will definitely determine our rebirth; besides* shōmyō *there is no right karma that will definitely determine our rebirth; besides* shōmyō *there is no meditative recollection that will definitely determine our rebirth; besides* shōmyō *there is no transcendental wisdom that will definitely determine our rebirth. Further, there is no threefold mind apart from* shōmyō; *there is no four modes of practice apart from* shōmyō; *there is no fivefold recollection apart from* shōmyō. *Amida's Original Prayer is no other than* shōmyō; *the mind that loathes this world of defilement lies at the bottom of this* shōmyō. *We should believe in the unrestricted and unconditional power of Amida Nyorai deriving from none other than the Other-power of the Original Prayer of Dharmakara Bodhisattva of ages past. Even if you are aware of*

154

*matters more profound and erudite than this, if you keep to them
and do not do the Nembutsu, then you will be subject in this life
to greater and smaller punishment within the sixty-odd provinces
of Japan. You will be deprived of the forty-eight Vows, and you
will fall into a hell of incessant torment and suffering in the life
to come.*

Although the *Two Page Testament* cannot be said to strike home to
man's inmost heart as does the *One Page Testament*, its emphasis
of *shōmyō* gives it great significance. Though it may be said with certainty
that Nembutsu is *shōmyō*, in this passage Hōnen stresses the actual *utterance* of Nembutsu. Without confining it to meditative recollection in one's
heart, he exalts the importance of the act of speaking the words of the
Name. How can there be the kind of meaning Hōnen speaks of in the
"Namu-Amida-Butsu" "Namu-Amida-Butsu" that flows forth from the
mouth? He himself is reported to have repeated the Nembutsu tens of
thousands of times each day. Whether Shinran said such great numbers
of Nembutsu I do not know, but he did recognize its profound meaning,
and the practice of the Nembutsu was not discontinued among his disciples and fellow-believers. Some of them were even suspected of harbor-
ing heretical beliefs because of this practice.

In modern times, for example, Shichiri Gōjun, Murata Jōshō, Teishin-
ni, and other believers like them all continued Nembutsu *shōmyō*. If
faith has already been attained, then why Nembutsu? It has been stated
that Nembutsu is an expression of one's gratitude for the Buddha's Compassion, but what exactly does that mean? Were it simply a matter of
gratitude, why the need for a continuous succession of Nembutsu? There
is little difficulty attached to the interpretation that views *shōmyō* in terms
of Self-power, but the Nembutsu as an act of thankfulness for the Buddha's Compassion—particularly the 'continual' Nembutsu—how are we
to interpret that?

I have considered elsewhere the question of Nembutsu *shōmyō* in more
detail, though still in insufficient measure. I shall have to return to it at
a later time.

2. Becoming the Master of Namu-Amida-Butsu—Gratitude for the Buddha's Favor

In Rennyo's (1415–1499) *Goichidaiki Kikigaki* ("The Writing of Things Heard during a Life") it is written that "one becomes the master of Namu-Amida-Butsu when one accepts Amida. To become the master of Namu-Amida-Butsu is to have faith." Stated conversely, to acquire faith is to become the master of Namu-Amida-Butsu. "To become the master" means to accept Amida. Ordinarily, to become the master of Namu-Amida-Butsu would necessitate becoming Namu-Amida-Butsu itself. Which is to say that oneself and Namu-Amida-Butsu must not be two. If they are, then whichever becomes the master renders the other subordinate. To "become Namu-Amida-Butsu" is for one to become one's own master. It means casting away the ego-self of the individual, thereby awakening to a spirituality which transcends the ego-self. Here faith is established. In this "relying upon Amida" the self that relies on Amida and Amida who is relied upon must not be two; it must be as if one is relying upon oneself. Or we might say that Amida awakens to the existence of Amida. In other words faith does not come about in the two, but where the one is realized as the one. For this reason repeating "Namu-Amida-Butsu" is nothing else but Amida calling out to himself through himself. The "oneself" calling out is the spirituality that transcends the self; the "oneself" who is called upon is the individual self. When Amida thus halves himself the materialization of the Original Prayer occurs. When the Prayer is manifested the attainment of faith arrives. In the *Anjin Ketsujō Shō*[10] we find, "Therefore, it should be understood that although the Nembutsu samadhi just referred to is a reverential calling out of Nembutsu on our part, it is not our act. We are performing Amida's act." This is the same as was previously stated. If the self of the individual self is the direct embodiment of Nembutsu samadhi and the master of Namu-Amida-Butsu, then what is the meaning of *shōmyō*—vocal Nembutsu—as an act of thankfulness towards the Buddha? Rennyo says,

> *After attaining faith, your gratitude for the Buddha's favor, by means of the recitation of the Name, should not be neglected. But it would be a great mistake for you to think that heartfelt reverence and gratitude are due to the Buddha's favor, and not to*

give your attention to the actual reciting of Nembutsu that comes from the mouth as if unintentionally. The natural and unrestricted recitation of the Name is caused by the Buddha's Wisdom, and is nothing else but the Nembutsu of thankfulness for the Buddha's favor. (Goichidaiki Kikigaki)

According to the above, one must say the Nembutsu after attaining faith, as a Nembutsu of gratitude for the Buddha's favor. Mere thankfulness or reverence is not expressive of one's regard for his favor. After attainment of faith there must be uttering of Nembutsu, which is itself a praising of the Buddha's favor. If this is true, it would follow that to experience the Buddha's grace is a revelation that comes naturally upon the attainment of faith. In this case the form of the revelation happens to be "Namu-Amida-Butsu." Nembutsu cannot be forced from without, it must emerge naturally. Then it is something in which faith is acquired in the simple repetition of "Namu-Amida-Butsu," without consciousness or anything else derived from thoughts of reverence or thankfulness for the Buddha's mercy or favor. Nembutsu that is not so must, in a certain sense, be called artifical. A mere thoughtless, loud-voiced "Namu-Amida-Butsu" must be said to have no relation whatsoever to the faith of Pure Land tradition. And indeed, it cannot be identified with a heart that is grateful for the Buddha's favor.

In *Songōshinzōmeimon*, Part I[11], there is this inscription in praise of the Chinese Pure Land patriarch Zendō:

> *Zendō is the incarnation of Amida Buddha. Recite the Buddha's six syllables and you praise the Buddha, you confess and repent, you issue the vow to attain Ōjō and to save all beings, and all your good deeds adorn the Land of Purity.*

Regarding this inscription, which was written by Chih-yung (J. Chiei), Shinran comments:

> *Chiei was a saint of China. He praised Zendō's special virtues, calling him the incarnation of Amida Buddha. "Recite the Buddha's six syllables" means to recite the six syllables Na-mu-a-mi-da-buts(u). The next phrase means that to recite "Namu-Amida-*

157

Butsu" is to confess and repent one's sins that extend back to be-
ginningless time. The next means that to say Namu-Amida-Butsu
is to aspire to attain Ōjō in the Pure Land of Restful Bliss and
to transfer one's good merits to all living beings. The last sentence
means that since all good deeds are contained within the three
syllables A-mi-da, to repeat the Name is to adorn the Pure Land.
Thus Chiei Zenji praised Zendō.

The Nembutsu of gratitude does not appear in these comments. However, on this point Murata Wajō comments simply and briefly:

> *Nembutsu is Namu-Amida-Butsu.*
> *Namu-Amida-Butsu is Amida Sama.*
> *Amida Sama saves us.*
> *Say Nembutsu in gratitude for this.*
> *That is all that is needed.*

Here indeed the essence is apparently grasped. Still it seems to me that
in order to express "gratitude" it should not be necessary—as Murata
Wajō advocated—for people to gather together in one place and send out
loud choruses of "Namu-Amida-Butsu," "Namu-Amida-Butsu."

3. The Nembutsu Sōzoku ("Continuous Nembutsu") of Murata Jōshō
Wajō

Murata Jōshō Wajō of Isshinden in Ise Prefecture was a prominent
Nembutsu practitioner of recent times. He was raised by Shichiri Gōjun[12]
of Hakata, Kyushu. Some of his words and deeds are recorded in a book
entitled *Negusari*. It is indeed a welcome book, for those not only of the
Pure Land, but for all men to read deeply and take to heart. Murata
Wajō brought people together and had them do nothing but repeat Nembutsu aloud to no specific purpose, while he himself would speak his
thoughts as they occurred to him or answer questions put to him. For
this reason he has been pointed out as being heterodoxical by those of
the Shin sect. The following description should give some idea of the
manner of his 'assemblies.'

Wajō Sama, why do we come here and yell ourselves hoarse with all this loud reciting? Listen . . . from some directions we hear "Na Na Na . . ." from some directions, "Da Da Da Da . . ." from other directions, "Nan Nan Nan . . ." That one nun in particular seems to be saying "Ise Ise Ise . . . Yamada Yamada Yamada . . ." no one seems to be reciting the six syllables of the Name.

This brings the assembly into sharp focus, enabling us to imagine the cacophonous clamor of the voices. Wajō himself remained unconcerned with the goings-on and just gave out a continuous stream of "Namu-Amida-Butsu," "Namu-Amida-Butsu." Judging from this there would seem to be something in the repeating of "Namu-Amida-Butsu," "Namu-Amida-Butsu," either softly or loudly, which is not simply a matter of thankfulness for the Buddha's favor.

Did Wajō really have some aim or purpose in this? Wondering if the ways of his teacher Shichiri Gōjun[12] were "in disagreement with the sacred teachings," Wajō asked a scholar if they really were, and received the reply: "That is Gōjun's greatness." This he reported to the assembly, and added, "We are all crawling infants, and thus have no need to get caught up in reason and logic." He then took up the litany again, "Namu-Amida-Butsu."

It is without any gratitude to the Buddha, or anything else, that he just repeats "Namu-Amida-Butsu" "Namu-Amida-Butsu" and gets others to do the same? However one may say that something will be forthcoming if only we utter the Nembutsu, the leader of the assembly still repeats a continuous Nembutsu and entrusts everything to the power of the Buddha. And that is all right, though people like me want to theorize about it. Before the war we heard about a religious movement in England called the Oxford Movement, which seems to have had considerable success. This somehow reminds me of it.

Suzuki Shōsan enumerates five different kinds of Nembutsu in his *Roankyō*. Though presumably only meant as suggestions, they can also serve as points of reference. They appear in response to a farmer's question concerning the essence of Nembutsu. First Shōsan describes a Nembutsu of merit, done while mindful of the profound meaning of the virtue in each of the six syllables of the Name. Second, there is a Nembutsu of shame and repentance. Next, a "cutting-off" Nembutsu, that is, a Nembutsu which clears away both good and bad thoughts with the sword of Nembutsu, "Namu-Amida-Butsu" "Namu-Amida-Butsu. . . ." The fourth he calls the Nembutsu of the time of death. The fifth is a Nembutsu of sameness, Nembutsu that flows out completely unhindered like breeze rustling through pine trees. This explanation greatly pleased the farmer. "All of them," he said, "are fine, but I think I will choose the 'cutting-off' Nembutsu alone. It will do for everything." He left exuberant with joy. Six years later he was reported to have attained a magnificent *Ōjō*.

Though the meaning of the "cutting-off" Nembutsu appears to be quite far removed from the Nembutsu of Pure Land tradition, the ability to remain unfettered by good or evil cannot be understood unless one becomes the master of Nembutsu. Nevertheless, Shōsan's case might also be called different from becoming the master of Nembutsu upon the acquiring of faith, because he establishes the idea of "cutting-off" from the very beginning.

There is yet another case given in *Roankyō*, and it does not seem to fit into any of the previously mentioned five types of Nembutsu. It resembles Hōnen's practice of Nembutsu repetitions, which sometimes reached as many as 60,000 a day. Or perhaps it might be likened to the *koan* studies in *Kanna* Zen.

> *Once a man told of a remarkable event which had taken place recently in his town. There was a sixty year-old man who had a very avaricious nature and who was completely indifferent to religion. His son was so grieved at this state that when he found what he thought was a way to correct it, he resolved to try. He said to his father, "Here I am, I have found a way to get some money, but I don't have the time to do the work. If you were interested in religion, I think it would be a fine opportunity for you." Hearing the mention of money, the father badgered the son for more details, until finally the son assented. "There is a man who will give ten ryo to anyone who will repeat for him, for a period of three years, 60,000 Nembutsu each day." His father said, "It's just the work for me. Don't let anyone else have it. Get the money. I will do it." The son made sure of the promise, then happily gave the money to his father. From morning until nightfall he did the Nembutsu as promised without ever*

160

putting down his rosary. This went on for almost two years. Then one day he summoned his son and said, "I am old and my end is near, I have no need of anything anymore. I don't know why I took that money—what a miserable thing to have done. Now it is too late for me to work for my own future life, to which I have been oblivious. I have wasted all my time working for someone else's future. I want to turn the Nembutsu I repeated during the past year to my own salvation, and to return the money I received. I will even add my own to it. Give it back with my deepest certain apologies." He was sad and repentant. The son said he wasn't certain what the man would say, but promised to return the money. His father is said to have awakened to the truth in increasing measure, and to have become a remarkable man of faith.

There is a similar story involving one of Hakuin's disciples.[13] That does not mean, however, that Hōnen's 60,000 daily Nembutsu necessarily has the same meaning as the Nembutsu *sōzoku* of the Zen-man. Murata Wajō's "continuous Nembutsu" cannot be placed in the same category as the Nembutsu of either Shōsan or Hakuin. Each must be given separate and detailed study.

4. *Nembutsu and "Sitting with Stable Trunk"—The Subjugation of Wild Animals—Charging the Enemy Camp*

The author of *Negusari* writes that "At his peak, he [Murata Wajō] was marked by a strictness and severity; it was just like the training of the Zen sect. When you come across someone who passed under his guidance during that time, you still can feel his influence." "Wajō taught that when doing the Nembutsu you should straighten up and allow your strength to flow to the lower trunk of your body." Naturally, we cannot know the whole of Wajō's Nembutsu from the above words, but they do give a feeling that is somewhat indicative of it.

A tea-master once said, "In the tea ceremony it is necessary to sit with a stable trunk." Here are some of Murata Wajō's own words regarding this instruction. "Namu-Amida-Butsu . . . there is nothing wondrous about the way in which the great teaching spreads, because it is the wondrous teaching of Amida Sama. . . . It is not the spread of the

161

teaching, rather the Nembutsu done while sitting with stable trunk . . . Namu-Amida-Butsu . . ." "Sitting with stable trunk," "letting your power flow down into your abdomen," "like Zen training," these words show that the Nembutsu of gratitude for the Buddha's compassion does not stop at mere thankfulness. They are secondary matters, and not related to Wajō's true intention. That spiritual insight can include even such things may be seen, I think, as the reflection of something Japanese.

While thinking about Nembutsu *shōmyō*, I came across something in the *Negusari* I would like to relate. It is the story of nineteen year-old girl from Ecchū who passed a terrifying night in the wind and rain in the mountain forest behind the Inner Shrine at Ise, under threat of attack by wild animals.

Terribly frightened, she repeated the Nembutsu for all her worth. When her voice weakened, the animals began to close in, so she had to stay up all through the night keeping up a continual Nembutsu. This kept the animals at bay until she was finally rescued. There is another story, similar to this one, about a Mikawa woman named Osono, who while walking alone along a mountain path was suddenly set upon by a large dog. There was no visible way of escape so she took her rosary in hand, faced the onrushing animal and began to recite the Nembutsu. For some unknown reason the dog turned abruptly and disappeared into the forest. I believe many more examples similar to this must exist. In cases like this, it does not necessarily have to be the Nembutsu—"Namu-Amida-Butsu." Repeating the Nichiren sect's Namumyōhōrengekyō would do just as well, or perhaps repeating the *Heart Sutra*. When the seventh century Chinese priest Hsüan-tsang travelled to India it is reported that he never forgot to recite the Heart Sutra. For the Shingon sect there is *omuabokiya*, for those of Tenrikyō the words, *tenri-ō-no-mikoto*. All these I believe would obtain the same result. More than the miraculous power of the words, or the mysterious nature of their meanings, it is a kind of spiritual air which comes from the whole bearing and attitude of a particular person at a particular time that is able to ward off an adversary. Animals seem able to sense this instinctively. Swordsmen often speak of there being no "*suki*", no opening in their line of concentration for the opponent to take advantage of.

At the time of the Shanghai Incident some years ago, a group of Japanese soldiers engaged in battle charged an enemy position. At first they just rushed forward yelling, but before they knew it this cry had changed into "Namu-Amida-Butsu," "Namu-Amida-Butsu." With Nembutsu they rushed on to the enemy. This brings to mind Suzuki Shōsan's answer, "Wade right in, saying Nembutsu," addressed to a samurai's inquiry as to how he should say the Nembutsu. When you are about to be beheaded, "Namu-Amida-Butsu"; when you are about to dispatch your enemy, "Namu-Amida-Butsu"; passivity, activity, negation, affirmation—Nembutsu comes from all of these.

Although I have digressed in this discussion, let me just say that contained in Nembutsu *shōmyō* are, historically, various meanings. Here it is the appearance of spiritual insight and there it is the training that tries to open up the road to that insight; and again it might be something that aims at psychological efficacy, or a sense of gratitude for the Buddha's favor as is spoken of in Pure Land thought. There is one that attempts to arouse the consciousness of this gratitude as well. Others could be added in addition to these. Nevertheless, I will be content to reemphasize here that the growth and development of Japanese spirituality awakened by the "Namu-Amida-Butsu" of Hōnen was not a matter of only one direction or of a single aspect.

Further, independent studies of Nembutsu *shōmyō* will have to wait for another day.

NOTES

1   *Shōmyō* 称名 (literally, 'pronouncing or uttering the Name.') In the beginning of the history of the Pure Land school, the Nembutsu was practised in its literal sense, the followers thought of the Buddha in their minds, formed his images before their eyes, and perhaps recounted all the excellent virtues belonging to him. This is thinking of the Buddha, Nembutsu. The object of the Nembutsu, 'thinking of the Buddha' was to see him face to face so that the devotee could advance in his spiritual life and finally even come to the attainment of Buddhahood. But since this 'thinking of the Buddha' involves so much psychological energy, it cannot be practised by every Buddhist follower however devotionally minded he may be. He must be given a new way much easier than the 'thinking of the Buddha', and this was found in repeatedly uttering (*shōmyō*) the Name of the Buddha. Now the devotee while pronouncing the Name may not necessarily meditate on the Buddha with any degree of mental concentration, but the recitation at least directs his attention towards Buddha with all that follows from it. Thus the *shōmyō*, 'pronouncing the Name,' came to help the Nembutsu, 'thinking of the Buddha.' While the *shōmyō* is not the Nembutsu, the former, as time went on, came to be identified with the latter, and nowadays when we talk of the Nembutsu, it may not mean 'thinking of the Buddha' but 'pronouncing or reciting the name,' unless a reservation is made. In the Shin Sect, both Nembutsu, 'thinking of the Buddha,' and *shōmyō*, 'vocal utterance of the Name,' are regarded as synonymous, meaning invocation of the name of Amida.

2   The *Heike Monogatari* ("The Tales of the Heike") is the epic tale of the 12th century wars between the clans of the Minamoto and the Taira (Heike), chronicling the struggles of 1180–1185, in which the Minamoto finally triumphed, bringing an end to the Heian court culture and establishing the Kamakura Shogunate. The present translation is based on that of A. L. Sadler, in the *Transactions, Asiatic Society of Japan*, 46, 2 (1918) and 49, 1 (1921). Trans.

3   The episode of Taira Atsumori and Kumagai Naozane, during the battle of Ichi no tani, is described in Brinkley's *History of the Japanese People* (New York: 1915), as follows: "Atsumori, a stripling of fifteen, was seized by Naozane, a stalwart warrior on the Minamoto side. When Naozane tore off the boy's helmet, preparatory to beheading him, and saw a young face vividly recalling his own son who had perished early in the fight, he was moved with compassion and would fain have stayed his hand. To have done so, however, would merely have been to reserve Atsumori for a crueller death. He explained his scruples and his sorrows to the boy, who submitted to his fate with calm courage." Trans.

4   'One calling,' or 'one thought' (一念) is a momentous term in the philosophy of Shin and Jōdo. Its Sanskrit original is *eka-kshana*, meaning 'one instant' or 'one moment.' As we say in English 'quick as thought' or 'quick as a flash,' 'one thought' represents in terms of time the shortest possible duration, which

is to say, one instant. The one instant of faith-establishment is the moment when Amida's Eternal Life cuts crosswise the flow of birth-and-death, or when his Infinite Light flashes into the darkening succession of love and hate which is experienced by our relative consciousness. This event takes place in 'one thought' and is never repeated, and therefore is known here as 'the last moment,' 'the end of this world,' and I would say, it is even the coming into the presence of Amida. This moment of 'one calling' or 'one thought' is the one in our life most deeply impregnated with meaning, and for that reason must come to us in our 'ordinary moments of life' and not wait for the 'last moment' in its relative sense.

5 Plain or 'white-wood' 白木 Nembutsu—a Nembutsu completely uncolored by external elements. Trans.

6 See Chapter 2, Note 18.

7 The Discussion at Ohara—about the year 1186 Hōnen, at the invitation of Kenshin from Mr. Hiei, engaged in a debate on the Pure Land teachings with several scholars from Nara and Mt. Hiei. It is said, Hōnen so successfully defended the Pure Land teaching that three hundred learned priests present finally accepted his position and chanted the Nembutsu for three days and nights. Trans.

8 Dōshaku 道綽 (Tao-ch'o) 562–645; Chinese Pure Land patriarch and teacher of Zendō. His main work is the *Anraku shū (An-lo-chi)*. Zendō 善導 (Shan-tao), died 681, was a Chinese Pure Land patriarch who left several important works on the Pure Land teaching, the chief of which is a commentary on the *Meditation Sutra*. Trans.

9 The threefold heart (三心)—(1) sincerity of heart (至誠心); (2) a deep (believing) heart (深心); (3) desire to be reborn in Amida's Pure Land (回向発願心).

Four modes of practice (四修); (1) Treating with profound reverence and respect all sacred objects, such as Sutras, the Buddhas' Images, etc. (恭敬修); (2) practising nothing but the Nembutsu as all else is superfluous (無余修); (3) leaving no intervals of time between the Nembutsu repetitions, but keeping them up continuously (無間修); (4) the continued practice throughout one's whole life of the foregoing three (長時修).

Five modes of practice (五念); (1) prostrating oneself before Amida Buddha (礼拝); (2) praising His sacred Name in terms befitting the Buddha of boundless light and wisdom (讃嘆); (3) desire to be born into the Buddha's Land (作願); (4) meditation upon Him and things of his land (観察); (5) feeling compassion for the suffering of living beings and wishing to save them by imputing all one's own accumulated merits to them (回向).

10 *Anjin Ketsujō Shō* 安心決定抄 ("On the Attainment of Spiritual Peace"). A work of unknown authorship; one of the most important of all the Pure Land tradition.

11 *Songōshinzōmeimon* 尊号真像銘文.

12 Shichiri Gōjun 七里恆順 (1834–1900), a Shin priest from Hakata, Kyushu. Dr. Suzuki translated portions of his recorded sayings in "Sayings of a Tariki Mystic," included in *A Miscellany of the Shin Teaching of Buddhism* (Kyoto: 1949). Trans.

13 See *Essays in Zen Buddhism* (*2nd Series*), Rider, London; 1958, p. 149. (Trans.)

CHAPTER 4 THE MYŌKŌNIN

I. DŌSHŪ

1. His Life and Relation to Rennyo

Among Pure Land believers those particularly rich in faith and goodness are called Myōkōnin, literally, the "wondrous good men." A
Myōkōnin does not excell in scholarship or in discussing fine points of
religious teaching; he experiences the thought of the Pure Land tradition
personally and it lives in him. Though all Jōdo believers, including
scholars, should be so, it is the Myōkōnin who is especially blessed in
this respect. Since he is a rare person, the term Myōkōnin can be applied
truly to few people. Any Life of the Myōkōnin would have to consist of
the individual life histories of these devout people.

Heading the list of Myōkōnin is thought to be one who served as escort-
guard to Rennyo Shōnin (1414–1499)[1] with devotion bred of deep faith.
This man was Dōshū, of Akao in Etchū (Toyama) Province. Of his life
we know in fact very little; in Rennyo's *Goichidaiki Kikigaki* he is mentioned or quoted in two or three places, and in the *Zoku Shinshū Taikei*
there is something as well.

Myōkōnin would make fine material for any work concerned with the
historical development of Japanese spirituality, in which we would have
to examine the contents of their faith. As one small such study, no more
than a suggestion and extremely unsystematic, I would first like to turn
to Dōshū, and then to another Myōkōnin, Asahara Saichi. I think with
that I will have generally shown how I view spirituality, and how I would
search for evidence of its development.

In spite of our limited knowledge of Dōshū, he appears as a seeker
after truth possessed of excellent and persevering mental ability. While
the exact substance of his faith cannot be clearly seen, there is no doubt
that he worked for Rennyo with utmost spiritual devotion, in this way
attempting to thank the Buddha for his favor. He compiled 21 "Resolu-

tions," which, although not containing the essence of his faith do give us a glimpse of it. The following is based on information supplied me by Mr. Seiji Iwakura, and from letters sent to Mr. Yasushi Kusunoki by Rev. Shizuo Dōshū, the head priest of Dōshūji Temple. This has been assembled by Mr. Iwakura into a book which I have learned will soon be published. It delves deeply into Dōshū's life and I am sure that readers will find it well worth reading. I for one am eagerly awaiting its publication.

Dōshū's birth date is unknown. He was born in Etchū in a small valley village named Akao, near the upper reaches of the Shō River. To reach Akao one must travel a distance of over twenty miles after leaving Jōgahana, a dangerous journey through valleys and high mountain passes. I heard recently it can now be reached by bus. The mountain road is so perilous the slightest mistake would mean a thousand-foot fall. In winter the region is covered with more than 20 feet of snow, and a trip between Akao and the Honganji Branch Temple at Jōgahana would literally be at the risk of life and limb.

Legend has it Dōshū's ancestors were retainers of Go-Daigo's Southern Court that survived the dissolution of that house. If true it would mean he had samurai blood in his veins. It is said he accompanied Rennyo to various parts of the country during the difficulties of the Sengoku period. Thus in a sense his role was one of bodyguard, and he was probably well versed in the martial arts. According to Mr. Iwakura, Dōshū's handwriting closely resembles that of Rennyo, except that it is even stronger and more skillful. This in itself tells us something of the man.

His secular name was Yashichi. His parents both died while he was young and he was raised by an uncle named Jōtoku. Because his parents had been very dear to him he wished to find someone like them. He was told to go to the Temple of the 500 Arhats in Tsukushi (Kyushu) where he was assured he would find one among the Arhats who would resemble his parents, and that when that particular Arhat saw Yashichi there would be a smile of secret understanding whereby he would know him. So Yashichi resolved to travel to Kyushu, and went as far as Asōzu in Echizen Prefecture where tradition says he met a priest who led him to Rennyo Shōnin, under whose guidance he then fell. That Dōshū possessed a discerning eye in matters of spiritual insight is made clear in the 131st part of Rennyo's *Goichidaiki Kikigaki*.

168

"Dōshū said that though he heard a certain word constantly, he always felt as grateful as if he heard it for the first time." In part 130, Rennyo holds up Dōshū as an example in explaining why spirituality is always fresh and new, an experience like hearing the first note of the *uguisu*. "Most men wish to have something new and novel; but a man of faith feels each thing new and fresh, even though he might have heard the same thing many times before. No matter how many times you hear something, it should be heard as fresh and as new as if hearing it for the first time."

It is curious that in spiritual insight each thing is always experienced as if for the first time. Therefore no matter now many times it comes, it is always fresh and new, even as the changing times roll on. Since Dōshū achieved this spirituality, his words are transmitted in Rennyo's *Goichidaiki Kikigaki* as those of a saint.

> *Dōshū of Akao said, "As a matter of daily concern, you should never neglect the morning service at the family altar; you should make monthly visits to the nearest sub-temple to worship the Sect founder, Shinran; and each year you should make a pilgrimage to the Head Temple. . . ."*

Here Dōshū shows himself to be the Confucian gentleman, "respectfully attentive all day long." He was intrepid and resolute in seeking the way and then in continuing along it. In him we see something of the spirit of the "Period of Wars" of 15th century Japan. When he was in his native place, he never missed the early morning services at the Inami Branch Temple. The path from his residence in Akao to the Inami Temple was strewn with mountain peaks, piled one after the other. Only an extremely strong hiker would be able to come and go without difficulty, especially in winter with its 20 or 30 foot-deep snowdrifts, when a misstep could send one thousands of feet to the valley bottom. Yet this did not deter him in the least. How long did he continue these exploits? Even after making allowance for legend's exaggerations his deeds are still extraordinary. They gained for him the respect and admiration of all. Two or three times each year, without fail, he would travel to the capital Kyoto, paying no attention to his master Rennyo, who told him it was unnecessary to come so often from so far away. It seems he considered Rennyo an incarnation of Amida. Legend even tells of him worshipping a ray of light that shone forth from Rennyo's body. He once said he would fill up Lake Biwa with mud by himself if ordered to do so by Rennyo. This statement in its religious ardency shares a common spiritual ground with Shinran's avowal that he would gladly go to Hell together with Hōnen.

Dōshū's actions may be said to possess an almost ascetic element. Most Jōdo followers appear to be lacking in just this sense of self-control or discipline. This is probably because they tend on the one hand to depend on Amida's Other-power, and on the other not to arouse the effort of self-control which would keep a tight rein on the passions. But Dōshū applied himself to a honing process of severe austerity. That does not mean, of course, he was trying to achieve approbation and thus gain birth in the Pure Land. He devoted himself assiduously to remaining mindful of his graditude toward the sect patriarchs and urged himself continuously against laxity or backsliding. He never sought severe ascetic practice for its own sake. At home in Akao he would stack up wood—forty-eight sticks—and sleep upon them. The forty-eight were for the forty-eight Vows of Amida. He did this to keep himself from sound sleep, to enable himself to keep clearly in mind and *taste* the fact that Amida accumulated numberless eons of practice for the sake of sentient beings. Another report has him hanging down from the branch of a Zelkova tree he found growing out over a swift current of water. To admonish himself against negligence he would repeat to himself, "Below lies the torrent of the three evil courses, should I be irresolute. . . ." In this concrete way he drove his admonitions into sharp relief before his own eyes. While travelling he would sleep on grain husks he spread on the floor of his shelter.

He took great pains to collect the *Ofumi* (*Gobunsho*, "Honorable Letters"),[2] letters written by Rennyo to his followers. This was not merely because he wished them for his own sake, to help him attain faith, he wanted them to show to the villagers of Akao as well, to help instruct them in the Way. Number 281 in Rennyo's *Goichidaiki Kikigaki* states: "Dōshū, begging Rennyo to give him some written instruction, was told: 'You may lose a letter, but faith kept in the heart can never be lost.' Nevertheless, the following year he acceded to Dōshū's request."

The next story tells how once, while he was setting out for Kyoto, his wife asked that he obtain from Rennyo some instructions for her concern-

170

ing the acquiring of faith. After a long and arduous return trip from Kyoto, before even stopping to take off his straw sandals, he produced a piece of paper on which was written the six letters, Na-mu-a-mi-da-butsu. This brought a look of some disappointment from his wife, who had obviously expected something more detailed. Seeing her reaction, and still without having taken off his footwear, he said, "All right," and set off for Kyoto once again, many miles, days, and hardships distant. Though he had that very moment returned from a more than ten day trip through the mountains, he began the same journey once more. I think this story —even if only legendary—enables us to understand the extent of Dōshū's purity and honesty, such that hardship and privation could make no inroad.

There are preserved in Dōshū's temple three handscrolls in his own hand, containing copies of twenty-three of Rennyo's letters. That and the fact that the temple in Akao has been maintained to the present day by his descendants clearly reveal the great influence of Dōshū's teaching among the people. The story of his giving his wife the 'letter' from Rennyo also ties in here, perhaps. He was the object of veneration in his village.

At a time Dōshū's goodness was widely known, a Tendai priest from a neighboring village thought to test this man about whom he had heard so much. Finding him bent down weeding in the fields, the priest came up behind and kicked him over. Without even changing his expression, Dōshū got up and began to weed again. The priest gave another try, kicking him over again. The reaction was the same. At this the priest could not contain himself. "For no reason at all someone comes up and kicks you down, yet you don't show any anger. In what region do you exist?" Continuing to smile, Dōshū answered, "It was to pay the debts of my former existence. I probably have many more still to pay."

The notion of debt for a former existence comes originally from the idea of karmic retribution in the three periods (past, present, future), but it is my belief that in this form, payment of debt from a former existence, it is something that originated in China. The second Chinese Zen patriarch Hui-k'o (Eka) speaks of it. Since Zen places much faith in the assertions of the *Diamond Sutra*, the expression often appears from the mouths of Zen-men. This is what is called 'using up karma.' In the *Diamond Sutra* we read:

Furthermore Subhūti, if a good man or good woman who is about to fall into evil ways due to evil karma from former existence is belittled by others, the evil karma from his former existences will be exhausted and he will attain Supreme Enlightenment.

We all shoulder the burden of this debt, and it must at some time be paid. The debt is this present existence—the individual self. Therefore, at some point this existence must be overturned and penetrated to its core. We must at some point succeed in jumping from the individual self to the supra-individual self. This is called *ōsō-ekō*, receiving the blessing of being born in the Land of Bliss. When it is achieved there is *gensō-ekō*, "return and transfer," the return to this life and the dedication of all one's merits toward the enlightenment of one's fellow beings. But it is not a process of achieving rebirth, followed by the transference of one's merit. Rebirth is the return and transfer, *Ōjō* is *gensō*, between them there is a mutual relation. "Paying the debt" is speech from the consciousness of the individual self. Actually, there are no debts to be paid, no debtors, no debtees. The debt and man appear and disappear in the universe of the supra-individual self. Buddhists call this *hokkai engi*, and also "sportive" samadhi.[3] But it is in the existence of the individual self that the karma must be exhausted. At this Dōshū was a truly resolute master, reminiscent of Suzuki Shōsan, who lived long after him during the first years of Tokugawa rule.

Since Shōsan was a man of Zen his attitude toward Buddhist teaching naturally was different from that of Dōshū, but there is somehow a close resemblance in their characters, their indomitable wills and resolute temperaments. I do not remember Shōsan speaking of "payment of debt," but for teaching purposes he does talk of exhausting karmic hindrances, of exhausting self, of self-abandonment, of "not being deluded by this putrid flesh." To pilgrims who were making the temple pilgrimage around the island of Shikoku, he said to mourn at each temple for those who died without descendants to mourn them. He taught those chanting dāhrani that karmic hindrance would be naturally removed through the intent repetition of the dāhrani's words. He said that even in the invocation of Nembutsu one should simply have faith in the Buddha's grace; he taught that to worship for all one's being would consume karmic hindrances; to exhaust the

172

self and not to harbor the thought that through such acts one would become a Buddha. Concerning those who say, "I do not fear karma in the least" he answered they were proof of the words, "Those who do not fear karma are those with the greatest karma." He said:

> It would be best for a beginner to pray for faith first of all, and then to repeat mantras and dharanis, using up his mind and body. Or, if one invokes the eight-syllable dharani 100, 200, or even 300 thousand times, he can use up karmic hindrances, deepen his faith, and awaken to the truth. He should discard any wish to become a venerable priest and work earnestly to become one with the earth.[4]

The self, in any case, must be consumed. The self is the karmic hindrance. It is the debt of one's former existence. Because of this encumbrance one cannot arrive at the supra-individual Person, one cannot awaken to spiritual insight. It is not necessary to wait for a kick from someone to pay the debt. One must advance himself, and test and realize the truth that he is a self of burning passions and desires. This cannot be concretely experienced in this body simply by hearing of the existence of such passions from another. When the existence of the passions and desires is experienced as reality in one's own body the opportunity to attain the Believing Heart (faith) appears naturally. To the degree of the former's earnestness, the latter will be firm and clear. First realize the former without taking into account beforehand the arrival of the latter. Otherwise, you will be honoring the Buddha and expecting thereby to become a Buddha yourself.

Dōshū was really travelling along the road of spiritual awakening while undergoing his intense self-training. Superficially, the realms of austerity, hard work, diligence, absolute passivity, absolute trust, etc., seem to contain many disparities. But with a little thought one may feel at their depths the spiritual awakening that is common to them all. And the shape of this feeling may be said to bear a Japanese character.

Dōshū's "21 Resolutions," which will be given in the following section, were drawn up the third winter following the death of Rennyo, and were intended as personal directives. There is no doubt, however, that they were used chiefly to indicate the right path to the villagers, Dōshū's fellow believers. Since these "Resolutions" were none other than those practices he himself had followed up until this time, there would seem little need for him to have taken the trouble of enumerating them then. It may be conjectured, however, that after Rennyo's death the villagers asked Dōshū to write something, and that he just dipped into his past experience and came up with these directives. Nothing in particular pertaining to faith itself is found therein. We may regard them as guides for conduct for his fellow-believers (and for himself as well), both to encourage correct practice and to help prevent a tendency to slide into negligence. If there is any section concerned with faith, it would have to be the last part of article twenty-one: "Never breach the laws and rules of society. In your heart preserve the reliability and blessedness of the 'One Thought,' while externally acting with deep prudence toward others." Followers of Jōdo often speak of compliance with the laws of the world and of faith without ostentation; one is simply to keep the reliability and virtue of the 'one thought' deep within one's own heart. Though it should not necessarily be taken in an extreme sense of keeping one's faith a secret, the admonition against flaunting one's faith under any circumstances may be interpreted to mean that spiritual insight should not be approached lightly. Such insight, in some cases, may tend to disregard the laws of the world—society's morality, customs, and written laws. Some among the Christian mystics of the European Middle Ages committed highly dubious acts under the pretext that "I am God. My will is God's will. I may act just as I wish." This is something always to be guarded against, and it applies to all religions. It was probably this both Rennyo and Dōshū were concerned about.

2. Dōshū's Twenty-One Resolutions

(1) Do not be forgetful of the One Great Matter [of your rebirth] as long as you live.

(2) Should something other than the Buddha dharma enter deeply into your heart, consider it shameful and dispatch it forthwith.

(3) You must resolutely break through and sweep away any tendency to indolence, laxity, or self-indulgence.

(4) If you feel something to be shameful in light of the Buddha dharma, you must sever immediately and without hesitation all connec-

174

tion with it.

(5)   Hold no favoritism in your heart. Do no evil to others.

(6)   You are always being watched, therefore do not think you may do evil just because no one is watching your actions.

(7)   You must always respect and honor deeply the Buddha dharma, be ever modest yourself, and behave with prudence.

(8)   However you look at it, it is shameful to consider trying to use others by means of the Buddha dharma. Should such an intent come to your mind, consider that there is no other reason for having faith in the Buddha dharma than to assist you in the One Great Matter of this one life, and reject such thoughts.

(9)   If you find yourself somewhere evil is being committed, regardless of its relative merits, you should leave.

(10)   The very thought Amida knows the wretchedness in my heart brings me deep sadness and pain. Though I am well aware he has forgiven me all my prior actions, the fact that he knows my inner state is cause for shame and sorrow. When I think that my heart was anchored in wretchedness in the world before and is now still so, I know a wretchedness beyond description. Even though I chanced to meet Amida my heart would still remain in wretchedness. Oh, wondrous compassion! I beg forgiveness for my prior transgression. I must entrust myself to your compassion.

(11)   If you are still alive today or tomorrow and you become lax with regard to the dharma, you must consider it shameful, sweep the laxity aside, and attend to the dharma.

(12)   If wonder does not rise fully in your heart you should consider it shameful and wasteful, and resolve that though you starve to death or freeze to death you will attain Ōjō and decide the One Great Matter in this present existence, the fulfillment of your desire from beginningless kalpas in the past, and press yourself resolutely in order to recover your sense of wonder. If even then wonder is not obtained, consider you are probably being punished by the Buddha; break through your laxity and praise the dharma to fellow devotees, because those acts at least should be matters of wonder.

(13)   You must not make the mistake of being self-indulgent, of sleeping away your life in vain, failing to consider the One Great Matter.

(14)   Do not make excuses for not having friends. Encountering those

of your household, though they may not be conscious of the dharma, direct their attention to it as best you can, above all ask them about the One Great Matter and be attentive to retaining a sense of wonder in your hearts.

(15)   Keep fully in mind that the matters of the temple are important above all else.

(16)   You must not hold thoughts of hate or vengeance toward those who hate you.

(17)   You must simply keep the One Great Matter deeply and unceasingly in your heart, and follow the suggestions given you by your fellow believers.

(18)   Do not become attached to the myriad things of the world, just keep deep in your heart this One Great Matter.

(19)   As I write in this way, because my heart is so incorrigible and shameful, even though I consult with it deeply and gain resolve, I wonder if something will be forthcoming. I must follow without fail the advice of others.

(20)   I think of nothing but the hope you will give me your incomparable compassion, keep me from going astray, and correct what is in my heart.

(21)   Oh, this wretched heart! If I am to resolve the One Great Matter I cannot think of the fate of this existence. Wherever I am ordered to go I must go. I must resolve even to journey to China or to India in search of the dharma. Compared with such resolution, is there anything so easy as following the way of Amida? Consider deeply the transience of the world. One is not long upon this earth. Death from hunger, freezing to death, make little difference. Do not think twice about such considerations, and constantly work for the One Great Matter. Do not go against these resolutions; strive, be attentive, never breach the laws and rules of society, preserve inwardly the reliability and blessedness of the one thought, and outwardly act with deep humility toward others.

II. ASAHARA SAICHI

1. Myōkōnin Asahara Saichi

I first heard of Myōkōnin Saichi from Professor Nishitani Keiji almost two years ago. I wanted very much to read his poems. Then this year I received a book entitled *Daijō Sōō no Chi* ("A Land Suited for Mahayana") by Rev. Fuji Shūsui, in which some of Saichi's poems were included. Upon reading them I felt that Japanese spiritual insight was here manifested in its pure form. In the following chapter some of his poems will be given, along with my own comments. I think it best to place Saichi's experience within the wider one of Pure Land thought, and not within that of the Jōdo or Shin sects in particular.

According to Rev. Fuji, Myōkōnin Saichi—as Asahara Saichi is called—lived in the small country town of Kohama in the province of Iwami, now Shimane Prefecture. He died in December of 1933 at the age of eighty-three. Until his fiftieth year he worked as a shipwright, at which time he became a maker of geta, a type of wooden footwear, the occupation he continued up until his death. His father was a deeply religious man who lived himself to be over eighty.

While working Saichi wrote poems on the wood shavings which fell from his planer. These poems gradually accumulated until they attained considerable numbers. Carrying on his work in the midst of a samadhi of religious joy, a Nembutsu samadhi, he wrote artlessly of the thoughts which chanced to enter his head, without in any way letting this interfere with his work. On the contrary, he did more work than any average geta-maker. Very often those immersed in the "ecstasy" of samadhi are least inclined for practical life—forgetting their work, dropping dishes, or stitches. Saichi was totally different from such people, his work itself was the blissful Nembutsu samadhi. But the human consciousness is self-reflective, and the words of poems cannot help but flow naturally from the mouth. Saichi's "poems" are completely unshaped, unpolished, without technique or artifice of any kind. He uses what small literary knowledge and skill he has and, like a spider weaving out thread, he produces a natural poetry, without style, and without adhering to 31 or any other set number of syllables. They are truly wonderful expressions of religious sentiment.

177

Rev. Fuji's book relates how from the time Saichi was eighteen or nineteen years old he was ardent in his desire to learn of the Way. Yet because he was unable to gain any kind of resolution whatever, he abandoned the search after five or six years. At age twenty-seven or twenty-eight he came to realize the impossibility of abandoning his great undertaking even for a single day, and began to advance once again along the Way, inquiring after the dharma. Were he able to travel to Kyoto and just listen to some great abbot he thought the Way would be revealed to him. But to go from his village in Iwami to the capital was an undertaking of such magnitude he could not even consider it. So he went to local country temples or to the houses of lay Buddhists whenever sermons were held, and listened to the expositions of the teaching. It was said only after he had passed the age of fifty did he finally attain *anjin*[5]. We can well imagine the hard struggle he underwent during that period, but at the same time we are very thankful his poetry does not smack of formal Shin sect terminology. Those who are too concerned with letters to give their attention to actual experience are apt to speak conceptually. This tendency does not appear in the Myōkōnin, who fall directly under the experience itself. It is the taste of this experience which must be known, thought systems may be constructed afterwards. To produce the system first and then try to squeeze the experience out from it is like trying to extract blood from turnips.

Due probably to Saichi's completely artless mode of expressing himself and to the lack of connective particles to indicate the relationship between words and phrases in his poems, it is at times difficult to grasp their meaning. We are unavoidably caught in the words. In such cases, we the readers will have to take the initiative as interpreters.

2. The "Namu-Amida-Butsu" Poems

What first strikes one about Saichi's poetry is the constant repetition of "Namu-Amida-Butsu." "I'm thankful, Namu-Amida-Butsu," "I'm miserable, Namu-Amida-Butsu," "Amida Oyasama, Namu-Amida-Butsu," "I'm blessed with Amida's Compassion, Namu-Amida-Butsu," "My breath flows in and out, Namu-Amida-Butsu," "The day is over, Namu-Amida-Butsu," "Night is here, Namu-Amida-Butsu," and on and on. Nembutsu wells forth in an endless stream. The "Namu-Amida-Butsu"

178

of his Nembutsu seems to contain many layers of meaning. Now, instead of trying to analyze them one by one, I shall plunge into "Namu-Amida-Butsu" itself.

As to what his "Namu-Amida-Butsu" means, my own answer is that Saichi's entire being has become "Namu-Amida-Butsu." Or rather, Saichi is nothing but "Namu-Amida-Butsu" itself. To say that his consciousness is completely filled with Nembutsu only perpetuates the dualistic view, for consciousness and Nembutsu have become two. Saichi's Nembutsu does not emerge from the dualistic viewpoint. His central identity is "Namu-Amida-Butsu" itself. His consciousness is one in which "Namu-Amida-Butsu" realizes "Namu-Amida-Butsu." When Rinzai's "true man" or Shinran's "I, alone" are realized, there Rinzai and Shinran are born. It is then "Namu-Amida-Butsu" rushes forth from the mouth. Saichi did not make the geta, "Namu-Amida-Butsu" made them. When this "Namu-Amida-Butsu" chances to return to the individual self, the uttering of the Name, the repeating of Nembutsu, "Namu-Amida-Butsu," "Namu-Amida-Butsu," comes about. It was to attain this experience Asahara Saichi spent thirty years of his life seeking. He was a lost child who had not strayed from his doorstep even a single pace, yet had he not been lost, he would not have understood.

The supra-individual Person that breaks through the consciousness of the individual self must tell us that it has been there. This exclamation is spiritual insight. It is the realization of "Namu-Amida-Butsu." Therein Saichi's poems all have their genesis.

It would be foolish for us to try to explain them by saying that "Namu" is *kimyo* in Japanese, which means "taking refuge," "adoration," "worshipping," etc., and that "Amida Butsu" is the Tathagata of Infinite Light. No doubt at times such explanations are needed, but for Myōkōnin, for ordinary religious men and women, such talk only tends to drive them into paths of illusion. Just "Namu-Amida-Butsu"—that is all that is needed. The oak tree in the yard does not state, "I am a tree of the cypress family," but simply grows up in the garden as it is. "Namu-Amida-Butsu" is "meaningless meaning," and if we try to give it some kind of meaning, or start to think that some significance should exist within it, then the six-syllable Name is no longer one's own, but moves away up to the highest clouds. Since "Namu-Amida-Butsu" transcends time and place, if even the slightest bit of discrimination, distinction, or computation is

179

allowed, the geta will not get made, the work will fail, and Saichi will disappear as Saichi. Contradiction alone will be felt, the mind will become turbulent, heart and mind will be obstructed, and joy, the emotion that flows from the supra-individual Person, will fly.

Whenever I meet with Joy,
I speak not of time or place;
I'm joyful, you're joyful—
That is pleasure, "Namu-Amida-Butsu."

Saichi's joy is not a conscious phenomenon of his individual self. The participation of the supra-individual Person in it can be perceived with utmost clarity. Neither is it of a temporal nature, nor can it be limited to any fixed place. It occupies Saichi's consciousness constantly. It is a continual joy without distinctions of time or place. For that reason Amida participates in it as well. Were it limited by the consciousness of Saichi's individual self, it would be an accidental and occasional thing, and moreover would be tinged with the character of the individual self. Were that so, it would be the same as ordinary joy, and would not be of the sphere of spirituality. Herein lies the distinctive feature of religious emotion.

3. Joy and Repentance

Nembutsu is the Buddha of unceasing joy and repentance,
The Buddha born with "Namu-Amida-Butsu."

Repentance is joy, joy is repentance. This constant mixture is immediately Namu-Amida-Butsu. Because of "Namu-Amida-Butsu," Saichi is, as he is, fully consciousness of his repentance and wretchedness and folly, and at the same time is the Buddha of joy. Spiritual insight realizes this contradiction and at the same time knows, intuitively, that there is no contradiction. This can be seen in the following:

When I encounter the opportunity of repentance,
Time and occasion are utterly wretched.
This becomes the source of joy,
In "Namu-Amida-Butsu."

180

This is full of contradiction. Since this *bombu* is wretched, he is repentant. The possibility of realizing his wretchedness is in the "opportunity." If there is no opportunity realization is not possible. This realization is the source of joy. It is joy itself. Wretchedness—repentance
—joy—"Namu-Amida-Butsu": this is the chain of experience. It is not
a straight line sequence from any one to any other. They occur simul-
taneously. When analyzed by the consciousness of the individual self the
emotional image of a contradictory repentance and joy is incompatible.
But viewed from spirituality, repentance and joy, wretchedness and
"Namu-Amida-Butsu" are interfused, and are three-dimensional or circular. The true and appropriate form for this is "Namu-Amida-Butsu,"
"Namu-Amida-Butsu." "Namu-Amida-Butsu" rejoices in "Namu-Amida-
Butsu." Or perhaps we might say that Nembutsu says Nembutsu.

This dharma is the dharma of repentance.
If it is the dharma of repentance, it is the dharma of joy;
If it is the dharma of joy, "Namu-Amida-Butsu."

Repentance and joy and "Namu-Amida-Butsu" are tied together as in
an endless, beginningless circle. If you have any one of them the others
are there naturally. Repentance and joy, joy and repentance, are not two,
but one, one yet they are two. The one is the many and the many are
the one. This is uncontrollable when viewed from the aspect of the contradiction, but since there is another side where such is not the case, we
are able to carry on with our lives. This is compassion, the compassion
of "Namu-Amida-Butsu." Saichi's life until the end had this "Namu-
Amida-Butsu" at its center. When he experienced the momentousness and
grandeur of this center he experienced the momentousness and grandeur
of repentance and joy. He expresses it as follows:

Abundance of joy is wretchedness too;
Abundance of wretchedness, and abundance of mountain waters
    too,
Is due naturally to the abundance of the waters of the sea.
The taste of joy and repentance is thus known.
Shame and joy are an Ocean of Compassion. . . .
The six syllables, Na-mu-a-mi-da-butsu.

181

Saichi's poems are always "Namu-Amida-Butsu" from beginning to end, and it is also their center. There is little doubt that the opening of his enlightenment was profoundly and thoroughly grounded in the six syllables of the Name.

4. Receive Amida San from Amida San

By means of "Namu-Amida-Butsu" Saichi's individual self, heavily laden with sin and full of wretchedness, goes straightway to become a charitable Buddha in the realm of Amida Nyorai. This is the Great Compassion of the Nyorai. For Saichi it is Amida's great favor.[7] The Great Compassion of the Original Prayer and thankfulness for Amida's great mercy are but two aspects of the same thing. When the supra-individual Person starts to function, it is called Great Compassion. When this Great Compassion strikes the individual self of "wretched Saichi," the consciousness of the individual self calls it the (Buddha's) great favor. The worshipped and the worshipper are the same "Namu-Amida-Butsu." Saichi says:

> *I receive Amida San from Amida San,*
> *He has me say, "Namu-Amida-Butsu."*

"Receiving," "Accepting," "Has me say," are Compassion, the Buddha's favor, and the heart of joy. They are "Namu-Amida-Butsu" itself.

> *Compassion is Amida San.*
> *Compassion that makes me worship,*
> *"Namu-Amida-Butsu,"*
> *Is "Namu-Amida-Butsu."*

The meeting point of individual self and supra-individual Person is "Namu-Amida-Butsu." This point is invariably the beginning of all Saichi's poetry.

> *Great favor*
> *That makes my sin a virtuous Buddha,*
> *"Namu-Amida-Butsu."*

182

Again:

> *Great favor, great favor, oh, great favor,*
> *This Buddha is the Buddha*
> *Who makes Saichi Buddha,*
> *The great favor that says "Namu-Amida-Butsu."*

The Buddha makes this wretched, many-sinned, foolish Saichi a Buddha; through his great favor and Compassion, "Namu-Amida-Butsu" is accorded from the Other, immediately becoming one's own "Namu-Amida-Butsu." Saichi's insight of self-identity amid contradiction becomes more and more vivid. Let us look at the next poem:

> *Namu Buddha is Saichi, Saichi is the Buddha.*
> *Saichi's satori comes, "Namu-Amida-Butsu"—*
> *This is received, "Namu-Amida-Butsu."*

Where Saichi is the Buddha and the Buddha is Saichi there is "Namu-Amida-Butsu." He does not say, "Saichi is the Buddha; the Buddha is Saichi"; between there is the giving and receiving of "Namu-Amida-Butsu." When realization of this comes, Saichi's satori "opens up." The "Holy-Path" (*Shōdōmon*) may say that supra-individual Person = individual self, individual self = supra-individual Person, but with the insight of the Pure Land Path "Namu-Amida-Butsu" is included. It is the starting point and the goal as well.

5. Buddha's Saichi—Saichi's Buddha

What is this Namu-Amida-Butsu that has wretched Saichi on one hand, Great Compassionate Amida (or Oyasama the author of the great favor) on the other, and "Namu-Amida-Butsu" as the central point or connecting line? Is it not the six-syllable Name, simply a stream of sounds coming from the mouth? Doesn't it merely mean reliance upon Amida Buddha, seeking refuge in him? What incomprehensibility is this, which allows Saichi, the square handle, to be connected to Amida, the round socket.

Saichi is, as the ordinary man, an actual individual self. The Buddha does not possess the reality of the ordinary man as Saichi does, but has

183

a supra-individual reality that can be considered in opposition to it. At any rate, since these two confront one another from opposing extremities, they are at odds. What do the six syllables connecting them mean? Were they simply linked together in a line we might view them symbolically. But in the actual life of the individual self the working of the Name makes them into one, and that is something that cannot be comprehended by the ordinary discriminating consciousness. How then does the supra-individual Buddha, via the six syllables, enter into Saichi's individual self? Is it not true that the six syllables themselves are not to be found anywhere within the actuality of Saichi's wretchedness?

The problem returns once again to the root. What is "Namu-Amida-Butsu"? Saichi is understandable and the Buddha is understandable, yet what is this six-syllable Name? But in reality, neither Saichi nor the Buddha can be known. Is it not true that they can never be understood no matter how much searching is done via discrimination? For the Name of six syllables this would probably be even more true. Still philosophers will try in some way or another to elucidate it by means of logic. That is man's intellectual effort. For the rest of us the only way to settle it is through spiritual insight. Which is to say that in striking directly home to the six-syllable Name itself, we are able to comprehend Saichi and the Buddha cutting capers in self-identity and free intercommunion.

Granting lay thought must produce some kind of statement, it might be something like this: the moment the heart of Saichi—the ordinary man —turns to search for the Way, the six syllable Name makes its appearance. The appearance of the six-syllables occurs when Saichi comes into contact with the Great Compassion of Amida. When Saichi awakens to this he says " 'Namu-Amida-Butsu,' I am struck." This is the incomprehensibility spoken of before. It lies outside the bounds of ordinary thought. Here is a Buddhist's view of the Buddha-wisdom's incomprehensibility:

> *Namu is the Name of Amida,*
> *Amida is the Name of Namu—*
> *This is Saichi's "Namu-Amida-Butsu".*

Saichi does not speak of theory but expresses unadorned his insight as it comes to him:

184

It is not I who heard it,
It is not I who heard it;
"Namu-Amida-Butsu" strikes into my heart.
Now I am hit and taken by you.

The word 'strikes' relates plainly Saichi's experience of being struck by the Name. If you place the Buddha over there and yourself here and then try to connect them, it cannot be done, water and oil do not mix. If the realization that you are the Buddha is not present, then no matter how hard you may try, you cannot become the six syllables.

I do not become Amida,
Amida becomes me—
"Namu-Amida-Butsu."

The Name comes from Amida and 'strikes' Saichi. Although Saichi remains Saichi, he is no longer the former Saichi; he is "Namu-Amida-Butsu." Viewed from "Namu-Amida-Butsu" one side is Amida and the other side is Saichi, and moreover each side is retained. "Namu-Amida-Butsu" is another name for spiritual insight. It might be said that it is the substance or content of insight. Or couldn't we say that Amida, becoming the individual self, is "Namu-Amida-Butsu"? In going through Saichi's writings there is no other conclusion to be reached. A philosopher would have to erect some logical sequence; Saichi says:

My heart is your heart,
Your heart is my heart;
To become mine . . . is your heart.

To genuinely know this heart is "Namu-Amida-Butsu." Stated otherwise, if you become "Namu-Amida-Butsu" you will understand the meaning of the 'your' in the word, "To become mine . . . is your heart." The following situation,

Compassion and Light, all one.
Saichi and Amida, all one.
"Namu-Amida-Butsu."

185

in which all are one, is "Namu-Amida-Butsu." Here is "Namu-Amida-Butsu," Light, Compassion, and Saichi. I call this awakening, spiritual insight, and there seems to be something Japanese in its configuration.

> *How happy I am!*
> *Amida's seal is stamped on my heart.*
> *The seal of "Namu-Amida-Butsu,"*
> *The seal of Oyasama,*[8]
> *The child has received.*
> *I say simply "Namu-Amida-Butsu."*

I wish to consider the parent-child relation between Amida and Saichi later, but first a word concerning the "seal" of "Namu-Amida-Butsu." This seal is a bond which says that Saichi and the Buddha are contradictory yet have a nature of self-identity, which means that this seal is the six-syllable Name. To call the Nembutsu a seal is an unusual choice of words, yet it clearly shows Saichi's feeling.

If we say Saichi and Amida San are one, or that "Namu-Amida-Butsu" is a seal given as proof of the existence of this identity, the sense becomes wholly spatial, producing an inclination to regard the relation between them as a merely static one. When this happens Buddhism assumes a pantheistic view. Even today some Buddhist scholars might make such an assertion, I do not know, but there could be nothing more mistaken with regard to Buddhism. The self-identity of Saichi and the Buddha must be seen through a viewpoint in which spatial is temporal, where it might even be said that space is time and time is space. Space and time must be linked in what might be termed an active relationship. In any case, Saichi operates within Amida, and Amida moves within Saichi, and that is exactly the manner in which "Namu-Amida-Butsu" must exist. "Namu-Amida-Butsu" must be *uttered.* "Uttered" means spoken in the three activities of mouth, mind, and body. The Zen sect says, "the feet run, the hands grasp." Those of the Nembutsu schools do not address themselves to this point as distinctly as the Zen-man; on the other hand, they show more interest in the emotional aspect that speaks of the relation of parent and child, or of the all-pervading Light of Compassion.

> *Oyasama dwells in my fiery hands;*

Oyasama who says "Namu-Amida-Butsu."

The words "Oyasama dwells in my fiery hands" suggests the infinitude of hellish contradictions that seem to make up the boundless passion, the endless torment to which human life is subject. Within all this dwells Amida. Saichi's 'dwell' suggests passive non-action, something without emotion. But, actually, Saichi's feeling is not so, for it burns intensely together with the flame itself, though Amida is not touched by the flames. That is how I understand "Oyasama who says 'Namu-Amida-Butsu.' " It is not merely a matter of remaining quiet and motionless and repeating the Nembutsu. Uttering, saying is an act. As the fire burns "Namu-Amida-Butsu" burns with it, and "Namu-Amida-Butsu" is uttered. Each movement of the planer, sweeping wood shavings stroke by stroke to the floor, is the sound of "Namu-Amida-Butsu." Oyasama moves in Saichi's hands and feet, and the wood shavings fall away from the plane-strokes until they lie all around him at his work table—the hands and feet are not Saichi's. He is empty-handed yet grasping the handle of the hoe, on foot yet riding the bullock—the feet and the hands are Oyasama's. This in itself is the "Namu-Amida-Butsu" uttered by Oyasama.

Prior to his fiftieth year Saichi, who had been striving hard to attain the Way, would probably have said, "Saichi says the Nembutsu." Until "Saichi" was blown about and knocked down by Amida's great wind he was too conscious of "Saichi." "Saichi" was buffeted about and struck onto something—"Namu-Amida-Butsu." From that time forth he dwelled in fire; no, he dwelled together with the fire, and came to "taste" fully the life of Nembutsu samadhi.

Though we speak of the sameness of illusions,
Illusion in illusion
And dharma in illusion
Are different—
Here Tariki and Jiriki are known.

Here Saichi becomes objective and critical, which is rather unusual. But as he rightly says, insofar as illusion exists in illusion, that is, insofar as it has not yet emerged from the plane of discrimination, a Nembutsu uttered by Oyasama will be necessarily incomprehensible. One has to be

187

knocked down by the wind. He must have broken the threads of discrimination and been cast into the immense Void of non-discrimination. Yet by itself that will not suffice, for he must strike on the dharma, he must run up against the dharma, or rather, he must be struck by the dharma. Since this will come from the Other (Amida), it is not his own act. While there is a question of karmic opportunity here, man's own part is completely passive. This is where the *Tariki* view materializes. The Oyasama of "Namu-Amida-Butsu" is the Oyasama who says "Namu-Amida-Butsu." They are one and the same. It is Nembutsu that says Nembutsu.

6. *Saichi's View of Rebirth (Ōjō)*

A salient characteristic of the poems included in Rev. Fuji's book— poems we might call Saichi's 'Nembutsu-Samadhi Poetry Collection'—is that Saichi's thoughts never refer to the idea of rebirth in the Pure Land after death. The idea that after death one is received into Paradise, therefore let the trials and sorrows of this world be as they will, never comes up even once. It is generally believed that the Nembutsu sects state the following: *shaba* (this world) is suffering; *gokuraku* (the Land of Bliss) is, as its name says, a place of happiness. Therefore, in this world one must above all else practice perseverance, obedience, etc., and meet the end in quiet composure. Simply believe in Amida's Original Prayer and without any doubt you will attain *Ōjō*. Thus all one's days should be spent repeating "Namu-Amida-Butsu." There is little more than this.

It is generally thought that the ideas that Amida's heart is your heart, and that you can receive the Pure Land in this *shaba* world, belong only to the Holy Path and are not found in the Pure Land or Tariki Path. In spite of this, there is no mention at all of future life in Saichi's poetry. His heart is filled completely with the Name of six syllables received from Oya, and there seems to be no room left over for anything else.

> *Saichi, where will you go in the next life?*
> *I'll be received into the native place of Namu-Amida-Butsu.*
> *"Namu-Amida-Butsu."*

This poem is the only clue for establishing Saichi's *Ōjō*-view, his view of future rebirths. Within it the idea of a Pure Land after death does not

appear. The home of "Namu-Amida-Butsu" is "Namu-Amida-Butsu";
whether it is in this life or the next is not clear. Saichi mentions the next
life, but his "Namu-Amida-Butsu" is always Saichi himself, now, the
present Saichi, and within this a future life apparently is not included.

You don't go to the Pure Land after death,
You go before the end has come;
Being entrusted to "Namu-Amida-Butsu,"
"Namu-Amida-Butsu."

According to this Paradise clearly comes before death. You do not go
there after death but while still alive. Saichi is there now. I have rendered
the word *sumete* in the third line as "entrust," although such an interpretation is not certain. It seems to imply that when you are entrusted
to or occupied with Amida you need not worry over this or that, or
something similar. For Saichi, all that is needed is "Namu-Amida-Butsu"
"Namu-Amida-Butsu," hence his unconcern whether he goes to Paradise
or to Hell. All is left to Amida San to do as he wills, it is not to be
calculated by this "wretched person"—this is Saichi's heart become
"Namu-Amida-Butsu." For Saichi is the new Buddha, and Amida is the
old Buddha, and Saichi the ignorant ordinary man is prepared to go anywhere Saichi the new Buddha takes him.

Saichi is the new Buddha, Amida is the old Buddha;
Old Buddha Oyasama is my Oyasama—
"Namu-Amida-Butsu."

To speak of "one's own Amida" is to utter the very words of the Holy
Path. But Saichi lives constantly with "Namu-Amida-Butsu," he does not
forget the central "Namu-Amida-Butsu" even when his expression seem
incomprehensible. In the following,

Wind and air two, but it is
One wind, one air;
Amida and I are two,
But the Compassion of "Namu-Amida-Butsu" is one.

189

two is one, one is two. The secret of this wonder is *"Namu-Amida-Butsu."* And "Namu-Amida-Butsu" is nothing but Compassion itself. Saichi existed in the Name's six syllables from beginning to middle to end. He is "Namu-Amida-Butsu," "Namu-Amida-Butsu" is Saichi. He is wholly embraced within Amida's Great Compassion.

> *Received [by Amida], my heart goes to the*
> *Pure Land for the first time.*
> *Returns again to the foul taste of the* shaba *world;*
> *Sent back, to work for the salvation of all beings.*

According to this poem, Saichi has already gone to the Pure Land for the first time, and here and now he has returned. This is the "return and transfer" for the sake of all beings. Saichi is truly the adopted son of Amida. Sweeping his planer, he surrounds himself with falling chips and shavings. Are they not the pieces of a sincere heart working for the salvation of all living beings? And after all is said, is it not quite obvious why he adds nothing about going to the Pure Land after death?

Saichi regarded himself as one who had long before finished the business of dying. Thus he naturally did not bother about after death. Neither was he wandering about in the region of birth-and-death. The next poem clearly reveals his own spiritual attitude.

> *You have stolen the end of my life,*
> *My passing, my funeral, finished.*
> *The joy afterwards, "Namu-Amida-Butsu."*

The expression "you have stolen the end of my life" is indeed fresh. It expresses marvelously transcendance of birth-and-death.

> *Death has not yet come . . .*
> *No wonder—*
> *It has already passed;*
> *The end of life is over,*
> *"Namu-Amida-Butsu."*

In the first of the above two poems he says his death is already past,

190

in the second he questions whether it might be still to come, and in the next, he says his end is now.

> *Now is the end . . . my end,*
> *Which is yours;*
> *Joyfulness, "Namu-Amida-Butsu."*

In a book entitled *Shūjishō* ("A Tract on Steadily Holding [to the Faith]" 執持鈔) by Kakunyo Shōnin (1270–1351), it is written:

> *When in accordance with the words of a good master you awaken in your ordinary moments one thought of trust in Amida, let this be regarded as the last moment, the end of this world for you.*

Saichi's expressions are vivid because they are not conceptual.

7. *The Salvation of Sentient Beings*

How did Saichi view the salvation of sentient beings? The line "Sent back, to work for the salvation of all beings," quoted above signifies clearly that this salvation is his present work. Yet how should the following monologue be intrepreted? Since Saichi is deeply immersed in the Nembutsu samadhi, and occupied with singing of his mental state, he would seem to have little time to worry himself with scholarly exposition on such things as the salvation of sentient beings. Yet since he does speak of the oneness of *hō* and *ki*,[9] of the thoughts that are irrelevant to a Believing Heart, of the inability of wise men and saints to enter the Pure Land, neither is he incapable of adopting an objective, critical attitude. This being the case, he probably did some thinking about the salvation of living beings as well.

> *Saichi san, are you in?*
> *Yes, I'm home.*
> *The head of the house isn't in.*
> *He's gone out, to the salvation of living beings . . .*
> *He'll be back shortly, please wait.*

191

"Namu-Amida-Butsu," "Namu-Amida-Butsu."
He's back, he's come back!

How should we understand this salvation of beings? Amida has now left to engage in the salvation of sentient beings, and Saichi feels he is not at home. Is Amida's work of salvation different from Saichi's present business? Could "not at home" mean that Saichi's work and Saichi's self have separated, and that outside, irrelevant ideas have intruded between them? Is this a monologue of self-examination, as to whether a fissure has developed in Saichi's maintenance of Right Mindfulness? Is he examining himself, pressing the needle to himself, testing his ability to continue in Nembutsu samadhi, that is, testing the unconscious consciousness of his attainment of faith? This is different from the constant diligence in someone not yet possessed of established faith, put forth as a device to perpetuate Right Mindfulness. Is it not rather a playful question and answer with the master, Amida Buddha? All of us have this playful spirit. Human consciousness is not always dashing forward, it is also good at sightseeing. To leave after fragrant grasses and return following the falling flower petals is the privilege of man alone. He thus sometimes wanders from illusion to illusion. Nevertheless, Saichi's salvation of living beings is not something that needs to be planned and then carried out elsewhere, he should have no need to strive in this or that specific act to work for salvation. There is no doubt Saichi's life was passed in the manner of a sportive samadhi, examining the constancy of his faith, all the while doing his work fashioning geta. In short, for Saichi, salvation of sentient beings was not accomplished by emptying, going outside of himself, but by leading a life of Nembutsu samadhi, giving life to his everyday mindedness; that is, doing, acting, was for him the salvation of living beings. The next poem may be read in this light as well.

> *The Believing Heart is the principal*
> *Of the salvation of living beings;*
> *I receive it, "Namu-Amida-Butsu."*

The Believing Heart is the "principal" received from Amida, thanks to which this life is spiritually moved. When one reverently and thankfully receives the Believing Heart and becomes "Namu-Amida-Butsu,"

192

that is the salvation of living beings. The salvation of sentient beings is our everyday life itself, and no others acts in addition need be considered. The "capital funds" for a life devoted to the salvation of living beings is granted upon attainment of faith, upon the receipt of the Believing Heart. Life without "Namu-Amida-Butsu" is life of empty promise, extremely unstable and insecure. Most of us are creatures of just such lives, our actions never attaining the level of effortlessness and purposelessness, of life unaware of conscious strivings (Skt: *ānabhogacaryā*). The salvation of living beings is none other than this kind of purposeless life. It has to be a salvation within a sportive samadhi. Saichi's planing and fashioning of his geta woodblocks is an act of sportive samadhi, the purposeless act of the salvation of all beings. Saichi's life was that of a saint, though he himself calls it playing with Oyasama. Playing he goes hand in hand with Amida, and playing he goes to the Pure Land. As Saichi puts it, "By playing you are taken to the Pure Land." In Zen, this is said to indicate the stage of enlightenment where one is able freely to enlighten others.

> *This wretched one is now playing with Oyasama,*
> *In this* shaba *world.*
> *I will be taken into the Pure Land of Amida,*
> *Playing with Oyasama.*

In this present *shaba* world, this wretched self just as it is, I lead a life of sportive samadhi together with Amida; the Pure Land is but the extension of this sport: such statements could be made with authenticity only by one thoroughly possessed of a Believing Heart. With a bit of logic someone might produce something similar, but Saichi's straightforward, artless declaration is something no amount of ordinary training could produce. In Asahara Saichi Japanese spiritual insight can be said to have formed a crystal of utmost brilliance and purity.

I think the following poem helps clarify the meaning of Saichi's previous words about the salvation of living beings:

> *This evil person takes delight in Buddha, "Namu-Amida-Butsu."*
> *Buddha takes delight in Saichi's ki, "Namu-Amida-Butsu."*
> *Sending me to the salvation of living beings,*

193

Joyfully, "Namu-Amida-Butsu."

With this, "Namu-Amida-Butsu" becomes the main constituent of all conceivable things. The evil person delights in the Buddha through its mediation. The Buddha delights in Saichi as a *ki*, in the evil person, through its mediation. Here, and nowhere else, is this joy; the acts of the evil person, Saichi's everyday mind, the geta shavings, the toil in the rice-fields—"Namu-Amida-Butsu" is doing "Namu-Amida-Butsu." This is the salvation of sentient beings. Going away from oneself, one leaves behind "Namu-Amida-Butsu." It means being absent from one's home, and that could not be the salvation of living beings. "Living beings" is singular. This wicked person, this *ki*, Saichi himself, this must be saved, for otherwise there would be no meaning in the salvation of living beings (in the plural), in the supra-individual, or in an other. And this salvation is the joyous sportive samadhi.

8. Saichi's Satori

Saichi was a master of enlightenment. He does not brandish it about like a Zen-man. He uses terms such as gratefulness, joyfulness, happiness, pleasure, etc., instead of intellectual expressions. This is a distinctive feature of those associated with the Pure Land tradition, who express themselves in emotional or affective language. Yet of course things of an intellectual nature appear in their vocabulary. Even Saichi must speak of satori.

> *Namu Buddha is Saichi's Buddha—he is Saichi.*
> *Saichi's satori opens up, "Namu-Amida-Butsu."*
> *He has received it, "Namu-Amida-Butsu."*

The meaning of the first line is unclear, but as a whole the poem means: Saichi is the Buddha, the Buddha is Saichi. "Namu-Amida-Butsu" is the agent for this realization. Through it the Buddha and Saichi are linked in a circle; that is, Saichi's satori is received from the six letters of the Name. All is Namu-Amida-Butsu, there is nothing else. It is not Saichi equals Buddha, Buddha equals Saichi, it is "Namu-Amida-Butsu." "Namu-Amida-Butsu" must not be thought of as an intermediary connecting Saichi

194

and the Buddha. The idea of the three is that they are three and they are one. When the discriminatory intellect speaks, they become three, but with spiritual awakening there is nothing but "Namu-Amida-Butsu" alone, there is no Buddha and no Saichi. This is apparent in the following:

> *Impermanence is me, this impermanence*
> *Attains the enlightenment of Nirvana,*
> *"Namu-Amida-Butsu."*

Saichi dissolves the opposition of Nirvana and impermanence in "Namu-Amida-Butsu." In personalistic terms, since impermanence is Saichi himself, Nirvana is Amida Butsu. The self-identity of these two is "Namu-Amida-Butsu." "Namu-Amida-Butsu" is always employed by Saichi with absolute independence. It is his Person, "the only one in all the universe," Shinran's "one person," the "man" of Rinzai's true man of no title. Saichi lived constantly within "Namu-Amida-Butsu's" Right Mindfulness. He lived in it and acted in it. Gutei has his one-finger Zen that he could not use up in a lifetime. Saichi's one finger is "Namu-Amida-Butsu." If we are to call Gutei a man of enlightenment, we must say the same of Saichi. He speaks of "walking, standing, sitting, lying, Namu-Amida-Butsu." He is the enlightened man himself, who dwells with the Buddha, rising with him and retiring with him.

The *Anjin Ketsujō Shō* tells us that "Namu-Amida-Butsu" is the form in which we accomplish *Ōjō*. Saichi actualizes this form.

> *Not listening to it as something as it should be,*
> *Listening to "Namu-Amida-Butsu" as for the first time.*

Even here Saichi's enlightenment is clearly perceived. Something as it should be has no relation to what is present *now*, actually manifest before one's eyes. It is limited to conceptual reasoning. Saichi's Name is not such a feeble concept. It is an actual "Namu-Amida-Butsu" heard here and now this very instant. It is thus always new and fresh, each time it is new, everyday it is new, always felt as if for the first time.

To live is not to have lived, nor is it an expectation to live. It is not the potential to live or "ought to live." It is *living now*, instant by instant, thus it is continual creation. In Saichi's words it is "Namu-Amida-

195

Butsu heard as for the first time." Saichi was definitely a man smitten by "Namu-Amida-Butsu."

He often uses the word *ataru,* meaning to hit, to strike, or to smite, yet with profound meaning, the meaning of "encounter" or "clash" that Zen men often speak of. It describes well the experience Saichi had.

"Namu-Amida-Butsu hits me."

"Namu-Amida-Butsu strikes my heart."

"You strike my heart."

"The Name of Amida hits my heart, Namu-Amida-Butsu."

"Strikes my heart."

"Namu-Amida-Butsu strikes my heart."

Such lines are frequent in Saichi's poetry. "Strikes" (*ataru*) means Saichi and Namu-Amida-Butsu meet like two arrows head-on, and their meeting can in no way be avoided. It means something that has until now moved continuously straight ahead suddenly has its movement stopped and changed to a new direction or movement. It means advancing beyond the end of a hundred-foot pole, where something unanticipated and unplanned by the discriminating intellect suddenly opens up. *Ataru* denotes discontinuity, breaking-out, fortuity, intuitiveness. Though it can have various meanings, with good and bad connotations, here it speaks of a region beyond reach of discriminatory wisdom. Saichi searches and questions, "Is 'Namu-Amida-Butsu' this? Is it that?" but these all miss the mark completely, and he is "struck" unexpectedly. After all, Saichi's *ataru* is a kind of *magure-atari,* "changing to hit," a chance or fortuitous encounter.

9. Taste—Experience—Now

Saichi also uses the word "taste". Taste is experience. One knows by tasting whether something is sweet, bitter, or otherwise. One knows cold and warmth by oneself. To man who exists by means of words all things are ideas and concepts, and he does not taste. With someone like Saichi, whose relation to words is only remote, word examination is avoided, and all things are spoken of through experience. For this reason his words penetrate to the quick. It is highly refreshing, even exhilarating, to see him put so easily into words what is beyond reach of the scholar's imagination. I am not at all certain his jottings should be called poems, in any case, they read like the *Anjin Ketsujō Shō*. Or we might even compare them with Ippen's *Sayings*.[10]

Saichi's poems, according to Rev. Fuji, begin with this:

> *Namu Amida, on the way to Amida Butsu.*
> *Tasting Namu, "Namu-Amida-Butsu."*

His notebooks, which appear to have been kept over a period of many years, are a genuine chronicle of his experience. They note unreservedly, simply, innocently, without affectation or calculation, as a spider spins out its thread, how Saichi 'tasted' Namu-Amida-Butsu according to his daily mood. Like the Zen "lunatics" Kanzan and Jittoku, who used to write their poems on tree trunks and the broad leaves of plantain trees, Saichi took up his brush and sang of "Namu-Amida-Butsu" as the natural poet of spirituality. Clouds, it is said, rise up mindlessly in the mountain peaks, and if the mountains are high, clouds will be naturally abundant. If one's spiritual insight is deep enough he cannot help but try to express that experience in words. And because his words are artless and shorn of technique they touch all the more the true nature of his experience. Saichi's three lines,

> *A heart of joy tasting today,*
> *A Believing Heart bred of "Namu-Amida-Butsu."*
> *"Namu-Amida-Butsu."*

contain boundless meaning. "Namu-Amida-Butsu" is the incomparable Iron Hammer wielded by the Buddha's all-conquering power. Knocked down by this hammer, Saichi attains faith. Now, this very instant, his faith, his Believing Heart, is tasted. Now is the eternal present, the absolute present. It is not the now that continues in the straight line of past,

197

present, and future. It is the present unattainable in the three periods of past, present, and future. Its center is found only within the infinite circle. Here is where Saichi stands. No, Saichi is the center. And here spiritual insight is grasped, overflowing the emotional plane as the heart of joy.

Jōdo followers in some respects are men of simplicity. They themselves call it simple-heartedness or genuine-mindedness and go no farther. Compared with them, Zen men might even seem philosophically-minded. They are not professional philosophers of course, but somehow there is an odour of reason about them, and they understand the charge of literary expression as well. In illustration of this, let us see what Saichi's "heart of joy tasting today" would become in the hands of a man of Zen, in this case the well-known founder of Daitokuji Temple in Kyoto, Daitō Kokushi (1282–1337).

Daitō Kokushi lived the life of a beggar for more than twenty years and tasted the lowest levels of human life. In his day the beggar's lot might not have been as bad in some ways as it is today. But they no doubt were despised as being less than human. I think Daitō's life as a beggar was an attempt on his part to experience the wretchedness of the outcast, rather than a desire for material poverty.

He received a call from the Imperial Court requesting him to found a temple in the north of the capital, which he did. In spite of his many years as a wandering beggar he was very learned, and this turned out to be very helpful later when he became a distinguished abbot. I frankly wish he had left some record of his daily life, in addition to the writings which reveal his learning, literary ability, and Zen genius. In the case of Saichi, whose utterances come straight from the heart in the language of everyday speech, without undergoing any carving or polishing whatever, it is possible to see his character in each and every word, whereas Daitō, or any other Zen master, uses words and phrases not always readily comprehensible at first encounter. Even though the written word is addressed to the eye, if one does not possess some knowledge of Chinese literature and Zen literature as well, such writings are quite incomprehensible. It is not only because one does not have the necessary Zen experience that they are incomprehensible, but because to break through the shell that covers this experience—which is very thick—and get to the taste within is an arduous task. Since Saichi's verses are made much as

198

he threw off his roughhewn geta, we are pretty well able to discern at a glance what they are about. Objects of art highly ornamented or finely finished are destined for the *tokonoma*. This is not to slight Daitō Kokushi's writings in any way, for as the Kokushi, the "National Teacher," he was naturally confined by the influences· of accumulated convention and the background of the age in which he lived. The following quotation appears in Part Four of the *Kaian Koku Go* ("Words from Dreamland"), a collection of Daitō's poems and sermons with commentary by Hakuin. It is a sermon for New Year's Eve.

> *New Year's Eve. The sun rises, and the moon rises. The morning comes, the night comes. Twelve months, three hundred and sixty days are here culminated. The new and the old are intermingled and tonight come together. If any man puts his body in the old year, he will not discharge his newly decided potential in the new.' And if he puts his mind in the new year, he will lose his primary function. Therefore, Hokuzen roasted the big white bullock [the symbol of Highest Reality] that used to roam in the monastery courtyard, and Soō shouldered the midnight lantern. Though things are so, I do not enter such caverns. Why? "The December snows filling up to the horizon make all things look white, while the spring winds blowing against the doors are still severely cold."*

There are some traditional allusions in this, but there is no reason to explain them in detail now. The aim of the sermon is that the past year is going, the new year is about to come, how are we to view the *now* of this moment, this juncture? New Year's Eve is the intersection where the old and the new blend together, and the past and future change places. This is the point of the question, "Now, this very moment, what is it!" Tōin Iida, a Zen master, comments on the sermon as follows in his *Kaian Kokugo Teishō Roku:*

> *In the present there is no new and old. The past perishing, the future being born—that is the work of the present, which does not cease even for an instant. If you are diligent, there will be no time for the water-wheel to freeze to a stop. One must enjoy*

199

a life in which each day is new, every day new. A man's death is like the final day of the year, the following day, the new year, is immediately the beginning of life. There is not an instant's stop. Even though we attach the provisional names of life and death the time is always the same time. Its activity has gone along since beginningless time. Death is located among the activities of time too; without death there is no life. In other words, the present; except for the present there is nothing. The eternal past is also the present, and it is beginningless. It is said in the Lotus Sutra, 'Many kalpas have passed since I attained Buddhahood.' Eternity throughout the whole future is the present as well, and it is endless. So if you would know the beginningless and endless present, simply look at the present. Eternity is becoming the present. If you would know the eternal future, look at the present. The present extended is the future. Miroku billions of years in the future is but another name for us here in the present . . . (Kaian Koku Go Teishō Roku, IV)

It would be interesting to compare the criticisms of Daitō or this modern Zen master regarding "A heart of joy tasting today" with Saichi's own simple remarks on the same subject. Since Saichi spent his eighteenth through fiftieth years listening to expositions of the dharma, it can be supposed he was fairly conversant with the vocabulary of Pure Land thought. In spite of this we find no literary or scriptural words among his notations. His writing is extremely colloquial, simple, and natural. The words *ki* and *hō* do appear, but they are commonly known to Pure Land believers.

> *Don't listen to reason and logic,*
> *Be captured by the taste, listen to the taste;*
> *"Namu-Amida-Butsu."*

Saichi lived from beginning to end a life of "tasting." His words, "Be captured by the taste, listen to the taste," have a wonderful freshness. All expressions should enable us to see Saichi living immersed in a "Namu-Amida-Butsu" samadhi. He had from the first no interest in reason or logic. From the age of nineteen or so, when his sincere heart first resolved

200

to seek the Way, the voice of Japanese spirituality was constantly whispering in his ear. He determined that one way or other he would understand this voice in all its clarity. For a while, it seems he had a touch of laxity. But spirituality is not something that always appears on the surface of consciousness, it operates constantly hidden in the unconscious area of the heart. Saichi had to throw back his ears with a new determination and plunge on ahead in the direction of the whisper. Prior to his fiftieth year he must have undergone much hard struggle. Yet there is no record whatever of that period of his life, and there is really no reason for him to have written any, for he was too busy tasting the samadhi of his Believing Heart. He was living *now*, by the "unborn" the Zen master Bankei speaks of. Saichi did not cling to his past experience and repeat it in vain. To follow the memory is to reconstruct experience. Indeed, that is needed too, for the salvation of all in the world would be impossible without it. But it entails great harm. It is separated from the world of true existence and experience. That is why Saichi adopted *taste* and excluded logic. There was no special reason for this, it was simply the natural thing for him to do.

10. The Buddha is the Ordinary Man, the Ordinary Man is the Buddha —Guchi (Ignorance)

I would now like to speak of Saichi's view that the Buddha and the ordinary man, the world of purity and the world of defilement, are identical. Because this is a view that has issued from experience we should concern ourselves with its disparity from the concepts of scholars and teachers who tend to calculations and conclusions. We must not summarily reject what is so calculated, for the human consciousness has need of the mind's logic if it is rooted in a life experience. There should be no singleminded disparagement of teachers and scholars. The key is to investigate the degree to which the logic of the mind is firmly entrenched in the reality of life. Although Saichi listened presumably for many years to the expositions of Buddhist teachers, he on his part noted down on wood-chips his own experience in his own manner of expression. It is to these we must look. Saichi says:

The death anniversary of the sect founder

The anniversary is for the death of Shinran, the founder of the Shin sect, and is at the same time the "death anniversary" of Saichi the geta-maker. This is certainly a bold statement. Bold, that is, from an ordinary Pure Land follower, for Saichi it is nothing out of the ordinary. With a cavalier unconcern he says it no differently than he would state that a cat is a cat. It is not easy to speak so with such artless simplicity. The line "This is Saichi, isn't it?" is a bit difficult to understand. What does "this" refer to? Although there are various interpretations possible, I wonder what Saichi was trying to say. We must separate ourselves from the text and try to put ourselves in his place.

Since he is standing within the realization that today's anniversary for the death of Shinran is his own, 'this' must be the realization Saichi the geta-maker and Shinran the sect-founder are different, and at the same time one and the same. This very experience is Saichi's own self, at the same time it is "Namu-Amida-Butsu." "Isn't it?" added to "This is Saichi" is his own playful charm. A Zen man would have nothing of it. He would immediately tweak his opposite's nose, or give him a shove, exclaiming, "What's 'this'?" Saichi belongs to the Jōdo tradition. He cocks his head to one side, questions "is it not?" and goes on sweeping his plane through the wood-block before him, repeating "Namu-Amida-Butsu" all the while. It is interesting how this brings out his personality.

We might recall the lines quoted before: "Namu Buddha is Saichi's Buddha, it is Saichi." The Namu-Amida-Butsu that is moving within Saichi's heart, the six syllables of the Name that have been granted from Amida have an incalculable force here. Were it an insight of the discriminating intellect Saichi would be raised to a vain exaltation, and become a lump of unmanageable egotism. But since his insight in "Namu-Amida-Butsu" is one that sees the contradiction between Saichi and the Buddha as sameness, it is non-discriminatory discrimination, discriminatory non-discrimination. Saichi repeats "Namu-Amida-Butsu" whenever he says anything, and uses it to end his poems, because the center of his entire consciousness is constantly controlled and guided by "Namu-Amida-Butsu."

202

I don't listen as an ordinary man,
The ordinary man is a fraud.[11]
You strike my heart.

Being "heart-struck" is nothing other than "Namu-Amida-Butsu." In short, "Namu-Amida-Butsu" recites "Namu-Amida-Butsu" and listens to it as well. From someone like Ippen Shōnin this would sound quite convincing, but from the lips of Myōkōnin Saichi it comes as something of a surprise. Still, on second thought, isn't an experiential reality such as Saichi's an Oriental one, that shows in particular the spiritual insight of the Japanese?

I do not become Amida,
Amida becomes me,
Namu-Amida-Butsu.

I—the ordinary man—Saichi, all are a result, a product, an idea of the discriminating intellect. This is the "fraud." It is not based upon truth. Fraud—that which is produced by discrimination or analyzation—is what is hypothesized as the objective world by the consciousness. It is what Shinran calls hollow apparitions or unreality. Therefore, there is nothing at all in the I of Saichi or in the individual self of the discriminating intellect capable of becoming Amida. To be able to say as Saichi does that Saichi is the Buddha, that the death anniversary of Shinran is his own, is something that must be conferred from an Other, from Amida. It must be Compassion from Amida, the working of *Tariki*. Such a self-realization materializes in spiritual insight. This is the truth, there is no other. It is concrete reality in the ultimate sense, and the reason "Namu-Amida-Butsu alone is true." Saichi, Shinran, and Hōnen all lived within this consciousness.

Both Compassion and [Boundless] Light are one.
Both Saichi and Amida are one,
"Namu-Amida-Butsu."

The truth of Pure Land thought rests here, in the experience of becoming one through "Namu-Amida-Butsu." Since Hōnen, Shinran, and Saichi are one in this experience, the death anniversary of the founder is Saichi's own death anniversary. Christians are told, "For as in Adam all die, even so in Christ shall all be made alive." Pure Land followers die in Amida and live in Amida. Therefore, Saichi is Amida's Saichi and Amida is Saichi's Amida. Realization of this is "Namu-Amida-Butsu." Eternal illusion and eternal enlightenment, Saichi doomed to Hell, and Amida Buddha abiding in perfect purity, are inevitably and indissolubly opposed, they are contradictions that reject any idea of resolution. They are absolute opposites, and that is how it must be. The contradiction is a contradiction yet there must be free and unobstructed interpenetration. To attempt to insert a third party would only perpetuate the opposition into a limitless succession. Since the ordinary man is beyond help, Saichi cannot excape eternal illusion and ignorance. This, by means of Japanese spiritual insight, he easily dissolves away as follows:

> *Though I am in eternal illusion,*
> *My Oyasama is an eternal Oya;*
> *Joyous gratitude, "Namu-Amida-Butsu."*

If ignorance is eternal one cannot be rid of it in an eternity. If enlightenment is eternal one cannot enter into ignorance in an eternity. However, this enlightenment is the eternal Oya, the embodiment of Amida's eternal Prayer. Therefore, in the light of this Prayer alone enlightenment and illusion become one. One caught in ignorance receives this as the great favor or Buddha's favor, and here is where the materialization of free and unobstructed interpenetration occurs. Saichi scribbled down on his shavings the reality of his own experience as he fashioned his geta. That is the great meaning of his poetry collection. I believe it is for the logicians to erect something new upon this reality.

Saichi's poems gained in profundity as they poured out. The following could only come from someone with Saichi's experience, from a scholar's lips it would be a piece of logic, and would carry with it the aura of a second-hand clothing box.

> *The world is foolish, I am foolish,*
> *Amida is foolish too;*
> *No matter, Oyasama relieves foolishness,*
> *"Namu-Amida-Butsu."*

204

"Amida is foolish too" is a daring assertion. Perhaps only Saichi could have made it. When Vimalakirti said "I am ill because all beings are ill," he inserted the word "because" between "I" and "all beings." Saichi inserts nothing, he simply enumerates: "The world is foolish, I am foolish, Amida is foolish." There are no words connecting these three. Then he shifts his tack, "no matter, Oyasama relieves foolishness." Only then is it known that Amida's foolishness and the foolishness of all beings are different. But from Amida issues no requirement that Saichi and the rest of the world relinquish their foolishness. All is *as it is*. That foolish people are saved as they are is the characteristic of Japanese spiritual insight. The contradiction is not dissolved, it remains as it is. Still the remaining contradiction is not the original one. It is a contradiction which has become tinged with a free and unobstructed interpenetration. It is "Namu-Amida-Butsu."

The external phenomena of the prior Saichi's ignorance are the same as those of the present Saichi, but the present Saichi's ignorance is supported by "Namu-Amida-Butsu." It is foolishness taken in hand by Oyasama, not foolishness of Saichi's discriminatory consciousness. Of course, Saichi's individual self is not lost; yet it is the Person of the supra-individual. It cannot be said the foolishness has been purified, yet the foolishness no longer emerges from the individual self. There is no purification of the foolishness, for it is eternal, but it must not be forgotten it is a foolishness which is in contact with the eternal Oyasama. It cannot exist in ordinary logic or language, but in spiritual insight the contradiction is accepted as it is, and is given life.

11. Saichi and Jōshū[12]

It should be interesting to compare Saichi's *guchi* (ignorance) and Jōshū's view of *bonnō* (desires and passions); Saichi's "Namu-Amida-Butsu" and Jōshū's crystal. Once Jōshū said to the assembled monks:

This is like holding up a transparent crystal in your hand. When a stranger comes it reflects him as such; when a native Chinese comes it reflects him as such. I pick up a blade of grass and make it work as a golden-bodied Buddha 16 feet high. I again take hold of a golden-bodied Buddha 16 feet high and make him act

as a blade of grass. The Buddha is what constitutes human de-
sires (bonnō) *and human desires are no other than Buddhahood."*
A monk asked, "For whom are the Buddha's desires roused?"
"His desires are aroused for all sentient beings."
"How does he get rid of them, then?"
"What is the use of getting rid of them?" answered the master.

Jōshū's crystal is Saichi's "Namu-Amida-Butsu." All of Saichi is reflected in this Name. If a stranger comes, a stranger is reflected as such, if a Chinese comes, he is reflected as such. We may view the Chinese and the stranger as *bonnō*, we may view them as the world of discrimination. There is nothing which cannot be illumined by this crystal (spiritual insight). The consciousness itself is one harmonious "Namu-Amida-Butsu," which becomes a blade of grass as well as a sixteen-foot Buddha. Whereas a Zen-man uses many naturalistic and objective expressions, Pure Land followers speak of the psychological phenomena of the individual self. They do not speak of Buddhas, or of grass, but of hate or sweetness, wretchedness or wrongness, or, opposed to these, of love, prayer, etc. The crystal is the all-seeing eye. It views both within and without, sees Saichi and the Buddha. It sees wrong views and it also sees enlightenment. Let me repeat: the crystal is "Namu-Amida-Butsu."

> *I received the eye from you,*
> *The eye to see you,*
> *"Namu-Amida-Butsu."*

"The eye to see you" is none other than the eye that sees Saichi himself, and that is "Namu-Amida-Butsu." Therefore the Buddha's ignorance (*guchi*) the ignorance of Saichi and the world's ignorance are all felt, and the fact of Buddha=*bonnō*, *bonnō*=Buddha is possible. If the eye is one-sided, free and unobstructed intercommunion cannot come into play. Thus *bonnō* cannot be excluded. *Bonnō* is the Buddha, the Buddha is the Buddha because he too has *bonnō*. Because of his *bonnō* the Buddha becomes aware of, appreciates, and experiences the *guchi* and *bonnō* (the ignorance and desires) of Saichi and all other living beings, and draws from within them a purposeless work. This is the working of the sixteen-foot Buddha. The function of the blade of grass is to be blown and rustled about by the wind, for this body of egoism to be accepted and embraced by the parent Oyasama. It is this body of egoism which, becoming hungry, is embraced by Oya. It wants milk, it is bothered by mosquitos, it itches.

> *The child held by Oya is here,*
> *Embraced by Oya,*
> *"Namu-Amida-Butsu."*

The use of the phrase "the child is here" should be noted. It means the child Saichi is here. Saichi who is here, is the blade of grass. And while he makes his geta is he not working purposelessly for the salvation of all beings as well?

In saying this I have no desire at all to join or fuse Pure Land thought and Zen. Those who would do that are the professional educators and scholars. Mine is only an attempt to compare their ways of expression from the standpoint of Jōshū's crystal and Saichi's "Namu-Amida-Butsu" themselves. To the end Zen is Zen and Jōdo is Jōdo. Looking at their differences, their similarities are not to be forgotten, and while looking at their points of similarity we are also to keep in mind the existence of their differences. I simply wish to call attention to the existence in both of what I feel deserves to be called the awakening of Japanese spirituality.

12. Shaba and Jōdo—The Corrupt World and the Pure Land

Passages such as the previously quoted "I am foolish, Amida is foolish too," and "my thoughts are your thoughts," give us an understanding of the relationship between Saichi and Amida, as well as a comprehension of the general by corresponding relation of *Shaba* and *Jōdo*.

> *Where is Saichi? In the Pure Land?*
> *Here is the Pure Land, "Namu-Amida-Butsu."*

His "Namu-Amida-Butsu" is the Pure Land. This is no doubt a matter of course. Since Saichi is not found apart from "Namu-Amida-Butsu," where he is found—in the *Shaba* world—there also must be Namu-Amida-Butsu. There can be no Pure Land except for this. It must be that the

Shaba world is the Pure Land, the Pure Land is the *Shaba* world. Only *Shaba* is not the same as Jōdo, for here there is "Namu-Amida-Butsu." By means of it *Shaba* is the Pure Land, and by means of it the Pure Land is removed to this world. The two are not simply one, it must be the two are one, the one is two. That is "Namu-Amida-Butsu."

> *I go to and receive Paradise,*
> *"Namu-Amida-Butsu."*
> *In this* Shaba *world I receive it—*
> *The moon of the Believing Heart.*

Though he states that he goes to and receives Paradise he does not say he will go there after death. With the moon of the Believing Heart, *Shaba* is illuminated and the Pure Land is received. *Shaba* and *Gokuraku* do not separate and become completely disparate, but neither are they regarded as one. It is "Namu-Amida-Butsu" of the *Shaba* world, "Namu-Amida-Butsu" of *Gokuraku*. Since Saichi exists in the *Shaba* world and Buddha exists in *Gokuraku*, if Saichi becomes Buddha it is natural that the *Shaba* world should become Paradise.

> *I hear the Name of Amida Buddha.*
> *That is the Buddha who becomes Saichi;*
> *That Buddha is "Namu-Amida-Butsu."*

Again,

> *Oyasama makes Saichi Buddha;*
> *The Amida of "Namu-Amida-Butsu."*

The connection of *Shaba* and *Gokuraku*, joined by "Namu-Amida-Butsu," bears no further repetition. Yet I would reiterate, in hope it should not be forgotten, that the six syllables of the Name must not be thought to intervene between two contradictory extremes, or that the Name is at some position above, and connects them. The Name conforms to "is" (*soku*) in "one is two, two is one." The *Shaba* world and Paradise are not spatially connected. The meaning of this "non-connection" is usually difficult to grasp, so I like to put it another way: it is the continuation of non-con-

208

tinuation, what Shinran calls leaping or passing crossways. Thus stated it might be interpreted as being spatial, as a continuum, leaping from one point to another. But these are all notions of the discriminating intellect. This is where spiritual insight works. Without it the meaning of the Name cannot be grasped under any circumstances. Saichi does not speak of such complexities, but says simply,

> *This is the Buddha that becomes Saichi.*
> *That Buddha is "Namu-Amida-Butsu."*

which is a direct utterance of spiritual insight.

> *This darkness is caught by the bright moon*
>   *Of the six syllables;*
> *While in a* Shaba *world, I live in the six syllables,*
> *How joyful!*

Saichi lives always in the moonlight of the six syllabled Name, though this does not imply the darkness of the *Shaba* world has dissipated. Hence he says, "While in a *shaba* world. . . ." He uncharacteristically fails to say "Namu-Amida-Butsu," and says instead that he is "living in the six syllables." The next poem quickly clarifies this point:

> *Shaba is the dawn, the dawn of the Pure Land.*
> *It opens, it's my joy, "Namu-Amida-Butsu."*

It might be speculated that the dawn of *Shaba* is the Pure Land, but that is not right, it is the dawn of the Pure Land. The joy at the dawning is no other than the awakening of "Namu-Amida-Butsu." Without the realization of "living in the six syllables" there can be no joy or happiness and hence no wretchedness. This realization is called *ichinen hokki*, the awakening or arousing of the one thought. The next poem is a rare instance when Saichi uses a technical term of the Pure Land tradition.

> *There is no eternity elsewhere,*
> *This world is the world of eternity,*
> *Here as well is* ichinen hokki,

209

"*Namu-Amida-Butsu.*"

We may say *Shaba* is the Pure Land, the Pure Land is this world, but unless this is based on the experience of *ichinen hokki* it is only an empty Nembutsu. One must run straight to the truth of "Namu-Amida-Butsu." That is the awakening of the one thought, and spiritual insight. It is not possible to grasp this unless one has already experienced "the end of the world." Only when the golden carp has broken through the net will it know what to feed upon. He who would say Namu is *ki* and Amida Buddha is *hō*, and that *ki* and *hō* together are "Namu-Amida-Butsu," is a preacher, not a Myōkōnin. The latter confines himself to "Namu-Amida-Butsu" and nothing else, without paying the slightest attention to whether it is the cause or condition of Pure Land *Ōjō* or the cause of a fall to Hell, and he lives within its reality.

> *When Buddha's six syllables, six essences,*
> *Come to me—"Namu-Amida-Butsu."*
> *Oya, who informed me of this,*
> *Is "Namu-Amida-Butsu."*

The Saichi who is aware that "the six syllables come to me" is the "Oya who informed me." Informing and being informed are experientially the same reality. Therefore,

> *If the eye that sees evil is the eye of Namu,*
> *It is possessed by Amida Butsu;*
> *That is the six syllables of "Namu-Amida-Butsu."*

This has come before—the eye that see Saichi and the eye that sees the Buddha are the same "Namu-Amida-Butsu." This eye does not only look without or look within; like the "eye" of Eckhart, it looks both within and without at the same time. The time you know is the time it is made known to you. *Ken* (見 seeing) is *shō* (性 nature), *shō* is *ken*.[13] I said this is simultaneous, but in fact it does not have a temporal nature. And it is not to be understood as a spatial sameness of place either. The I—Saichi—who "receives Amida San from Amida San" is this wondrous and incomprehensible eye.

210

If Saichi's verses were taken as a whole and classified into groups according to ideas, they would help ascertain the contents of a splendid Japanese spiritual insight. The next poem has been given before, but it makes a fitting conclusion to this section.

> *This wretched one is now playing with Oyasama*
> *In this* Shaba *world.*
> *I will be taken into the Pure Land of Amida,*
> *Playing with Oyasama.*

13. Emotional and Intellectual

What must be seen as Pure Land thought's most characteristic element is its view of Amida Buddha as Oyasama. Saichi's verses, in which he is constantly in a parent-child relationship with Amida, reveal this. The center of Pure Land thought is placed naturally within spirituality, but its insight is manifested mainly through the emotions. It contrasts in this respect with the intellect in Zen.

> *Amida San—*
> *You . . .*
> *You're eager to help me, aren't you?*
> *Thank you.*

This is not one of Saichi's poems. It was written by an elderly man in a remote area of Aki, and is quoted in Rev. Fuji's book. As this verse reveals, only in the Pure Land tradition is it possible to approach so closely to Amida. We do not find the same familiar, congenial attitude in Zen, which is invariably intellectual.

> *Jōshū once said to the assembled monks:*
> *"I do not like to hear the word 'Buddha'."*
> *A monk asked,*
> *"And yet do you work for the sake of men, or not?"*
> *Jōshū answered immediately, "Buddha Buddha."*

This laws of Chinese grammar allow the words "Buddha Buddha," to be interpreted in various ways. At any rate, Jōshū said he did not like even to hear the word "Buddha." When asked what he would do to save all beings, the voice of "Buddha" was heard from Jōshū himself. He might have said, "If you are able to help others, that is the Buddha." Or, "Call out the Buddha, 'Namu-Amida-Butsu' 'Namu-Amida-Butsu." The fact remains, one must not be captured by Buddha, or by No-Buddha. Existence and non-existence must be left as they are, and one must free himself from them. One must go on living within the contradiction, that is, one must become Buddha itself. Though Pure Land and Zen are here the same, in Zen negation comes first. Thus Zen speaks of *prajñā* that is not *prajñā*. The way of the Pure Land is to walk forward from the affirmation that follows this negation. Then it becomes natural for man to walk along as parent and child hand in hand with Amida. The intellect always wants to separate itself from things, the emotions live together with them. Here a surface difference between Zen and Jōdo appears. When it is fully understood that this is only a surface difference, then either affirmation or negation will depend only upon one's own particular tendency or insight.

> *Joy, joy's abundance is wretchedness too.*
> *This wretchedness is illuminated by the mirror of Compassion.*
> *Now it is a mirror within a mirror.*

Some points here are obscure, but I think the overall meaning is this: mere bounding excess of joy is not yet sufficiently separated from the consciousness of self. When this joy becomes genuine and pure it is embraced completely within Amida's Compassion. At that very moment it attains to the supra-individual Person, and the mirror of the individual self is received within the mirror of Amida so as to be like two facing mirrors with no image between them. And the joy in the consciousness of the individual self leads immediately to the Great Mirror Wisdom, where there is neither joy nor anxiety.

The line ". . . mirror within a mirror" is not often seen in Pure Land thought. The *Sutra of Eternal Life*, one of the three main Pure Land texts, has a simile in which something is likened to seeing one's face in a bright mirror. In the same sutra we also find allusion to the Pure Land and the corrupt *Shaba* world facing like mirrors reflecting one another.

212

But among Pure Land followers themselves there seems little concern with this aspect.

Saichi's poem here has a Zen flavor. I would emphasize how unusual it is to find this expression "the mirror within a mirror," among the usual Compassion, parent and child, gratitude, thankfulness, etc. Anyhow, it deserves special note when we find it in Saichi, with his "taste of 'Namu-Amida-Butsu'."

NOTES

[1] Rennyo 連如 (1414–1499). The great Shin teacher and restorer of the sect of the Middle Ages. The eighth chief priest of the Hongan-ji Temple. His works include the *Ofumi* (*Gobunsho*; 御文書), his letters edited by his grandson Ennyo, and the *Goichidaiki-Kikigaki* 御一代記聞書 (literally, "The Writing of Things Heard during a Life"), the records of his lectures compiled by his disciples.

[2] 続真宗大系 15.

[3] *Yuge sammai*—a conception describing the life of a Bodhisattva which is free from every kind of constraint and restraint. It is like the fowls of the air and the lilies of the field, and yet there is in him a great compassionate heart functioning all the time freely and self-sufficiently.

[4] *Dahrani*—a Sanskrit term which comes from the root *dhri*, meaning "to hold." In Buddhist phraseology, it is a collection, sometimes short, sometimes long, of exclamatory sentences which are not translated into other languages. It is not therefore at all intelligible when it is read by the monks as it is supposed to "hold" in it in some mysterious way something that is most meritorious and has the power to keep evil ones away. Later, *dharanis* and *mantrams* have grown confused with one another.

Mantra—a formula to be recited. Both *dharanis* and *mantrams* have an esoteric character, though when compared with the *dharani* the *mantra* holds a relatively greater esoteric quality, the *mantra* being comparatively more exoteric.

[5] *Anjin* 安心, literally, "mind pacified," meaning "faith confirmed."

[6] *Bombu* is the unenlightened man and stands in contrast to Buddha, with "Bombu-hood" in contrast to Buddhahood.

[7] Of this "favor" or "gift" (*on* 恩) as he sometimes called it, Dr. Suzuki commented, "The Favor or Gift coming from Amida is a free one, for he never asks anything in exchange or in compensation. When the sinner (*ki*) utters "Namu-Amida-Butsu" in all sincerity he is at once made conscious of his being from the first with Amida and in Amida. There has never been any sort of alienation or estrangement between Amida and the sinner. It was all due to the latter's illusive ideas cherished about himself." *Mysticism: Christian and Buddhist* (New York, 1957), p. 198. Trans.

[8] *Oya* has no English equivalent. It is both motherhood and fatherhood, not in their biological sense but as the symbol of loving-kindness. *Sama*, an honorific particle, is sometimes shortened to *San*, which is less formal and more friendly and intimate. *Oya* or *Oya Sama* is the title given to Amida by Shin devotees.

[9] *Hō* 法 is the dharma and *ki* 機 the recipient of the dharma. *Ki*, originally meaning "hinge," means in Shin especially the devotee who approaches Amida in the attitude of dependence. He stands as far as his Self-power is concerned against Amida. *Hō* is "dharma," "Reality," "Amida," and the "Other-power." This opposition appears to our intellect as contradiction and to our will as a situation implying anxiety, fear, and insecurity. When *ki* and *hō* are united in the

214

myōgō as "Namu-Amida-Butsu," the Shin devotee attains *anjin*, "peace of mind."

10 Ippen 一遍 (1239–1289) is the founder of the Ji Sect of Japanese Pure Land Buddhism. His *Sayings* are noted for their Zen-like trenchancy. Trans.

11 Fraud; *bakemono*, "something unreal," "something temporarily assuming a certain shape but not at all genuine."

12 Jōshū 趙州 (C. Chao-chou; 788–897), Chinese Zen master.

13 *Ken-shō*—literally "seeing into one's nature"; satori.

GLOSSARY OF SELECT TERMS

AWARE	See *MONO NO AWARE*.
BELIEVING HEART	Faith; heart or mind which receives without doubting.
BOMBU	The ordinary, unenlightened man in contrast to Buddha.
BUSHI	Samurai.
FAVOR	[Amida's] favor, free gift, grace. The principle of Shin teaching is "just ask and you will be saved," and not do this and salvation will be its reward." Nothing is imposed on one as the price of salvation. Amida's gift has no conditions attached to it. The believer and his mortal weaknesses just as they are absorbed in the infinite grace of Amida.
GOKURAKU	See JŌDO.
GRACE	See FAVOR.
GUCHI	Ignorance (the ignorant), folly, in contrast to enlightenment.
HELL	The Buddhist Hell (*Jigoku*; *Naraka* or *Nirriti*) is divided into compartments. Unlike the Christian Hell, sinners undergo suffering herein only as long as their karma is effective.
HŌ	The dharma, Reality, Amida, the Other-power. Note 9, Ch. 4.
HOKKAI ENGI	The Law of Dependent Origination in the Phenomenal Universe. The idea that the phenomenal world is produced by the mutual influence of all things.
HOLY PATH	See *SHŌDŌMON*.
JIRIKI	Self-power salvation through self-effort. Note 9, Introduction.
JŌDO	The Pure Land; the Land of Bliss, Paradise, *Gokuraku*.
JŌDOMON	The Path Land Path. See *SHŌDŌMON*.
KANNAGARA	The Way of the Gods; Shinto.
KI	The recipient of the dharma, the devotee who utters Nembutsu.
LATTER-DAY	*Masse*, the world of the latter period of the Buddha's teaching (*mappō*), when the doctrine alone is still alive, but there is neither practice nor enlightenment. Note 13, Ch. 1.
MAPPŌ	See LATTER DAY.
MONO NO AWARE	"The things around us that make us feel the pathos of things." Note 8, Ch. 1.
MYŌGŌ	See NAME.

216

NAME	The Name of Amida Buddha; often interchangeable with Nembutsu. Both refer to the six syllables "Na-mu-a-mi-da-butsu."
NAMU-AMIDA-BUTSU	See NEMBUTSU.
NEMBUTSU	Nembutsu literally means "to think of Buddha." *Nen* (*nien* in Chinese and *smriti* in Sanskrit) is "to keep in memory." In Shin, however, it is more than a mere remembering of Buddha, it is thinking his Name, holding it in mind. The Name consists of six characters or syllables, na-mu-a-mi-da-butsu. In actuality, the Name contains more than Buddha's Name, for Namu is added to it. Namu is *namas* (or *namo*) in Sanskrit and means "adoration" or "salutation." The Name therefore is "Adoration for Amida Buddha," and this is made to stand for Amida's "Name." In the Japanese Pure Land schools, Nembutsu usually refers to invoking the Name, "Namu-Amida-Butsu."
NEMBUTSU *SENJU*	Exclusive practice of Nembutsu; Nembutsu done to the exclusion of all other practices.
NEMBUTSU *SŌZOKU*	Continuous repetition of Nembutsu.
ŌCHŌ	"Side-wise leap." The experience by which, according to Shinran, one's rebirth in the Pure Land is absolutely assured. Note 8, Introduction.
ŌGEN-NISŌ-EKŌ	The two aspects of merit-transference, going and coming, (*gensō-ekō* and *ōsō-ekō*) as taught by Shinran. Note 16, Ch. 2.
ŌJŌ	"To go and be reborn," i.e., assurance of rebirth in the Pure Land. Note 15, Ch. 1.
ONE THOUGHT	"One Thought" or "One Calling" represents the one instant of faith-establishment. Note 4, Ch. 3.
ORDINARY MAN	See *BOMBU*.
ORIGINAL PRAYER	The eighteenth of Amida's forty-eight prayers or vows, which sets forth Amida's strong resolve to save all beings without exception, if they call upon his name even only once in sincerity of heart.
OYA-SAMA	The title, bespeaking informality and friendliness, by which Shin devotees refer to Amida. Note 8, Ch. 4.
PRAYER	See ORIGINAL PRAYER.
PURE LAND	See JŌDO.
REBIRTH	See *ŌJŌ*.
SEISHIN	Spirit, mind.
SENJU	See Nembutsu *senju*.
SHABA WORLD	"This world" as opposed to Hell, and to Jōdo, the Pure Land.

217

SHIN SECT	See Shinshū.
SHINSHŪ	The popular name for the Jōdo-Shin Sect of Japanese Pure Land Buddhism. The Shin sect of Buddhism founded by Shinran. Note 10, Introduction.
SHŌDŌMON	The "Holy Path," as distinguished from the Jōdomon, or Pure Land Path. The Holy Path leads to salvation through self-help; the Pure Land Path brings salvation through Amida's grace.
SHŌMYŌ	Pronouncing or uttering the Name of Amida Buddha. Note 1, Ch. 3.
TARIKI	Other-power, salvation through Amida's power or grace. Note 9, Introduction.

INDEX

Absolute Compassion: see Compassion
Absolute Love: 109, 111, 116
Absolute One: see Amida
Amakasu Tarō Tadatsuna: 51, 150, 151
Amida: 20, 21, 39, 51, 77, 79, 81, 83,
  90, 93, 119, 136, 151, 154, 156, 157–
  158, 161, 175, 176, 180, 182, 183,
  184, 185, 186, 190
ancestor worship: 64
asagao: see morning-glory
Asahara Saichi 浅原才市: 167, 177 passim
Anjin Ketsujō shō: "On the Attainment
  of Spiritual Peace" 156, 195, 197
Avatamsaka Sutra: (J. Kegon-kyō) 69
Awanosuke, diviner: 147
Believing Heart (faith): 173, 191–192,
  197, 201, 208
Birth (in the Pure Land): see Amida
Boundless Compassion: see Compassion
Buddha-wisdom: 184
Bukkō Kokushi, Zen master 仏光国師: 21
bombu (ordinary man): 181
Catholicism: 122, 124
Central Asia: 61, 67
Chiie (C. Chih-yung): 157
Chih-i (J. Chigi): 66, 79
Chokushū goden: see *Hōnen's Life*
Christian mystics: 174
Christianity: 61, 100
chrysanthemums: 60
Chuangtzean: 104
Chūron: 68
Compassion (Amida's Great): 21, 50,
  53, 54, 155, 175, 176, 181, 182, 190,
  203, 212
Compassionate One: see Amida
Confucianism: 22, 35, 103, 105
courtiers: 37, 71, 86, 129
dahrāni: 172
Daijō Sōō no Chi ("A Land Suited for
  the Mahāyāna"): 177

Daitō Kokushi: 198, 200
Dannoura: 128
Dengyō Daishi: see Saichō
Diamond Sutra: 171
Discussion at Ohara: 139
Dōgen: 119–122, 124
Dōshaku (C. Tao-ch'o): 139
Dōshū of Akao 赤尾の道宗: 167–174
Eckhart: 210
Eight Sage Drinkers: 30
Elegies: 30
Fa-tsang (J. Hōzō): 66, 79
favor, Amida's: 83, 156, 157, 159, 163,
  182, 183, 204
feminine culture: 72, 73, 85, 128
Fuji Shūsui, Rev.: 177, 178, 188, 197,
  211
Fujii Yoshizane: 86
Fujiwara Kanezane, ex-Regent (Tsukino-
  wa no Zenkō): 147
filial piety: 64, 65
Five Classics: 69
Five Confucian Filial Piety Relation-
  ship: 69
Five Confucian Virtues: 69
Four Books: 69
Gandhi: 65
Genji monogatari: 37
Genshin 源信: 51, 89, 100
gensō ekō: see *ōgen nisō ekō*
Go-daigo, Emperor: 168
Goichidaikikikigaki: 156, 167, 169
gokuraku: see Pure Land
grace, Amida's: see favor, Amida's
guchi (ignorant): 140
Gutei (Chu-chih), "One-Finger Zen" of
  Zen master: 91, 195
gutoku (bald-headed, simple-hearted man):
  82, 86
Hakuin: 161, 199
Hatakeyama Kagesue: 96

Heart Sutra: 162
Heike, the: 128
Heike monogatari: 127–129, 130
Hekiganroku (C.*Pi-yen lu*): 76
Hell: 53, 77, 81, 87, 92, 93, 121, 132, 142, 204, 210
  certain Hell: 53, 83
hiragana syllabary: 37
hō 法: 119, 191, 200, 210
Hōjō Tokimune 北條時宗: 21
hokkai engi 法界縁起: (Law of Dependent Origination in the Dharma-world): 114, 123, 172
Holy Path: see Shōdōmon
Hōnen 法然: 14, 15, 16, 19, 55, 56, 91, 92, 94–97, 103, 104, 106–110, 121, 132, 142, 145, 152, 153, 158, 161, 165–169, 171–173, 195, 198, 206–207, 210, 214, 255
Hōnen's Life: 52, 93, 145, 147, 149
Hongan-ji Temples: 86
honji suijaku (traces of descent from the original soil): 117
hōsshin seppō (the Dharma-body preaches the Law): 78
Hsüan-tsang: 162
Hui-k'o (J. Eka): 171
Hyakujō kōwa zuimonki: 88
Ichimaikishōmon ("One Page Testament"): 89, 138, 152, 155
ichinen hokki: 209, 210
Inari (the Shinto diety): 32
inga (retribution): 66
Ippen (*Sayings*): 197
Izumi Shikibu: 71
Japaneseness: 59, 104
jinen hōni (naturalness): 100
Jinnō Shōtōki: 97
Jiriki (Self-Power): 119
Jōdo: see Pure Land
Jōdomon (Pure Land Path): 83, 183, 188
Jōshū 趙州 (C. Chao-chou): 205, 211
joy, repentance: 180–182
kami 神: 28, 32, 33, 34, 35, 36, 49, 118

Kaian koku go ("Words from Dreamland"): 199
Kakunyo Shōnin: 191
kana literature: 72
kannagara: see Way of the gods, the
Kannon: 102
Kashiwadebe, Prince: 31
Kegon 華厳: 22, 65, 67, 79, 114
Kenreimon'in: 127
Kenshin: 139
ki 機: 119, 191, 193, 194, 200
Kichibei, Myōkōnin: 213
Kimmei, Emperor: 18, 38
Kitabatake Chikafusa: 116
Kōbō Daishi: see Kūkai
Kōkinshu: 37
kokoro 心: 11, 12, 14
kompaku 魂魄: 11, 12
kontai ryō mandara: 113
Kūkai 空海 (Kōbō Daishi): 38, 43, 46, 69, 79, 89
Kumagai Naozane: see Renshōbō
Kusakabe, Crown Prince: 35
Kusha: 67
Kusunoki Masashige 楠 正成: 21
Kyōgyōshinshō ("Teaching, Practice, Faith, Attainment"): 80, 82, 85
Kyorai, haiku poet: 109
Kyōshin: 82, 109
Land of Bliss: see Pure Land
Lactzean: 104
Latter-day (*masse*; *mappō*): 48–49, 51, 140, 145
Lectures on National Morality: 95
Lotus Sutra: 200
Love songs: 29
love poems: 29, 34
Mahābhārata: 69
mantra: 173
manyō-gana: 72
Manyōshū: 28, 29, 31, 33, 34, 36, 37, 38, 88
Manzei, Buddhist novice: 31
mappō: see Latter-day

masse: see Latter-day
Minamoto Yoshiie: 96
Minki 明極 (Zen master): 22
Mongol Invasions: 40, 70, 74
monogatari: 37, 39, 42, 44, 49
mono no aware: 39, 73, 74, 95
morning-glory: 60, 65
Motooti Norinaga 本居宣長: 23
Mu-ch'i (J. Mokkei): 22
Murasaki Shikibu: 71
Murata Jōshō Wajō: 155, 157–161
myōgō: see Name, the
Myōkōnin: 86, 141, 210
Name, Amida's (*myōgō*): 51, 90, 135, 136, 141, 151, 153, 154, 157, 158, 159, 182, 183–186, 190, 208
Namu-Amida-Butsu: see Nembutsu
Namumyōhōrengekyō: 162
Nansen (Nan-ch'uan): 76, 113
'National Learning' (Kokugaku): 71
Negusari: 158, 161
Nembutsu: 44, 53, 66, 69, 77, 80, 81–87, 91, 92–93, 109–111
Nichiren: 47, 54, 75
Nimaikishōmon ("Two-Page Testament"): 154–155
Nirvana: 32, 195
obedience: 120, 124
ōchō 横超 (leaping sideways): 20, 101
Ofumi (Gobunsho): 170
ōgen nisō ekō: 88
Ōjō (birth in the Pure Land): 50, 53, 82, 88, 93, 134, 135, 136, 138, 139, 140, 141, 142, 143, 148, 149–151, 153, 158, 160, 170, 172, 175, 188, 195, 210
Ojōyōshū (The Essentials of Salvation): 89
Okisome Azumabito: 34, 35
One Great Matter: 174–176
"One Page Testament": see *Ichimaiki-shōmon*
"One Thought" the awakening of (*ichinen hokki* 一念発起): 136, 174, 176, 191,

209, 210
onna-moji (woman's writing): 71
Original Prayer (Vow): 51, 78–80, 81, 84, 86, 92–93, 116, 135, 137, 140, 144, 146, 150, 153, 154, 156, 188, 204
ōsō ekō: see *ōgen nisō ekō*
Other-Power: see *Tariki*
Oxford Movement: 159
Oyasama: 183, 186, 187, 189, 205, 207, 208, 211
Ōyōmei 王陽明 (Wang Yang-ming): 22
Person, supra-individual: 76, 85, 86, 88–89, 90, 101, 102, 108, 114, 173, 180, 182, 183
Pillow Book, The (Makura no Sōshi): 37
prajñā-wisdom: 32, 50, 212
Prayer: see Original Prayer
psyche: see *seishin*
Pure Land (Jōdo): 17, 19, 22, 27, 46, 49, 50–52, 53, 65, 71, 77, 79, 82, 85, 93, 103, 107, 110, 129, 135, 137, 138, 144, 147, 148, 157, 158, 207, 212
Pure Land Path: see Jōdomon
raigō: 51
rebirth: see Amida
reisei: 11, 14, 15, 55, 59, 68, 69, 70, 71, 73, 75, 76, 79, 85, 86, 88, 94, 99, 102, 103, 107, 111, 112, 127, 129
religious consciousness: 16, 17, 28, 38, 42, 75, 78, 91, 100, 116, 118
Rennyo 連如: 156, 167–171, 173
Renshōbō Kumagai Naozane: 96, 133–134, 149, 152
repentance: 180–182
Right Mindfulness: 136, 192, 195
Rikkō (C. Lu Kêng): 113
Rinzai (C. Lin-chi): 77, 141, 179, 195
Roankyō ("Donkey-Saddle Bridge"): 84, 141, 159, 160
Ryūkan, priest: 153
Saichō (Dengyō Daishi): 38, 43, 48, 69, 80, 89
Saint Francis: 122
salvation of living beings: 190

221

samadhi: 177
Nembutsu samadhi: 177, 191, 200
samurai (*bushi*): 23, 42, 45, 46, 70, 87, 96, 132, 133, 145, 149, 150, 163, 168
Sanron: 65, 67
sarpirmanda: 69
scholars of Mt. Hiei and Nara: 82, 89, 90, 139, 143
School of Reason 理学 (Li-hsüeh): 22
Sei Shōnagon: 71
seishin: 11–15, 17, 19, 27, 47, 48, 118
self, individual: 76–78, 99, 119, 182
self, supra-individual: 78, 101, 119
"Seven Article Pledge": 145
Seven Wise Men of the Bamboo Grove: 30
Shaba world: 188–189, 193, 207–208, 212
Shichiri Gojun: 155
shimo (thusness): 100
Shin Sect: see Shinshū
Shingon (C. Hua-yen): 64, 65, 66, 69, 78, 82
Shinra Saburō: 96
Shinshū (Shin Sect): 19, 20, 46, 50, 53, 54, 77, 88, 101
  Shinshū experience: 20, 21
  Shinshū faith: 20
Shinran: 19–23, 51–53, 77, 78–82, 84–90, 100–103, 104, 107, 113–115, 119, 121, 122, 123, 127, 137, 147, 151, 152, 169, 179, 202
Shinto 神道: 18–19, 23, 35, 36, 39, 47, 48, 54, 104–106, 107–109, 112, 114, 118
  Ancient Shinto: 18
  Five Classics Shinto (*Gobugaki Shinto*): 47–48, 54
  Ise Shinto: 32, 103–104
  Ryōbu (Dual-Aspect Shinto): 47
  Sectarian Shinto: 108
  Shrine Shinto: 18, 108
Shōbōgenzō zuimonki: 119
Shōdōmon (Holy Path): 83, 153, 183, 189

Shōkōbō: 147
shōmyō (vocal) Nembutsu: 127, 129, 135, 136, 154–156, 162, 163
Shōtoku Prince: 16, 21, 75
Shōshoku shū: 52
Shugendō: 69
  yamabushi
Shūjisho ("A Tract on Steadily Holding to the Faith"): 191
"shut out all your thoughts!": 21, 23
six paths of transmigration: 30
Sōjō (Sêng-chao): 113
soku-hi, the logic of: 50
sōmonka: 31
Songoshinzōmeimon: 157
spirit, supra-individual: 115
spiritual awakening: 114, 120
spiritual insight: 72, 87, 108, 109, 111–116, 118, 121–123
spirituality, Chinese: 66
spirituality, Japanese: 11, 17–19, 20–23, 36, 38, 49, 50, 53, 61, 66, 67, 69, 71, 73, 77, 78, 79–80, 83, 87, 88, 89, 91, 92, 93–95, 99–103, 104, 106, 112, 114–116, 127, 128, 139, 142–144, 147, 151, 163, 167, 200, 207
Suzuki, Shōsan: 84, 137, 141, 142, 143, 144, 159, 161, 163, 172
taigi meibun: 97
Taira Shigehira: 130, 132, 149
  Taira Kiyomori: 127–128
  Taira Atsumori: 96
  Taira Tadanori: 95
Takakura, Emperor: 127
tamashii: 12, 13
Tannishō ("Tract Deploring the Heterodoxies"): 80, 81, 119
Taoism: 35, 103
Tariki (Other-power): 20, 21, 46, 50–52, 53, 54, 83, 119, 123, 124, 170, 188
Temmu, Emperor: 34, 35
Teishin-ni: 155
Tendai 天台 (C. T'ien-t'ai): 20, 22, 65, 66, 67, 69, 79, 82, 116, 139, 145

tenri-ō-no-mikoto: 162
Three Pure Land Sutras, The: see Pure
Tso Chuan: 11
"unborn", Bankei on the: 201
Upanishads: 69
upāya: 117
Vedas: 69
Vimalakirti (J. Yuima): 205
Wasan (Buddhism Hymns): 80
woman's literature: 72
Yamabe Akahito: 28
Yuge, Prince: 34, 35
Yuishiki 唯識: 22, 65, 67
Yuishikiron: 68

Warrior: see samurai
Way, natural accordance with the: 121, 122, 123
Way of the Gods, the (*kannagara*): 23, 74, 76, 100, 101, 110
will: 98, 99, 124
will power: 11, 15
wine: 29
Zen: 17, 18, 21, 22–23, 46, 54, 64, 66, 69, 70, 77, 84, 87, 88, 97, 122, 137, 141, 142, 160, 161, 198, 207, 211, 212
Zendō: 139, 141, 157
Zenshōbō: 152, 153